Global Communication

◍SAGE | 50 YEARS

SAGE was founded in 1965 by Sara Miller McCune to support the dissemination of usable knowledge by publishing innovative and high-quality research and teaching content. Today, we publish more than 750 journals, including those of more than 300 learned societies, more than 800 new books per year, and a growing range of library products including archives, data, case studies, reports, conference highlights, and video. SAGE remains majority-owned by our founder, and after Sara's lifetime will become owned by a charitable trust that secures our continued independence.

Los Angeles | London | Washington DC | New Delhi | Singapore

Cees J Hamelink

Global Communication

Los Angeles | London | New Delhi
Singapore | Washington DC

Los Angeles | London | New Delhi
Singapore | Washington DC

SAGE Publications Ltd
1 Oliver's Yard
55 City Road
London EC1Y 1SP

SAGE Publications Inc.
2455 Teller Road
Thousand Oaks, California 91320

SAGE Publications India Pvt Ltd
B 1/I 1 Mohan Cooperative Industrial Area
Mathura Road
New Delhi 110 044

SAGE Publications Asia-Pacific Pte Ltd
3 Church Street
#10-04 Samsung Hub
Singapore 049483

Editor: Mila Steele
Assistant editor: James Piper
Production editor: Imogen Roome
Proofreader: Bryan Campbell
Indexer: Martin Hargreaves
Marketing manager: Michael Ainsley
Cover design: Jen Crisp
Typeset by: C&M Digitals (P) Ltd, Chennai, India
Printed and bound by
CPI Group (UK) Ltd, Croydon, CR0 4YY

Library of Congress Control Number: 2014941015

British Library Cataloguing in Publication data

A catalogue record for this book is available from
the British Library

MIX
Paper from
responsible sources
FSC
www.fsc.org   FSC® C013604

ISBN 978-1-84920-423-1
ISBN 978-1-84920-424-8 (pbk)

To Seija – with more loving memories than one mind can process

CONTENTS

PREFACE

With this book I want to invite you to study a phenomenon that is becoming increasingly central to your daily life and to the world in which you pursue your studies. I hope to assist you in developing the capacity to study global communication by stimulating your interest in the investigation of complex questions about this field and thus to explore your own ways of reflecting on its various dimensions. Throughout the book I want you to learn the art of asking questions. I am convinced that the essence of any academic and intellectual project begins with asking questions.

In this book I will introduce global communication, describe its global context and its history, and ways of studying this field. I will also propose the analytical and normative perspectives that could direct the study of global communication. These perspectives reflect obviously my personal preferences and you can exchange them for other angles if you find these more enlightening and helpful for your understanding of the field.

In the following chapters I will invite you to look at the economic, political and cultural dimensions of global communication. Each chapter will have questions for reflection and discussion. There will be short lists of selected titles with annotations and suggestions for further reading. These selected readings are useful to cite in the papers that you may have to write and would like to see well graded!

At the end of each chapter I have suggested a research assignment. In dealing with these assignments try to combine the standard academic requirements about referencing and citing with the possibility of creative thinking, innovative exploration and the art of posing questions.

In university education it is very common to judge students' intelligence by their capability to answer questions posed by their teachers. The conventional examination format checks whether students can give smart answers to smart questions. I have never felt at home with this dominant tradition that equates intelligence with the talent to give answers. This gives academic education the appearance of a popular TV Quiz. I do believe that intelligence is best measured by the talent to pose thought-provoking questions. When Socrates stood before his judges in Athens, he admonished the court that, "the unexamined life is not worth living".

The suggestion that science equates finding smart answers to questions is fatal for the development of creative and critical thinking. In the reflexive mindset, intelligence is measured by the capacity to ask questions. Reflexive pedagogy allows students to have questions and uncertainties and thus develop their own visions and dreams about the world. To enable the art of asking questions inevitably implies that uncertainty is given space. It is very promising for scientific development that today, cosmologists are willing to accept that the universe consists of some 96 per cent of invisible dark energy and dark matter that we do not understand and cannot explain. In the same vein, it is an important step that advanced genetics research looks at itself as primarily "driven by ignorance".

The choice of books for your reading reflects my personal choice, just like the selection of individual scholars that I consider are important inspirational sources. Mentioning their names does not exclude others who have played essential roles in the understanding of global communication. But the inspirational thinkers I selected served me well during over 30 years of teaching global communication. Their names are modest statutes for those who enlightened me as I wandered through the – often amazing – complexities and challenges that global communication in all its various dimensions offers.

You can also find more sources, materials from Sage Publications, and an impression of my teaching in global communication on a special website: http://study.sagepub.com/Hamelink

We owe it to ourselves as self-conscious beings to be reflexively critical. I would like to see that you critically reflect on the phenomenon of global communication that will touch upon your lives in many different ways. And take nothing for granted, including the way I will talk to you about global communication. If you as students can point at flaws or omissions in my thinking, I will be very happy to learn from your critiques. The beauty of the scientific endeavor is that it remains a life-long learning experience.

This book would have never been written if Mila Steele – my favorite publisher – and Julia Hoffmann – for many years my favorite student and assistant – had not persuaded me to reflect on a long career in university teaching. It was a good but at times nerve-wrecking exercise since I always taught without notes and power points and had to find the lecture material from various sources. Among those were entries in Wikipedia where students –without my knowledge – had posted their lecture notes and – inevitably-parts of the present text lean heavily on materials that I wrote and published earlier.

Much gratitude is due to all the students and PhD candidates from whom I had the privilege to learn. In the end though, the manuscript would never have been completed if Seija – my Muse for 38 years – had not encouraged me to do so in the last days of her journey on our planet.

Cees J. Hamelink, Amsterdam, 2014

COMPANION WEBSITE

This book is supported by a companion website (**https://study.sagepub.com/hamelink**). On the site you can access the following video content in which the author further explains the topics covered in each chapter:

1. Global Communication: The Field
2. Studying Global Communication
3. Global Communication: History & Rules
4. The Global Communication Industry
5. Global News
6 & 7. Global Politics
8. The Global Divide
9. Propaganda and Spin
10. Global Conflict
11. Intercultural Communication
12. Global Communication Online
13. The Future of Global Communication

The site also offers links to a range of relevant journal articles, helping you to take your studies further.

Look out for the following symbols in the **Online Resources** section of each chapter:

▶ video content

 journal articles

WHAT IS GLOBAL COMMUNICATION?

Because of his comprehensive view of global communication, the intellectual depth of his writing and the engaging nature of his critical analysis, the essential inspirational source of this chapter is:

Armand Mattelart (1936–)

Born in 1936 in Belgium, Mattelart studied law and political science at the University of Louvain and completed his studies in Paris. In 1962 he travelled to Chile where he taught at the Catholic University, co-founded a Center for the Study of National Reality, and published, together Ariel Dorfman, the bestseller *How to Read Donald Duck: Imperialist Ideology in the Disney Comic* (1975), which was censored in the USA. After the military coup of Pinochet, he returned to Paris and began lecturing at the University of Paris VIII.

Among his major publications are: *Multinational Corporations and the Control of Culture* (1982); *Transnationals and the Third World: The Struggle for Culture* (1983); *International Image Markets* (1984); and *Mapping World Communication: War, Progress, Culture* (1994).

For the study of global communication, Armand Mattelart has taught us to critically reflect on the issue of power and power-relations in global communication.

- First, we need to find a good name for the field of study that this book addresses.
- Then we need to identify the essential building blocks of "global communication": the flows and stories.
- We should also raise the question of why we should study global communication.
- Finally, we need to analyze the key dimensions of the contemporary context of global communication.

What's in a name?

Juliet tells Romeo that a name is an artificial and meaningless convention: "What's in a name? That which we call a rose by any other name would smell as sweet."

William Shakespeare, *Romeo and Juliet* (Act I, Scene II).

Indeed, we could call a rose "cow-dung" and its smell would not change. We would still enjoy its beauty and put the dung in a vase. It may be, however, that names are less insignificant than Juliet suggests. Romeo only has to change his name – she thinks – but it is precisely their names that doom the lovers from the very beginning. Many of us have experienced the association of judgments – pleasant or negative – with names of people. The names that parents choose for you may haunt you throughout life. Yet, Juliet is right in proposing that names are conventions. But, the conventions are not meaningless. If the surgeon asks for a scalpel and gets a chisel the patient is likely to have a problem.

Communication among human beings is made possible largely by conventions about how to name things, people, and experiences. Part of all scientific projects is the naming of the phenomena that we investigate, interpret, and hope to understand.

This book proposes that its field of study bears the name "global communication". The same field has also been named "international communication", "world communication", and "trans-border communication". Scholars have offered good arguments for these different names.

- International communication. International usually refers to processes that occur among states, like in international relations. Although it has been suggested that the state is withering away, we have to acknowledge that they are still a formidable reality and – often – powerful agents in facilitating, promoting, or hindering communication across their borders. However, it also needs recognition that the international arena increasingly involves interactions between both state and non-state actors. The international political arena has multiple actors. Particularly since the Second World War, we find such agents as intergovernmental organizations (IGOs), international non-governmental organizations (INGOs), transnational business corporations (BINGOs) and international public service organizations (PINGOs).
  Studies of international communication are often inspired by the nation-state as the key concept. This has been seriously challenged by the development of diaspora communities around the world: de-territorialized "imagined" communities that are made up of a great variety of migrants that keep moving back and forth between home and host countries or that settle in host countries but often with strong attachments to their countries of origin. Diaspora communities also will often develop media that produce and distribute content related to their specific experiences.
  International communication is in fact communication among states and inter-state communication would be a more appropriate term.

- World communication. This term has a broader meaning than international communication. It remains a somewhat nebulous term, though, and conjures up romantic associations with the "family of man". Its translation in non-English idioms is not always easy, although one could use in some languages (like French) the word "mondial".
- Transborder communication. The term sounds awkward but does suggest precisely what the core phenomenon of our explorations will be. The form of communication we will investigate is a "glocal" process in which "messages" flow across national borders.
- Global communication. This is the most fashionable term today. It also has its disadvantages both in translation and in its suggestion that we have achieved the creation of a one-world community. Global represents rather an aspiration than a reality. Communication globalizes but it also remains local. Most TV and film production is not global, but local in origin. Global and local belong together. We do not live in the globe but in specific locations. However cosmopolitan one may be, one's identity is primarily defined by "locality": the locus of birth, family, language, jokes. Attachment to the place where you experience the greatest cultural "comfort" – often referred to as cultural proximity – is an essential experience. We are global and local citizens and our communication could possibly best be termed "glocal". This notion connects the global (e.g. a product for global marketing) with the local (e.g. local tastes and experiences).

Almost inevitably when global communication is mentioned, thoughts are directed towards its largest contemporary infrastructure: the Internet. The Internet as a network is not only a material concept, it is also a psychological concept that brings home to its users the world as a very diversified whole. The network is decentralized, horizontally structured, de-territorialized, but also localized. We are globally interconnected from bounded places! As Appiah has phrased it, we are "cosmopolitan patriots" (1998: 290–328).

Obviously, the "we" in such statements does not include all the world's people. Global communication has a normative connotation as it suggests the existence of a global society in which all the planet's habitants participate and equally matter. In the early twenty-first century many people continue to be excluded from global connections.[1] Today, communication can be seen as an "agent" of globalizing processes in economic, political and social-cultural fields that interconnect large numbers of people across the globe. And, equally, as an (institutionalized) process, global communication itself is considerably affected by these processes.

? Is "global communication" the best descriptor of the phenomenon that is the central topic of this book?

Flows

Whatever adjective we may prefer, at the core of our interest is "communication". Yet another "name" that covers a great variety of meanings. As the student of communication knows, the ever-expanding literature offers an almost endless list of definitions. But do we really have to begin with a definition? Do psychologists define the psyche? Do biologists define life? Do mathematicians define number?

The best approach may be to begin with the observation of human behaviour. Seen from another planet, human societies probably look very much like ant hills: permanent movements by little animals that run around moving all kinds of things from A to B and from B back to A. A seemingly senseless perpetuum mobile. If we take the observation of "motion" as a starting point, the extraterrestrial observer would probably agree with Manuel Castells, who wrote that "our society is constructed around flows" (1996).

Flow is a useful concept since it suggests a multidirectionality of movements: linear and circular, top-down and bottom-up, engineered and spontaneous.

Stories

The messages that the human species transports around the globe are in fact stories. Stories are the key sources of human knowledge and, as Greek philosopher Plato observed, "Those who tell stories rule society". We learn through stories. Stories provide patterns and structures and thus help us to adapt to our environments. Global communication is a complex multilayered process in which dominant and counter-stories flow cross the globe. The most important producers of TV stories, with hundreds of millions of people watching their products, are the US-based MTV, CNN and Discovery Channel. There is not yet a non-Western TV soap with the global popularity of *Sex and the City*, *Friends* or *Desperate Housewives*. However, counter-stories develop as a result of local production, storytelling in diasporas, and the emergence of new storytellers. New social networks such as YouTube expand the community of global storytellers. YouTube, with all its contemporary "bards", emerges – from an evolutionary perspective – as an essential instrumental of human adaptation to a complex environment. Surviving in the midst of complexity demands networks through which ever more actors exchange stories among each other. The essence of human communication is its narrative structure. We are "storytellers" and all the global flows of ideas, opinions, observations, knowledge, information, data, sounds, and images can be brought under the umbrella concept of "storytelling".

Human beings have throughout their history always told stories over large distances and Chapter 3 deals with this.

Does the study of global communication matter?

Why would one dedicate time and energy to the study of global communication? Why would we study cross-border flows of stories? What is so important about this phenomenon?

Global communication is the basic flow

Throughout much of recorded history there have been flows of people, flows of goods, flows of money, and flows of stories. The flow of stories deserves special attention since it has developed into the type of movement that is essential to the other flows. Flows of people (such as in tourism and business travel) are today unthinkable without massive volumes of stories about airline tickets, hotel reservations, or purchases by credit cards. The same holds for the traffic of goods, which is impossible without an extensive network of computerized message transmissions. Flows of money have become streams of electronic bits. Banks transport messages about transfer and reception of funds to other banks, to governments, and to clients but do not move the funds themselves.

The cross-border flows of stories provide the essential supporting infrastructure to trading across the world and to global financial transactions. Worldwide transport of people, goods, and money is today unthinkable without global communication.

The contents of global communication provide news, advertising and entertainment to numerous people around the globe. The stories that news providers, ad agencies and entertainment companies produce contribute significantly to how people see other people and how they frame and interpret the world in which they live.

People have always lived with images of the others who lived in distant places. Usually the images were reflections of distorted realities. Atilla the Hun was already aware of the critical importance of images. As a skilled precursor of modern propagandists, he spread wildly exaggerated stories about the supranatural powers of his army in his campaigns throughout fifth-century Europe.

We perceive the world through the stories that we are told! As Alexa Robertson wrote, "Through the agency of storytelling, our situation in the political and cultural landscape, and that of everyone else, is set out, maintained, negotiated and adapted to new circumstances" (Robertson, 2012: 2). And Kenneth Boulding helped us to understand this even better by saying, "It is what we think the world is like, not what it is really, that determines our behaviour" (Boulding, 1959: 120). The international political arena is largely dependent upon stories that nations and their representatives tell each other for diplomatic, propagandistic, public relations or war-mongering purposes. Global communication today is a crucial source for our perceptions of the world and for our sense of belonging to this world.

- Global communication is a key player in the global economy
  As I will discuss in Chapter 4, global communication is facilitated through the industries that manufacture infrastructural equipment, that provide connectivity services and that produce content.
- Global communication is essential to global politics
  Politics provides an important argument for the relevance of global communication as flows of stories build discursive power. This will be detailed in Chapter 9.
- Military operations depend upon global communication

Military activities have worldwide become dependent upon command, control and intelligence systems, and the use of unmanned predator planes ("drones") as well as the possibility of cyberwar, all of which demonstrate the significance of global communication. This will be discussed in Chapter 11.

- Global communication is a carrier of cultural expressions
  Global communication distributes globally essential cultural icons, is crucial to the development of cultural mélanges and is a major cause of local resistance against foreign cultural impositions. These issues will be addressed in Chapter 11.

The globalization of communication

The rise of a global media system first became visible in the late eighteenth and early nineteenth centuries with the early development of a global infrastructure of telegraph and wireless connections and global news distribution (through Reuters, Havas, and Wolff). These forerunners were not so much driven by the interests of the imperial powers (Britain, France, Germany, in particular), but rather by commercial and trading interests. The expansion of global communication has often been documented as the history of the struggle of imperial countries to control communication infrastructures. However, Winseck and Pike (2007) have demonstrated – with considerable empirical evidence – that the companies active in these infrastructures were not as closely affiliated with national governments as was often believed. Moreover, "The web of interconnections and interdependence constituting the global media system of the late nineteenth century and early twentieth could also be seen in governments' willingness to rely on foreign firms to meet their foreign communication and military security interests" (Winseck and Pike, 2007: xvi). And, "the globalization of capitalism was actually a stronger influence on the organization and control of global communication than was imperialism". In this context, the authors made the interesting observation that "Most zones of empire (Britain) were some of the least connected, worst served places on the planet". At the same time "Communication networks and information flows, simply put, were densest in areas where world markets were most developed. And in this, the global media system was crucial in two ways: first, the media firms operating in times, and second, these firms provided the networks and supplied the informational and news resources upon which capitalism depended and thrived" (Winseck and Pike, 2007: xvii). There was certainly rivalry among the empires but also a large measure of cooperation. There was "shared hegemony"; some expression of this was found in international legal agreements, for example in the field of post and telegraph.

In the mid-nineteenth century many newspapers regularly published world news and they were served by transnational agencies such as Reuters, Havas and Wolff. In the first part of the twentieth century governments discovered the potential of international propaganda and the film industry emerged as an international medium, with the exports of Hollywood films. The recorded music industry also began early on to globalize.

The arrival of television satellites in the late 1970s broke the principle of national sovereignty of broadcasting space and made it difficult, and ultimately impossible, to offer effective resistance to television transmissions from outside the national territory. The driving forces were also primarily economic: the need in most countries for large volumes of imports, commercial/profit motives, and advertising. Markets for products became global and advertising went overseas. Media products that could fairly easily globalize (i.e. be sold in foreign markets) were news, cinema films, recorded music and TV serials.

> Television is still probably the single most potent influence in this media globalization process, partly because, as with the cinema film, its visual character helps it to pass barriers of language. Just as important, however, is the fact that its predominant form of organization and means of transmission are such that it cannot easily be contained within national frontiers or kept out. (McQuail, 2010: 217)

An illustration of the globalizing of communication is provided in the Discovery Channel.

THE DISCOVERY CHANNEL

The global media enterprise that is Discovery consists of a range of television channel networks launched in 170 countries, and a growing number of digital media offerings distributed via the Internet and mobile telephony targeting global segments of the world's television and media audience.

John Hendricks, the founder of the Discovery Channel, started to promote the plan to create a documentary television channel to potential investors in 1982. Hendricks talked to 211 venture capitalists before bankers Allen & Co, New York, agreed to provide $3 million in funding.

The Discovery Channel US went into profit in the 1980s and sought new international markets. Throughout the 1990s and 2000s Discovery expanded into Europe, Latin America, and Asia.

Although Discovery's global tier of television channels forms the backbone of the company's distribution of media content, at the beginning of the 21st century the company has increased its efforts to position itself in the digital environment such as the Internet and within mobile telephony.

Branding and marketing had a central role in the development of Discovery in the US and have also been vital to its strategy to globalize the brand.

Although Discovery Channel is a major global provider of factual information, the programs' account of the real world has a defined focus. This also includes a notion of 'government-friendliness' and a certain limit of critical portrayal of the real world in many programs. However, this gives the global television channel a crucial ability to cross cultural, political, and religious boundaries unhindered. There is a certain presence of entertainment

(Continued)

There exist today no real global media; there are hybrid forms based upon national contexts. There may be global connections but the *modus operandi* is determined by national standards, objectives, and expectations.

Jeremy Tunstall (2008) argues in *The Media Were American* that most people in the world do not speak English, that most prefer their own jokes, their own music, politics, and sports. In countries with large populations, national and local media are increasingly important and countries like India and China import little TV fare. International media productions are localizing. Major US studios are increasingly using local production facilities in Europe, Asia, and Latin America. Columbia TriStar, Warner Brothers, and Disney have set up international TV subsidiaries to produce English language co-productions, to be followed by country-specific programming. Sony has contributed to local-language film production in Germany, Hong Kong, France, and Britain, and television programming in eight languages. STAR TV, part of media mogul Rupert Murdoch's News Corporation, aggressively adopted the policy of indigenization in offering localized channels, including: STAR Chinese Channel (for Taiwan), and STAR Japan.

There is increasingly economic interdependence but not media-interdependence. One can observe media-regionalization (especially in Latin America and the Arab countries) but this is not the same as media-globalization.

In spite of the globalizing tendencies in the field of communication, the "national" remains essential (Tunstall, 2008: 450). The national level of media is still dominant in the countries where 90 per cent of the world's people reside. Audiences today prefer their own news, weather, sports, comedy, soaps, games, reality, and other cheap factual programming. By and large audiences, producers, and politicians agree that national content is to be preferred. In the Asian region, for example, we find Korean TV drama, Chinese pop-music, and Japanese comic strips.

Most national media cover significantly more local news than global news. There remains a North–South news gap. In the era of globalization one might have expected an increase in global news. However, this is not the case! The local framing of global news is paramount and global events thus become local stories.

Worldwide, nationalism continues to be a crucial factor in both news and entertainment. The nation-state is still a force to be reckoned with in the age of global communication. Mechanisms applied by national states are import restrictions, quota rules, and giving prime time to local products.

In connection with global communication, globalization occurs as homogenization, but also as an ingredient in a process of glocalization or hybridization, and as the driver of forms of fragmentation and polarization that can be subsumed under heterogenization. (These notions are further discussed in Chapter 11 on the cultural dimensions of global communication.) One reason for the proliferation of transnational channels is the physical movement of people that carry with them aspects of their culture. The issue of identity is central to the migrant's lifestyle, living as they often do "between cultures" (Bhabha, 1994). The nature of cultural mixing, as Martin Barbero has argued, can lead to a "hybridization" of cultures (Barbero, 1988). Iranian cable television in Los Angeles, for example, has had to tread a careful line between providing programmes which retain a traditional Islamic way of life with those which display the local consumerist lifestyle in the USA. New communication technologies have made it possible for broadcasters from many developing countries to export their media products successfully. Turkey's TRT launched TRT-INT in 1990 to transmit programmes via Eutelsat to Turkish-speaking populations in Western Europe, mainly aimed at the two million-strong Turkish population in Germany. There are new national and regional storytellers, like Al-Jazeera in the Middle East, the Brazilian TV soap industry, Mexico's Televisa, or Bollywood, the Indian film industry.

One of the most puzzling questions for the study of global communication is: Does global communication make the world a smaller place? Does it create a "global village", as Marshall McLuhan suggested? Or is Fortner correct in proposing that "Communication across distances, however, does not reproduce the intimacy that is the hallmark of village life" (Fortner, 1993: 24). As Fortner suggests, a better notion may be the "global metropolis". Characteristic of the big city is that most people do not know each other and that messages flows are highly unequal.

The context of global communication

- Trans-localization

  - o Globalization: the history
  - o Globalization: the analytical tool
  - o Globalization: the political programme

- Urbanization
- Institutionalization
- Inequality
- Global risks

Global communication does not occur in a vacuum. The flows and networks mentioned in this chapter, and the stories that form their substance, are part of a real world. Their habitat is life on planet Earth as it evolves and affects its individual and institutional inhabitants.

The study of global communication requires contextualization. This implies that we need to understand the real-world environment. To help this understanding we need a conceptual framework that brings together the most characteristic dimensions of today's world. Key elements of such a framework could be the processes of globalization, urbanization, the prevalence of the nation-state doctrine, institutionalization, large-scale inequality, and the global proliferation of risks.

Trans-localization

Global communication takes place in a context that is commonly described with the concept "globalization". It is almost impossible to discuss current social developments without reference to this term. It became one of the buzzwords of the last decade in the twentieth century. It is a popular, very fashionable, but also deeply contested concept. It is little understood and some authors even suggest that the concept has no meaning at all or that it merely gives a new name to old phenomena. This latter position warns us of the tendency to indulge in historical forgetfulness. This happens when we think that processes are the unique products of a new era whereas they may be part of evolving historical processes. When Marshall McLuhan launched the idea of the world as a global village, he in fact revitalized not only the thinking of Teilhard de Chardin (about, among others, "cosmic totality"), but "the old Christian myth of the great human family" (Mattelart, 2010: 315).

The first reference to the term "globalization" was probably in 1970 in the radical-leftist magazine *Sinistra Proletaria*, where the "mondialization" of capitalist imperialism was discussed. It gave the computer manufacturer IBM as an example. The concept gained popularity only in the 1980s. The *Oxford Dictionary of New Words* mentioned "global" as a new word in 1991.

It would seem a useful beginning to describe globalization in a simple way as a process in which the distribution of "X" across the globe takes place. In this process, X can be anything, such as goods, cultural artefacts, religious ideas, or trends in fashion. A first question that now pops up is when does this process begin.

Globalization: the history

There is an ancient phase of globalization which began with the journey of Homo Sapiens out of Africa (between 50,000 and 100,000 years ago) and matured between 500 BC and

AD 1500 with the silk routes that connected Asia with the Mediterranean and parts of Africa (between 200 BC and AD 200), the distribution of the "four great inventions" in China (the compass, gunpowder, papermaking, and printing) to the West, and the export of mathematics from the Arab countries. Between 1500 and 1800, a mercantilist, colonial form of globalization emerged with the adventurous expeditions of the sixteenth century that explored and exploited distant countries and forced foreign histories and religion upon indigenous people. After the industrial revolution (with the advent of steamboats and electricity) a modern form of capitalist globalization emerged in the eighteenth and early nineteenth century. The globalization phase of the nineteenth century was a process that had an enormous societal impact. Winseck and Pike wrote about this: "Globalization during the late nineteenth century and early twentieth was not just shallow and fleeting, but deep and durable. The growth of a worldwide network of fast cables and telegraph systems, in tandem with developments in railways and steamships, eroded some of the obstacles of geography and made it easier to organize transcontinental business" (Winseck and Pike, 2007: 1).

After the Second World War the pace and scope of global distribution processes rapidly increased. Important factors in this corporate globalization were the mobility of capital and the consolidation of markets through global competition. Characteristic of this phase is the global polarization between the industrial nations and the non-industrial nations, between the centre and the periphery, with the centre nations exercising control over the periphery through what Samir Amin has called the five monopolies of technology, finance, resources, weapons, and communication (Amin, 2000: 602). In the late twentieth century the scope of the globalization process was boosted further by technological innovations and the emergence of institutions that had the promotion of global expansion on their agenda (institutions like the World Trade Organization).

The two essential features of this twentieth-century global expansion are interdependence (e.g. in such fields as climate and health) and the spread of "modernity": in politics (the idea of parliamentary democracy goes global); in the economy (the free market economy gains massive popularity); and in culture (lifestyles, fashion models, pop music, and fast-food become global icons).

Globalization: the analytical tool

The concept globalization is used to describe and interpret contemporary social processes. In this application, the concept has both its protagonists and sceptics.

- The protagonists argue that from the 1980s onwards (with the deregulatory policies of Reagan and Thatcher and the demise of communism) more and more people around the globe are living in or are indirectly affected by free market economies. Capitalism has spread from some 20 per cent of the world population in the 1970s to over 90 per cent in the early twenty-first century. More and more people around the globe have become integrated in the global capitalist economy.

The sceptics respond that this is superficially true, but they claim that the "global economy" is in fact the economy of a few rich countries in the world, in particular the OECD countries. They point out that if the world were a global village of 100 residents, six of them would be Americans. These six would have half the village's entire income and the other 94 would exist on the other half.

- The protagonists argue that today there is more global trading than ever before.

Sweeping reductions in costs of air travel and shipping have facilitated the phenomenal expansion of cross-border trading. In the process, not only the volume of trade has increased enormously, but also its character has changed considerably. Firms are under strong pressure to take a global approach to their sales (e.g. through global brand names and global advertising), and thereby reinforce the globalization of markets.

The sceptics will protest that most world trading is not global but takes place within geographical regions. Moreover, the volume of international trading by the industrial countries has not dramatically increased since the early twentieth century. Actually, some sceptics even present trade figures which demonstrate that the nineteenth-century world economy was far more internationalised than today's so-called global economy.

- Protagonists will point to the growth of global financial markets and explain that this began in the 1970s with the rapid proliferation of offshore financial markets and the global circulation of vast amounts of money outside the jurisdiction of national authorities. And they will conclude that there is today an unprecedented global financial mobility. This is true, the sceptics agree, but these capital flows refer mainly to one type of capital: short-term speculative investments and not to productive capital. Financial mobility remains very limited where productive investments are concerned and the rapid money causes serious risks for Third World economies.
- Another argument for the protagonists is the increased global mobility of people: there are more refugees and there is more migrant labour around the globe. But the sceptics conclude that most people stay home, most refugees stay within their own region, and most labour is not mobile.
- For the protagonists, globalization as a social process refers to the intensification of global consciousness. The sceptics, however, say that at the surface there is a CNN-type global solidarity but the world is more a collection of many local villages than one global village. People may know the American president better than their neighbours, but in the end they will take sides with the provincial interests of their own tribe. Although more people may have become more cosmopolitan than ever before, this does not yet create a collectively shared cosmopolitan consciousness.

The protagonists argue that increasing economic interdependence leads to social interdependence. The sceptics will answer that this thesis lacks empirical confirmation and that while there may be some evidence of global solidarity, there are equal or even more demonstrations of the fact that people across the world do not feel part of the global family. Whereas the protagonist like to stress that current social processes lead inevitably to global integration, the sceptics think that the same forces propelling these processes may lead to integration as well as disintegration.

The protagonists and the sceptics therefore disagree about the appropriateness of globalization as an analytical tool. They are also divided on the question of whether the driving force of contemporary social process is primarily technological progress.

The protagonist side of the argument sees globalization as the inevitable consequence of modern technological developments in transportation and communication. The sceptical side argues that an explanation based upon technological determinism is too limited. Technologies undoubtedly play an enabling role, but the crucial variables are decisions made by public and private institutions. Related to this is also a serious disagreement about the significance of the national state. The protagonist argument suggests that the national state has lost its sovereign powers.

Economic processes, propelled by transborder finance flows, offshore electronic markets, and the worldwide marketing of cultural products, affect the decision-making powers of individual states. The sceptics say this is true, but only in a limited way. The financial capacities and political power of the major transnational corporations (TNCs) have certainly increased. Some of these corporations have revenues that exceed the Gross Domestic Products of important industrial nations. However, the sceptics find the claim that governments have become impotent greatly exaggerated. Many powerful companies could not survive without state subsidies (to such companies as Renault and McDonnell Douglas), or without the purchases by states from corporations for defence purposes (such as is the case with General Electric, Boeing, and IBM) or for more general purposes (e.g. Siemens and Alcatel). Moreover, for the efficient and effective performance of large companies the role of law enforcement institutions is crucial. National sovereignty helps the TNCs to avoid the creation of genuine supra-national regulatory institutions that might control their restrictive business practices. TNCs need national governments to guarantee safe investment environments, to create market opportunities through foreign aid or to promote the trade of their "national" companies through their diplomatic missions. They may also benefit from supportive national regulation on technical standards, patent and trademark protection, or acquisitions and mergers.

In the analysis of the sceptics, powerful governments have voluntarily delegated primacy to the marketplace. The state is still decisive in determining the quality of health care, social services, and education. The retreat of the state tends to be partial and from selected social domains, such as social services, and not from intervention on behalf of intellectual property right holders, for example. The sceptics may not deny that states play a lesser role, but they will argue that this is not an inevitable process.

? Is it helpful to describe our world as a "global village"? How can this notion be defended? How can this notion be refuted?

Globalization: the political programme

As a political programme globalization represents an agenda that has both its advocates and its critics. The advocates claim that globalization creates worldwide, open and competitive markets which promote global prosperity. The key justification of their political programme is that a global free market leads to more employment, better quality of goods and services, and lower consumer prices. For the critics, the globalization agenda is a neo-liberal political programme that primarily promotes the interests of the world's most powerful players. In their analysis, large numbers of farmers, workers, immigrants, youth, and women are very negatively affected by economic globalization.

The globalization advocates see the process as unstoppable and as ultimately beneficial. It will make all the world's people more prosperous. The critics disagree and say that if there is globalization at all, it is the globalization of poverty. Advocates and critics also disagree about the cultural dimensions of the globalization programme. The advocates defend that globalization promotes cultural differentiation and the critics claim it is merely a new disguise for old-fashioned cultural imperialism.

Both advocates and critics may have a point here, as the global landscape is made up of homogenizing global tendencies, heterogenizing local developments and hybrid forms that are sometimes referred to as "glocalization". The worldwide proliferation of standardized food, clothing, music, TV drama, and the spread of Anglo-Saxon business style and linguistic convention create the impression of an unprecedented cultural homogenization. Yet, in spite of the McDonaldization of the world, there remain forcefully distinct cultural entities to which the manifold inter-ethnic conflicts are ever so many dramatic testimonies. There is certainly an increase in cultural contacts and more cultural movements that go beyond national boundaries, but this does not yet bring about a global culture. Parallel with the homogenization of consumer lifestyles there is also local cultural differentiation. Although current globalization suggests integration, interdependence and homogenization, locality and nationality continue to play important roles in people's lives.

Globalization is often described as a transfer from the West to the Rest. Inspired by the Hegelian idea that the West is the source of rational thinking, there has certainly been an impressive flow of Western ideas, political constructions, and cultural lifestyles to other parts of the world. However, this Euro-American centrism is increasingly contested by the economic emergence of the new BRIC countries (Brazil, Russia, India, and China) and by proposals (particularly from Asian countries) to break through conventional dichotomous schemes that creates divisions between modern and non-modern, or the de-Westernizing of modern research (Wang, 2011).

Since processes of global distribution are often solidly embedded in localities, this component of the understanding of the world could be best referred to as "trans-localization".

? How cosmopolitan are you really? And how important is your local habitat in the definition of your identity?

Urbanization

In the twenty-first century the human species will for the first time in history become an "urban species". In 2009 half of the global population lived in urban areas and in the years to come this will be some 70 per cent. "According to current projections, virtually the whole of the world's population growth over the next 30 years will be concentrated in urban areas" (UN Habitat, 2011: ix). The city will be the locality in which people have to find ways to live together and to deal with all the conflicts that go with urban spaces. Latin America is the most urbanized region in the developing world, with 77 per cent of its population – 433 million people – living in cities. The urbanization of Latin America has yet to reach its peak. By 2015, it is expected that 81 per cent of its population will reside in urban areas. Equally, Asia and Africa are regions with a very intense urbanization. Asia alone will account for more than half the world's urban population by 2030 and in the same year the African urban population will be larger than the total population of Europe.

Global cities are becoming the world's centres of finance, fashion, the arts, and the media of communication. They are the key hubs in global economic activity and key actors in current processes of globalization. The January 28, 2008 issue of *Time* magazine had a cover story about how three connected cities (New York, London, and Hong Kong, aptly titled Nylonkong) drive the global economy. Their shared economic energy creates a powerful network that both illustrates and explains globalization. They are not only centres of money and high-finance, they are also centres of culture. Cultural production and consumption have become important elements of the economy of the world's big cities and this has introduced new ways to use urban space for public cultural performances. A variety of cultural roles merge, such as those of spectatorship, tourism, performance, and sales. The big cities have also become key places for all kinds of services, such as legal assistance, marketing, advertising, and architecture (Sassen, 2001).

The world has never before known so many cities and never such large cities as the massive conurbations of more than 20 million people that are now gaining ground in Asia, Latin America, and Africa. Many of these cities have populations larger than entire countries. The population of Greater Mumbai (which will soon achieve megacity status), for instance, is already larger than the total population of Norway and Sweden combined.

The quality and sustainability of life in the world's cities will largely depend upon the ways in which the urbanites manage to co-exist with each other. The way cities structure and manage their public space is obviously essential to any effort to enhance social interaction among urbanites. In addition to the management of the physical environment, there are also economic and socio-cultural elements that enhance or obstruct urban social interaction.

Understanding the world requires us to comprehend how urban populations will be able to cope... with such a characteristic of cities as heterogeneity.

Heterogeneity: the city is a place of heterogeneity, a place of differences. Dealing with the permanent provocation (Foucault, 2003) that heterogeneity poses is exceedingly difficult for many people.

Speed: the city is characterized by the tremendous speed of its movements and interactions. Social interactions demand time. For most city dwellers this means that they have to learn the art of slowing down.

Mindlessness: much of urban interaction is mindless. Running without seeing faces, passing others as strangers in the night, without feelings of responsibility towards others; speeding along the urban routes in cocoons that broadcast the signal that I don't mind you, please don't mind me!

It is more characteristic of urban life than of village life that numerous bystanders see a fellow human being beaten and kicked and don't intervene. They may even complain if other onlookers stand in their line of sight.

If the city is your natural habitat: how well can you deal with the challenges of heterogeneity, speed, and mindlessness?

Institutionalization

Like all other living species, the human being searches for adequate adaptive responses (in order to survive and reproduce) to complex problems. These problems stem from human experiences such as the desire to grow and to learn, the need to communicate or the concern about pain, suffering, and death. In the search for adequate adaptive responses, a wide range of institutions has been developed. It is arguably one of the critical distinctions with other species that humans "institutionalize" the satisfaction of basic needs. Not even our closest associates, such as chimpanzees or bonobos, design – for the satisfaction of their alimentary needs – agro-business conglomerates or mega meat-processing institutions! Humans institutionalize, among other domains, education, health care, and public communication.

Institutionalization is a social process of embedding human needs, ideas, values, and desires in organizational formats with objectives, structures, sets of rules, and procedures for assessment. The currently dominant type of institutionalization is the "delivery" institution. This encompasses all those organizations that transform the satisfaction of human needs into the delivery of (often addictive) commodities in the form of professional products and services. The characteristics of delivery institutions are that they commercialize the production and distribution of goods and services, that they are fiercely competitive, and that are run by professionals. The challenge this raises is whether these features enable human institutions to meet human needs.

Inequality

A standard feature of today's world is inequality in the access to resources, the experience of recognition, and the distribution of power. The inequality of resources can be illustrated with the observation that the 600 million best-off people have 60 times the income of the 600 million worst-off, or that for 1.2 billion people there is no access to safe drinking water. Worldwide, people's dignity is respected in highly unequal ways as the treatment of women, gay men and women, disabled people, older people, and people with darker skins illustrate.

In authoritarian countries, but also in democracies, the power of decision making is very unequally distributed. Around the globe this is also the case at work and in the family. Global communication functions in a deeply hierarchical and unequal set of power relations and is embedded in structural relationships that rob many people of their fundamental communication rights and that manage to create a culture of denial and silence about these abuses.

? What would be the implications for global communication if there was a more equal distribution of income, wealth, and power in the world?

Global risks

Ulrich Beck has coined the notion of the "risk society". An important dimension of the context of global communication is that we live in a global risk society. Human security is threatened by warfare (nuclear, biological, and chemical), terrorism, organized crime, changes in the environment (increasing ultraviolet radiation, rising temperatures, the disappearance of rainforests, a shortage of drinking water, desertification, the depletion of fossil fuels, and decreasing bio-diversity), carcinogen ingredients in food supplies, pollution by poisonous materials (acid rain, chemical products from insecticides or deodorants), series of natural disasters (asteroids, comets, volcanoes, or tornados), and genetic experiments. Much of the content of global communication adds to these risks!

There is hate speech around the world that incites people to ethnic, racial, and religious violence. There is the advertising discourse (Ad-Speech) that persuades people to indulge in a consumption fever that puts a dangerous burden on the planet's sustainability. There are news reports in the mass media that do little to help people understand the world they live in as they frame issues in ways that serve the interests of small, political, and economic elites.

Also, there are developments in information and communication technology (ICT) that facilitate an unprecedented invasion into people's private lives and that create very vulnerable societies. Added to this, there are the combined innovations in robotics, artificial intelligence, nanotechnology, and biomedical technology that fly humanity – blindly – towards a future that may not need human beings anymore. These developments also make a new type of global warfare in cyberspace possible.

In the following chapters I will address the different dimensions of global communication. It is important to keep the features of its context in mind and to consider the perspectives and challenges of global communication against the background of trans-localization, urbanization, institutionalization, inequality, and global risks.

Note

1. www.nua.com/surveys/how_many_online/index.html

Reading spotlight

Globalisation

Amin, S. (1976). *Un-Equal Development*. New York: The Monthly Review Press.
> In a provocative essay Amin analyzes how the advanced capitalist countries have strengthened relations of dependence and dominance between rich and poor countries.

Duchrow, U. and Hinkelammert, F.J. (2004). *Property for People, Not for Profit: Alternatives to the Global Tyranny of Capital*. London: Zed Books.
> This book takes up the core issue of capitalist globalisation: property. It offers a critical analysis of the neo-liberal notion of property and argues how this leads to worldwide impoverishment and devastation.

Giddens, A. (1990). *The Consequences of Modernity*. Cambridge: Polity Press.
> In this major theoretical statement, the author offers a new and provocative interpretation of institutional transformations associated with modernity. What is modernity? The author suggests, "As a first approximation, let us simply say the following: 'modernity' refers to modes of social life or organization which emerged in Europe from about the seventeenth century onwards and which subsequently became more or less worldwide in their influence."

Gray, J. (1998). *False Dawn: The Delusions of Global Capitalism*. London: Granta Books.
> John Gray argues that a global free market is an artificial construction that does not lead to universal prosperity but to chaotic problems. The book also offers a critical analysis of the Enlightenment faith in reason as a major cause of a laissez-faire capitalism that is presently collapsing.

Greider, W. (1997). *One World, Ready or Not: The Manic Logic of Global Capitalism*. New York: Touchstone.

> A challenging and penetrating analysis of the global economy that makes enormous accumulations of wealth possible as well as destroys lives of ordinary people around the world.

Global communication

Fortner, R.S. (1993). *International Communication. History, Conflict and Control of the Global Metropolis*. Belmont: Wadsworth Publishing Company.

> A book that offers a broad introduction to the understanding of global communication. The history of international mass media systems is described and their political, economical, legal and cultural dimensions are discussed. A concluding chapter addresses the future of the international communication system.

Golan, G.J., Johnson, Th. J., and Wanta, W. (eds) (2010). *International Media Communication in a Global Age*. London, Routledge.

> A reader that offers an overview of recent reseach on global communication. Attention for theoretical insights. Focusses on journalism, public relations, advertising and media ownership.

Kamalipour, Y.R. (2007). *Global Communication* (2nd edition). Belmont, CA: Thomson/Wadsworth.

> A reader with well-documented chapters on the history, theory, economics and politics of global comunication. There are also very insightful contributions about the Internet, national development, culture, propaganda and advertising.

Mattelart, A. (1994). *Mapping World Communication: War, Progress, Culture*. Minneapolis, MN: University of Minnesota Press.

> Mattelart analyzes historical, technical and theoretical aspects of global communication with the support of a broad range of documentary sources. The map he uses directs the reader to the service that communication renders to war-making, to the promotion of progress, and to communication as culture.

Thussu, D.K. (2000/2006). *International Communication: Continuity and Change*. London: Hodder Arnold.

> A textbook for students in media and cultural studies. The book offers an examination of important changes in the field of global communication. The author analyzes the expansion of media and telecommunication corporations and explores the impact on worldwide audiences. Case studies are found throughout the book.

Thussu, D.K. (ed.) (2010). *International Communication: A Reader*. London: Routledge.

> A comprehensive reader that offers essential academic texts (older and more recent) and policy documents in the field of global communication. References to relevant websites and a chronology of developments in global communication.

Online resources

Visit the book's companion website at **https://study.sagepub.com/hamelink** to watch the author discussing the theme of this chapter: **Global Communication: The Field**

Visit the book's companion website at **https://study.sagepub.com/hamelink** to access the following journal articles free of charge:

Bilcreyst, D. and Meers, Ph. (2000). The international telenovela debate and the contra-flow argument: a reappraisal. *Media, Culture & Society*, 22(4): 393–413.

Boyd-Barrett, O. (2006). Cyberspace, globalization and empire. *Global Media and Communication*, 12(3): 21–41.

Chalaby, J.K. (2005). From internationalization to transnationalization. *Global Media and Communication*, 1(1): 28–33.

Mattelart, A. (1992). An archaeology of the global era: constructing a belief. *Media, Culture & Society*, 24(5): 591–612.

Sparks, C. (2007). What's wrong with globalization? *Global Media and Communication*, 3(2): 133–155.

Sreberny, A. (2005). Contradictions of the globalizing moment. *Global Media and Communication*, 1(1): 11–15.

Further reading

Albrow, M. and King, E. (eds) (1990). *Globalization, Knowledge and Society*. London: Sage.

Appiah, K.A. (2006). *Cosmopolitanism. Ethics in a World of Strangers*. New York: W.W. Norton & Co.

Beck, U. (2006). *The Cosmopolitan Vision*. Cambridge: Polity Press.

Benhabib, S. (2006). *Another Cosmopolitanism*. Oxford: Oxford University Press.

Featherstone, M. (ed.) (1990). *Global Culture: Nationalism, Globalization and Modernity*. London: Sage.

Fisher, G. (1979). *American communication in a Global Society*. Norwood, NJ: Ablex Publishing.

Frederick, H.H. (1993). *Global Communication and International Relations*. Belmont, CA: Wadsworth.

Hamelink, C.J. (1994). *World Communication: Disempowerment and Self-Empowerment*. London: Zed Books.

Herman, E. and McChesney, R. (1997). *The Global Media: The News Missionaries of Global Capitalism*. London: Cassell.

Kaplinsky, R. (2005). *Globalization, Poverty and Inequality*. Cambridge: Polity Press.

Kofman, E. and Youngs, G. (eds) (1996). *Globalization Theory and Practice*. London: Pinter.

McPhail, Th.L. (2002). *Global Communication: Theories, Stakeholders, and Trends*. Boston, MA: Allyn & Bacon.

Mowlana, H. (1997). *Global Information and World Communication*. London: Sage.

Murphy, B. (1983). *The World Wired Up*. London: Comedia Publishing.

Nordenstreng, K. and Schiller, H.I. (1993). *Beyond National Sovereignty: International Communication in the 1990s*. Norwood, NJ: Ablex Publishing.

Schiller, H.I. (1982). *Who Knows: Information in the Age of the Fortune 500*. Norwood, NJ: Ablex Publishing.

Scholte, J.A. (2000). *Globalization: A Critical Introduction*. New York: Palgrave.

Thomson, J. (1998). Will globalization be good for Americans? *Futures Research Quarterly*, 14(3): 5–18.

Tunstall, J. and Palmer, M. (1991). *Media Moguls*. London: Routledge.

RESEARCH ASSIGNMENT

What does the growth of urbanization mean for global communication?

Collect data on the growth of worldwide urbanization. Use such sources as the United Nations Habitat Reports.

Write a well-argued assessment of how the process of urbanization may affect global communication: its players, its contents and its effects on global audiences.

Would you interview experts on this question? How would you select them? How would you approach them? What questions would you ask?

HOW TO STUDY GLOBAL COMMUNICATION

2

Jim Halloran could very persistently and eloquently plead for an approach to the study of communication that would comprehensively research the production, content, and reception of flows of media messages. He was in many respects an exceptionally inspiring friend and colleague.

─── James Dermott Halloran (1927–2007) ───

Halloran's interests were wide-ranging, covering policy-making, mass media effects, violence, television for children, journalism, development, media education, technology, and international issues. Halloran repeatedly reminded his colleagues that we need to define problems adequately so we can ask the right questions. He would famously remark that "if we ask silly questions we will get silly answers". He thought that many of the questions asked by communication researchers were indeed silly questions.

Halloran was Professor and Director of the Centre for Mass Communication Research at the University of Leicester from 1966 to 1991. He was also (from 1972 to 1990) President of the International Association for Mass Communication Research, now called the International Association for Media and Communication Research.

For researching global communication, his major publications are: "International democratization of communication: the challenge for research" (1986); *Mass Media in Society: The Need of Research*. UNESCO Reports and Papers on Mass Communication, No. 59 (1970); "Research in forbidden territory" (1973); and "The context of communication research" (1981).

For the study of global communication, James Halloran taught us to critically reflect on the societal context(s) within which global communication functions.

- Now we pose the question how can we study global communication?
- The issue of theorizing must be addressed.
- The most important obstacles that hamper the study of global communication will then be identified.
- The proposal that two analytical perspectives and one normative perspective may guide the study of global communication completes the chapter.

Approaches to the study of global communication

The academic interest in the phenomenon of global communication has two parents: the study of mass communication and the study of international relations. From the study of mass communication, the field inherited an empirical and normative interest in media contents, their effects, the practices of production and distribution, and the position and role of audiences. From the study of international relations, the field inherited such focal points as the power politics (hard and soft) of empire, the ideals of world peace, and the inequality of North–South relations.

What distinguishes the study of global communication from other forms of communication (local, national) is that it requires the analysis of the wider context of global realities. The study of global communication has travelled through a variety of theoretical approaches, such as were found in studies on propaganda, modernization, cultural imperialism, information society, and globalization. These different approaches were never combined into one comprehensive grand theory and in most cases there was even very little empirical testing of the hypotheses such studies implied.

The first studies on global communication were inspired by propaganda activities during the two world wars of the twentieth century. Intrigued by allied propaganda during the First World War, Harold D. Lasswell wrote his *Theory of Political Propaganda in 1927*. The widespread use of propaganda preceding and during the Second World War inspired studies about the significance of short-wave radio, such as *Propaganda by Short Wave*, by Harwood Childs and John B. Whitton (1942), and Hans Speier's *German Radio Propaganda* (1944).

In 1952, Paul Lazarsfeld noted in *Public Opinion Quarterly* an upsurge of interest in global communication research. That academic interest focused largely on the role of media in processes of national development, the inequality of global information flows, the relationship between mass communication and power, and normative questions about mass media practices. Researchers began to document that much international media content was being produced in the North, and specifically in the United States, and was disseminated across the globe in uneven quantities. They observed that there was more information traffic among the countries of the North than between the North and South.

The favourite theoretical explanation that was applied to this empirical reality used an "imperialist" conceptual framework. Its core message was that contents were "imposed" by stronger actors on weaker actors. There was at the time also a competing theoretical explanation that was based on the notion of "diffusion" (particularly elaborated by Everett Rogers (1962)) and that proposed that transfers of content were largely related to "cultural proximity": there would be more diffusion of cultural products, such as news or TV entertainment, among actors that shared similar values.

A first study that comparatively analyzed normative positions on mass media in a global context was presented in a book entitled *Four Theories of the Press* (Siebert, Peterson and Schramm, 1956). The authors divided the media into four categories: authoritarian, liberal, Soviet and social responsibility. They concluded that the social responsibility model was their preference.

To their four normative approaches (reviewed in, among others, Nordenstreng, 1997) Denis McQuail (1983) added later the development model and the participatory/democratic model. In 2009, Christians, Glasser, McQuail, Nordenstreng, and White took the *Four Theories of the Press* as the starting point for an exploration of the role of journalism in democratic societies.

In the post-1945 world politics (and particularly in the agencies of the United Nations) the issue of national development became a priority. In the 1950s, studies on the role of mass media in national development had emerged. Key authors were Daniel Lerner (1958), with *The Passing of Traditional Society*, and Wilbur Schramm, with *Mass Media and National Development* (1964).

Their theoretical approach conceived of processes of development as transitions from "traditional" societies towards "modern" societies with the mass media as crucial multipliers of social transformation. As Thussu wrote:

> This top-down approach to communications … was predicated on a definition of development that followed the model of Western industrialization and modernization. …
> The international communication research inspired by the modernization thesis was very influential, shaping university communication programmes and research centres globally. (Thussu, 2005: 44)

In the 1960s, a different approach to problems of development and under-development came up, with concepts such as "dependencia" (see especially Frank, 1969, and Amin, 1976) and cultural imperialism (Schiller, 1976).

Global communication was conceived as a process that – under the guise of a "free flow of information" doctrine – contributed to the economic, political and cultural dependence of receiving nations (mainly poor, "under-developed", Third World countries) upon sending nations (mainly rich, "developed", Western countries). Imperialism and dependency theorists proposed relationships between centre countries and peripheral countries, between which communication was characterized by the one-directionality of informational and cultural flows. The word "imperialism" referred to the politics of states to expand their empire and thus their sphere of power and influence. The word "cultural imperialism" referred to the historical fact that in imperial expansion cultural forces have always played a significant role. Illustrations are Christian missionary activities, the introduction of Western-style school systems, forms of colonial administration, modern conceptions of professionalism, and the use of European languages in overseas colonies. The essence of "cultural imperialism" is that in achieving the domination of one nation over other nations, cultural sources of power and influence are of key importance. Cultural imperialism will be discussed further in Chapter 11 on the cultural dimensions of global communications.

From the 1960s, yet another approach emerged that would turn out to be essential in the study of global communication. This was the political economy approach. Among its most important representatives were Nicholas Garnham, Peter Golding, Graham Murdock, Vincent Mosco, Robert McChesney, Herbert I. Schiller, Dallas Smythe and Janet Wasko (see the selected key texts and further reading sections of Chapter 4). The focus of their approach, which was rooted in the Marxist tradition, was upon the relations between communication and the structures of economic and political power. Much thinking in the political economy approach was inspired by Harold Innis (1972) and his study of communication and empire. Innis had demonstrated that communication was an essential organizational tool in imperial projects to expand power beyond territorial borders in order to protect imperial positions of power, to compensate for deficiencies in natural resources, or to achieve more wealth and more standing (respect, influence, glamour). Innis (1972) distinguished between time-biased media (e.g. stone tablets and parchment that could store messages for a very long time) and space-biased media (such as papyrus, which had less durability but more flexibility for transportation). Space-biased technologies favoured the monopolization of knowledge (for instance, by the Egyptian priest-scribes) and the expansion of political power (imperialism) and, in the historical process, lost against time-biased technologies that could more easily distribute access to knowledge.

Next to the political-economy focus on structures of ownership and control of global mass media, the Birmingham School (Stuart Hall) provided a different type of analysis that focused upon popular and mass culture and their role in shaping societal relations. The leading theorists of this cultural studies approach asked questions about how the media create globally shared values and meanings and how, with the spread of migration flows and diaspora communities, cultural resistance was developed through processes of hybridity or hybridization (Jan Nederveen Pieterse and Arjun Appadurai).

In the course of the 1990s a key concept in studies on international developments and trends in communication became "globalization". A host of studies appeared on media in a global context with authors such as Daya K. Thussu (2007), Joseph Straubhaar (2007), Ole Mjos (2010), and Alexandra Robertson (2010). Also, an important stream of studies emerged that were inspired by authors such as Marshall McLuhan (1964), Daniel Bell (1973), and Alvin Toffler (1980). These studied global communication from the perspective of the information society (Frank Webster and Manuel Castells).

It has become common practice to describe modern societies with the concept "information society" and it is important to give some attention to this attractive but also seriously contested analytical tool. In a general sense, it refers to increases in available volumes of information, the significance of information processing in ever more societal domains, and the fact that information technology provides a basic infrastructure upon which societies become increasingly dependent. However adequate this may be, it is questionable whether one can adequately describe societies with a single encompassing variable only, and even if this were possible it can be questioned whether information is a more precise category than money, crime, or aggression. In any case, it should be noted that societies pursue very different paths of development and if one insists on the reference to information, the plural notion of "information societies" should be used. There is no accepted definition of what the information society is. The meaning of the notion has been seriously challenged and it has even been suggested in the academic literature that the notion bears no relation to current social realities. For some observers, it only makes sense to speak in the plural sense about "Information Societies". For others, the reference to "society" raises the good old sociological questions of power, profit, and participation: who controls the information society, who benefits from it, who takes part in it? The Information Society means different things to different people: more telephones, or more money, or more regulation, or more empowerment. For all participants in the debate there is the feeling that important social and technical developments confront us with difficult questions and that our societies are struggling to find adequate answers.

There are undoubtedly "informational developments" in modern societies, and through interaction with other social developments these will have an impact on how the future of such societies shape up in different ways, dependent upon different historical circumstances.

In much of the current literature it is suggested – in "utopian scenarios" – that these developments have positive effects whereas negative effects are highlighted in "dystopian scenarios". In both cases, the analysts are driven by a deterministic perspective on social development: technological innovations have a direct impact on social processes. There is no space for reflection on the myriad complex ways in which technology and society are dialectically interlinked.

This is particularly serious since these informational developments often take place in the context of an uninhibited technological euphoria, propose political claims that are difficult to empirically substantiate, and ignore in their singular emphasis on information the more important social process of communication. Societies and informational developments interact with each other in many different ways. We can differentiate between the following four dimensions to these interactions.

There is a *technological dimension* to the interaction. Technology obviously plays a vital role in informational developments. The scope, volume, and impact of these developments is, to a large extent, shaped by technological innovations and the opportunities they create. The interaction is a process in which social forces and interests contribute to the shaping of technological innovations. With this dimension, issues are posed about the control over technology, the access to and benefit from technology, and the social risks that innovations and their applications entail.

There is also a *cultural dimension* to the interaction. The ways in which societies deal with the provision and processing of information are determined by cultural perspectives. Information contents are cultural products. Information is part of a society's cultural fabric. Among the important issues of this dimension are the sharing of knowledge and protection of cultural identity.

There is a *socio-political dimension* to the interaction. Information and communication technologies have an impact on society's development, progress, and political system. Among the important issues are freedom of political speech, protection against abusive speech, and information needs of societies.

There is an *economic dimension* to the interaction. Worldwide information markets have emerged. Economic interests are at stake in the protection of ownership claims to content. There are issues of corporate social responsibility and self-determination in economic development.

In the context of a widespread technology euphoria, it is quite common to find in information society debates the following expectations. Through harnessing the potential of information and communication technology, better responses to poverty reduction, equity, and social justice can be found. Knowledge and information constitute one of the fundamental sources of well-being and progress. There is a great untapped potential of ICT to improve productivity and quality of life. The benefits of the information society should extend to all and should be development-oriented. In building an information society, it should be ensured that women can equally benefit from the increased use of ICTs for empowerment and fully participate in shaping political, economic, and social development. The information society should be oriented towards eliminating existing socio-economic differences in our societies.

All the buzzwords from past decades are used in the current debate and literature: democracy, diversity, capacity, participation, gender, bridging the gap. However, the nagging question is why such aspirations have so far not been taken seriously by the international community. Why has the international community been unwilling in past decades to engage in real efforts to implement what it preaches? This is all the more problematic because the socio-economic and political conditions under which these claims should become reality are not at all encouraging. As a matter of fact, they are less amenable to the solution of the digital divide through the development of telecom infrastructures or access to knowledge than the conditions that prevailed during the time of the earlier UN efforts.

Before embarking on a new promising statement about the potential of the information society, it would be wise to analyze why at present the world is not an inclusive community, why there is no sustainable development, why there is no global transparent and accountable governance, why citizens cannot participate on an equal footing in their societies. There is much discussion on governance of the information society. The diplomatic and academic rhetoric uses notions such as multi-stakeholder participation, democratic decision-making, transparency, and accountability. Yet why would global governance of the information society have all the characteristics that other domains of such govern-ance do not have? Why would governments be trusted to want people-centred governance? Why would major global corporations strive towards greater transparency to the public and more accountability?

Information

Essential to the notion of the information society is obviously "information" itself. Much thinking about the future of information societies is based upon a series of popular myths, such as: more information is better than less information, more information creates more knowledge and understanding, open information flows contribute to the prevention of conflicts, more information means less uncertainty and more adequate choices, if people are properly informed they act accordingly, more information equals more power and once people are better informed about each other, they will understand each other and be less inclined to conflict. All very attractive assumptions but none is necessarily true!

A very popular assumption claims that information equals power. Information becomes a source of power only if the necessary infrastructure for its production, process-ing, storage, retrieval, and transportation is accessible, and when people have the skills to apply information to social practice and to participate in social networks through which information can be used to further one's interests. The assumption proposes that people were never able to exercise power because they were ill-informed and ignorant. However, too often people knew precisely what was wrong and unjust, and they were very well informed about the misconduct of their rulers. Yet they did not act, and their knowledge did not become a source of power because they lacked the material and strategic means for revolt!

A very attractive line of thought proposes that once people are better informed about each other, they will know and understand each other better and be less inclined to con-flict. However, deadly conflicts are usually not caused by a lack of information. In fact, they may be based upon very adequate information that adversaries have about each other. As a matter of fact, one could equally well propound the view that social harmony is largely due to the degree of ignorance that actors have with regard to each other. In many societies members engage with each other without having detailed information about the others. There may indeed be conflict situations because adversaries have so much information about each other's aims and motives. There are situations in which more information is not better than less information. If we all had detailed information about other people that we live and work with, the chance of raging civil war would be very great.

Most assumptions about the role and effects of information and knowledge are based upon seriously flawed cause–effect models. Information and knowledge are conceived as key variables in social processes and, dependent upon how they are manipulated, certain social effects will occur. Social science research has taught us, however, that information and knowledge-sharing do not occur in the linear mode of simple stimulus–response models that propose linear, causal relations between information/knowledge inputs and social outputs.

These processes are more complex, involve feedback mechanisms, and somewhere between the message and the receiver there are intervening black box variables that may create both predictable, expected and desirable as well as unpredictable, unexpected and undesirable effects. Even the best of peace-building information is no guarantee that people will behave peacefully!

Moreover, we have to be sceptical about all the expectations that are projected onto what more information does to human interactions. Such expectations are essential if one believes that social conflict is primarily caused by inadequate information. From this reasoning, it follows that conflicts will be resolved once adversaries have the correct information about each other. This suggests that if adversaries knew more about each other, it would be easier for them to reach agreement. It is, however, difficult to find empirical evidence for this suggestion and one could equally well propound the view that social harmony is largely due to the degree of ignorance that actors have *vis-à-vis* each other. As a matter of fact, many societies maintain levels of stability because they employ rituals, customs, and conventions that enable their members to engage in social interactions without having detailed information about who they really are.

The expectations about the power of information neglect the fact that conflicts often address very real points of contention and may be based upon the antagonistic interests of fundamentally divergent political and economic systems. There may indeed be a conflict situation precisely because adversaries have full and detailed information about each other's aims and motives. If disputes are about competing claims to scarce resources (as often is the case), it is unlikely that distorted communication is the crucial variable or that correction of this distortion would resolve the conflict. Moreover, precisely in situations of conflict, the problem is often the abundance of information rather than the dearth of it. The overload of messages may seriously impede rational decision-making since the means through which humans cope with information (selective filtering, stereotyping, and simplistic structuring) results in misperceptions and incorrect interpretations.

What happened to communication?

There is in current public debate, policy, and practice a strong emphasis on the importance of information and information technology. It is disconcerting that in much of this debate "communication" has practically disappeared. Yet, for the resolution of the world's most pressing problems we do not need more information processing but the capacity to communicate. Ironically, as our capacity to process and distribute information and knowledge expands and improves, our capacity to communicate and to converse diminishes. More and more people worldwide are interconnected through high-speed, broadband digital networks. However, connecting is not the same as communicating. The real core question for research in the coming years may be how to shape "communication societies".

The globalization of localized networks through network media such as YouTube promises new potential for global communication. Since in the early twenty-first century the reality of global communication is rapidly changing. With the emergence of global, digital social networks, consumer-generated content, and a host of new actors, researchers are challenged to explore new theoretical approaches that explain these new realities. Today, a conceptual framework is needed that encompasses notions such as two-way and interactive flows, empowerment, localization, and hybridization. A phenomenon like Web 2.0 can no longer be adequately described in terms of one-way flows, imposition, domination, and homogenization.

Is there a theory of global communication?

Scientists look in systematic ways at selected phenomena, collect information about the behaviour of these phenomena, and seek to develop theories on the phenomena they study in order to better understand and explain them. What we would like to understand and explain about global communication is:

- How it evolved over time and expanded in volume and actors.
- How it is organized (in what institutional forms) and how these are owned and managed.
- How discursive power is exercised by and through global communication.
- What (economic, political, or cultural) impact global communication may have and what specific functions it fulfils.
- How worldwide audiences respond to and deal with global communication.

There is not in fact an overwhelmingly large volume of theories that could help us to find valid answers to these questions. Actually, communication science is not very well equipped for this exercise. The field is haunted by a paucity of theoretical reflection, particularly in the area of global communication.

On theorizing

The basic ingredients of all scientific study are observation and interpretation. The main purpose of science is to understand phenomena in the social and natural world around us. We want to understand where these phenomena come from, why they behave as they do, and how and why they relate to other phenomena.

Marcel Proust wrote that "the act of discovery is not in finding new lands, but in seeing with new eyes". This is what the scientific exercise requires: "seeing with new eyes". The core business of all scientific work is observation. "Seeing with new eyes" can find guidance in the story of the child who asks his mother what she thinks about when she peels the potatoes. Her reflexive answer is: "I think about the potatoness of potatoes".

Early in the last century the Austrian engineer Viktor Schauberger predicted that the water management methods practised on the Danube would in time cause dramatic flooding. His ideas came from watching the Danube for hours and days trying to understand the nature of water: the "wateriness of water". On the basis of his seeing with new eyes, he made revolutionary water management proposals that were lost in the troubles of the Second World War but that do attract today a great deal of interest.

In order to interpret, understand, and explain the phenomena we study, theories are needed. Etymologically, the word "theory" comes from the Greek *theoria*, which means "vision". Science needs visions that put natural and social phenomena into a perspective so they become manageable and controllable. Theories can be explanatory (why does this happen?), predictive (what will happen next?), heuristic (what are the right questions), or normative (what should happen?). Theories are tools that may lead us to achieve validated knowledge. They consist of a set of concepts that enable us to formulate testable hypotheses. There is a multitude of theoretical approaches to assist the understanding of mass communication, ranging from theories about agenda-setting, framing, and priming to theories from structural, behaviourist or culturalist traditions (McQuail, 2000: 12). According to McQuail (2000), four kinds of theory relevant to mass communication can be distinguished:

- Social science theory, which is a set of ideas about the nature, working, and effects of mass communication.
- Normative theory, which is a set of ideas about how media ought to operate if certain social values are to be attained.
- Operational theory, which is a set of ideas assembled and applied by media practitioners in the conduct of their work.
- Common-sense theory, which is a set of ideas that we all have from our personal experience with the media.

For the study of global mass communication, McQuail (2000: 215–240) suggests the following domains: the new driving forces of technology and money; ownership and control of international media; cultural imperialism; dependency; national and cultural identity; transnationalization of media; international news flows; and the global trade in media culture.

McQuail's very useful overview convincingly demonstrates that the mass media are a valid object of scientific theorizing. However, as he notes, media theorizing is "still very fragmentary and also variable in quality. It often amounts to little more than a posing of many questions plus some empirical generalizations based on a disparate set of observations that are not fully representative of the enormous range of situations where the media are at work" (McQuail, 2000: 479). This does not sound like a summary statement that would inspire policymakers to look for responses to the problems they are expected to resolve. And yet, it could be argued that policymakers face a set of issues in the media field that might benefit from media theory.

Communication theory and communication policy

Prominent among communication policy issues are: the concentration of media ownership versus pluralism and access for multiple voices in the media; the protection of the constitutional value of free speech versus the possible damage of hate speech; the control of harmful media content (for example, in connection with children) and the risks of censorship; the professional responsibilities of journalists versus their professional autonomy; the cultural significance of media in relation to cultural diversity, the protection of cultural identity, societal integration, and the role of minorities; the protection of citizens against commercial advertising and political propaganda; the protection of intellectual property in relations to the knowledge society aspiration; the question of how to finance public media; and the confrontation between openness and secrecy in democratic societies. If one expects theorists and policymakers to engage in a productive relationship over such issues, we have first to signal that theory and policy – in a general sense – belong to different fields.

The theory–policy relation can be seen as a knowledge–political action gap. In the policy analysis literature, this has been analyzed in terms of conflicting sets of values, different organizational formats, and as a clash of knowledge versus power. Science and politics are often seen as worlds apart with their own organizing principles. Among others, Luhmann (1971) has suggested that science is driven by the principle of "truth" and politics is steered by the principle of "power".

However, as in the political world also in science, there is a competitive struggle for resources, credits, and public attention which certainly involves discursive (communicative, symbolic, and cognitive) modalities of power. And – to some extent – knowledge is power and power is knowledge. The relationship is often a producer–client interaction. This is the case when policymakers commission science to undertake research efforts. The research results may be used, but this is often unnoticed as policymakers may rewrite or edit results to suit the interests of their world.

Harold Lasswell (1971) wanted, through his media research, to make better information available to policymakers. Using the best available evidence as the basis of political decision-making may sound attractive, but political decision-makers are not necessarily interested in this rational approach to decision-making? Policy processes are not characterized by rationality but rather by emotional and subjective factors.

As Ithiel de Sola Pool observed, in the end media policy is guided by politics and not by academic reflection. Media policymaking is an activity with a (general or specific) purpose in mind or a problem to be resolved.

Policymakers have an agenda that is inspired by certain values and therefore seeks information that suits political decision-making. Research may produce usable or non-usable information. For the information to be usable the researcher needs to operate within the frame defined by the political system.

It is arguably a naïve expectation to want policymakers to be seriously concerned about the theoretical underpinnings of their proposals. Policies are made to achieve certain objectives and in case theory provides support for the means applied to reach these objectives it will be accepted as useful. The theory that does not fulfil this "alibi" function will be discarded. More important, however, is that implied in the expected use of theory by policymakers is the assumption that they want to be fully informed. In the practice of political decision-making, for example, the preference is often for a playing field with not too much information as this leaves the space for flexibility in manoeuvring conveniently open.

Where policymakers may want conclusive answers, they demand too much of the field of science. On many essential questions science is speechless and must admit to an ignorance and uncertainty that the policymakers are likely to experience as useless. Where policymakers may want strong theoretical and empirical evidence of the manipulative power of the media, academics may want to offer a set of qualifying footnotes that – at best – will lead practitioners and politicians to wonder whether any media policy is needed at all.

An additional problem is that policymaking in the field of the media is very controversial. Media are typically a domain where professional autonomy is considered to need no external rules or controls. The mass media – certainly in Western countries – fall under the protection of liberal claims to less state (policy) and more (uncontrolled) market. Communication plans and policies have always been more popular in so-called Third World countries. In the1970s, particularly in the United Nations agency UNESCO, there was a strong movement for the planning of national communication policies but relevant theoretical instruments were not available. Immediately after the Second World War there was considerable interest in media-related policy research. This was understandable because of the general sentiment of the engineerable society, the aspiration to create a better world, and the new available instruments for social sciences research. Media research developed in what came to be called the administrative, bureaucratic applied tradition that largely served dominant political and commercial interests. Its critical counterpart also emerged but this was not seen by power holders as useful to their interests.

Moreover, it should be questioned whether available research can provide the best evidence because the conclusions are usually incomplete, inconclusive, contestable, and they change in the course of time. Could a policymaker who would carefully study McQuail's textbook find sufficiently robust media theories that could help to design solutions for pressing policy issues? By and large, these studies fail to address such essential issues as what type of political institutions and practices we need to meet the challenges of the future. They provide little if any meaningful guidance to the choices we face. And therefore they do not seriously assist the task of public policymaking in the field of global communication.

Part of the blame for the unproductive theory–policy encounter can also be addressed to the policymaking field for its opportunism, lack of analytical rigour, and often anti-intellectualist hostility. Most studies undertaken on the impact of social research on public policy are rather discouraging. A constant finding is that a good 50 per cent of civil servants totally ignore research and some 40 per cent, even if hard pressed, find it difficult to point to research they would consider useful. Social scientific research, if used at all, mainly serves the improvement of bureaucratic efficiency, the delay of action, the avoidance of responsibility, or functions to discredit opponents, to maintain prestige, or to ask for more research.

Problems with theory

- Social science theories are underdetermined.
- Theories about human behaviour are influenced by theological notions.
- Theories about human societies have a European/American bias.

Underdetermined

As was earlier mentioned, most theories are "underdetermined", meaning that the empirical data are no definite arbiters on the validity of theory A versus theory B. We can never collect the data comprehensively. Empirical realities change over time. All social concepts are essentially contestable. The notion of contestability was introduced in philosophy by W.B. Gallie (1956) and was developed for the social sciences by, among others, W. Connolly and S. Lukes. This raises the question whether we can ever establish that a theory explains reality in a reliable and valid manner? We may do well to follow the advice of Thomas Kuhn (1996: 147), who proposed that theories should be compared (he calls this paradigm testing) through a "joint verification-falsification process". As he argues, "It makes a great deal of sense to ask which of two actual and competing theories fits the facts better". We should thus always try to identify competing explanations and find arguments for the best match with reality. This is, however, complicated by the realization that we do not have definitive standards to judge the superiority of one theory over another: the theory that all swans are white appears to be confirmed by our daily observation of white swans but is valid only until a black swan is found (Popper, 1959: 27).

There is no one single grand theory to comprehend global communication. The phenomenon "global communication" is extensive, complex, and fast-moving! Its study needs all the help it can get from ethnography, content and discourse analysis, audience studies, economic analysis, political science, (social) psychology, sociology, anthropology, and cultural studies. We have to rely on multiple sources of understanding and use them in eclectic ways.

Secular theology

In his book *In de schaduw van God* [*In God's Shade*], Harry van den Bouwhuijsen (2010) argues that theory in human and social sciences is in fact secular theology. The portrayal of the human being on which these sciences are based is derived from a tradition of monotheistic Christian thinking. Theological fictions not only determine the view of the "self", but also of the "other". The self is largely viewed as an individual person with a free will and with the capacity to account for his/her actions and to explain the intentions of his/her actions. Western social science searches for motivations and intentions of human behaviour, assuming that human beings can know themselves. This assumption is not universally shared.

For the Indian image of self (for example, in the Mahabharata epos), the question of why are you doing something makes no sense. You act in way X because you are X and there are no other motives. The Navaho Indians think that why-questions are foolish. The Mexican Zapotec say we look at the face, we do not know what is in the heart. On Papua New-Guinea and among the Himalayan Sherpas there is no interest in intentions of actions. Understanding the other means accepting what he does.

In the Christian tradition, the Other is seen as ultimately not different from the self. There is a strong drive towards discarding differences, and focussing on unity, universality and the conversion of those who think they are different. We are all descendants from Abraham, and differences are only temporal, eventually they will disappear.

St Paul declares, in his letters to the Colossians (3:11) and the Galatians (3:28), that there are no fundamental differences: we are all one. When the Amerindians had to fit into this biblical imagery, Pope Paul III (1537) declared them real human beings. They could receive the Christian faith and were potential Christians (van den Bouwhuijsen, 2010: 155). Of course, they were killed when the mission of conversion failed.

This secular theology, which is also dominant in communication studies, hampers a real, global understanding of communicating with "others" across the world. In studies on intercultural communication, for example, there is a general tendency to propose models ("tricks") that enable "us" to communicate with "them". They are in principle like us, only a bit different, and we need to learn how to deal with their deviance from us.

The concept of the Other as an exotic or deviant variant of the Self poses a deep obstacle to intercultural communication. Most studies in this field are based upon Western social science concepts that are taken to be universal, although they may not exist somewhere else.

Euro-American centrism

Across the world there has been a Euro-American dominance in media and communication research. In a rather uncritical way, models and theories with a British/American origin were accepted by students of communication in other parts of the world.

In recent years the growing recognition of Eurocentrism in communication theories has fuelled discontent among some Asian researchers (Wang, 2011: 2). The growing discontent and critical self-examination did lead to the emergence of an Asian communication paradigm and to a discussion about the need to "de-Westernize".

The critique of Western theories addresses such issues as the tendency to dichotomize (creating either/or divisions, e.g. between individualism versus collectivism in cultures), and to conceive communication largely as a linear, rational process of persuasion. According to Asante (2011: 21), the Western paradigmatic approach has distorted human reality. It suggested that the forces that drove European developments during the Renaissance and the Enlightenment, such as material conquest and domination over nature, were universal forces.

"The ultimate objective is not simply a critique of the West, but a suggestion of a way forward in our thinking and relating by detaching ourselves from a colonizing ideology" (Asante, 2011: 21). Asante does not want to replace the West with the East or the South, but wants to eliminate the hierarchical system in which Western philosophy claims its knowledge to be universal. What is needed is a "commensurable universality" in which diversity is recognized and there is an engagement in a global intellectual dialogue that enables comparison and evaluation.

For the study of global communication to become really global, this would require that theories and experiences from outside the Western world should be integrated in the global production of knowledge. It means that the prevalence of Euro-American ideas and methods about communication have to be broken open in order to move beyond such Western paradigmatic constructs as modernization, dependency, imperialism, and globalization. As was proposed earlier, the term "trans-localization" may be helpful here as it liberates us from the global–local dichotomy in which the West is largely conceived as "global and modern" and the Rest as "local and traditional". Genuine global communication studies would free the local from its eternal opposition and subordination to the global (Kraidy, 2011: 51). Its observations and analyses would, for example, conclude that there are modernities and traditionalities across the West–Rest divide and propose the notion of "multiple modernities" (Kraidy, 2011: 54–56). This approach necessarily implies the need for dialogue in which the disappearance of a dominant paradigm challenges researchers to produce new creative theories and methodologies. The dialogue can prevent that Western centrism is exchanged for other forms of centrism and the epistemological fundamentalisms are simply swapped.

?

How can we avoid one type of centrism and fundamentalism (e.g. the Euro-American centrism and the parochial belief in its intellectual superiority) being exchanged for another type of centrism and fundamentalism (e.g. Asian centrism and an equally parochial belief in its universal validity)?

Problems with method

If you did not find a satisfactory theory to help your understanding of aspects of global communication, you can turn to the grounded theory method. This means that you do not begin with a theory-based hypothesis that you apply to the phenomenon you study. Here you begin with the collection of data, and from the essential points in your data you develop categories that form the basis for the development of a theory. In fact, this is a process of reverse engineering. There is a good literature that will introduce this approach to you (for example, Charmaz, 2006). It is also possible that you found a theoretical perspective that looks promising (and, as I will argue later, the Darwinian evolution theory is a good candidate).

In both cases you will still need a method (from the Greek *méthodos* = along the road): you need a road map in order to validly check the reliability of the preferred theoretical perspective. It is to be expected that you turn to the standard protocol for doing scientific research: the scientific method. The essential elements of this method are systematic observation and measurement in order to test the validity of hypotheses that are formulated such as to base testable predictions on them. The steps you take should be repeatable, transparent, and documented. So far so good, it would seem. However, there may be some problems with the assumptions on which the road map is based.

The first problem that you encounter now is that this method is based upon the proposition that the observer and the observed are separated from each other as the result of detached and impartial observation. However, from quantum physics we have learnt that the detached observer does not really exist since observation always influences that which is being observed. Observation implies asking questions of an object and responses will be framed by the manner of questioning.

The conventional scientific method is also based on the notion that phenomena that are observed can be reduced to and understood from their parts. The analysis of components of a system (be it a human body or a society) suggest the possibility to look at separate parts of a system. Physics, however, suggests that the properties of these parts depend upon the properties of the entire system. And the entire system is usually beyond the scope of the scientific analysis.

The next problem is that objective measurement and the probabilist nature of the phenomena you study are on a collision course. From the study of nature we know that nature is probabilistic. Its randomness means that developments in nature are uncertain, unpredictable, and so much embedded in chaos that their description is practically impossible. In the sense of the currently dominant scientific method, nature is "unknowable" (Stein, 2012: 36).

One more problem you will encounter is the classical binary thinking of modern Western science (true versus false; either versus or; us versus them) no longer holds much validity. Against this it is discovered that in complex realities (such as global communication) "A" may also be "non-A". Moreover, when you want to engage with questions about the future of global communication (as will be discussed in the final chapter) you will have to accept non-linear thinking and contradictions if you are open to surprises.

Important internal limitations to the conventional scientific method are – in a globalizing world – also reinforced by the encounter of Western and non-Western cultures, such as in the meeting of Aristotelian logic with Confucian thinking (as will be discussed in Chapter 11).

You, as students, live in exciting times, in which you will experience very fundamental changes in the scientific method as science accepts that its very foundations need rethinking.

The study of global communication as a steeplechase

Several obstacles need to be overcome for a meaningful study of global communication.

- The boundaries of academic disciplines
- The obsession with causality
- The "national" bias

Disciplines

An impediment for a real global understanding of communication is the common institutionalization of science into disciplines.

In recent years, the discovery was made in different research fields that it was necessary to move away from mono-disciplinarity to the engagement of various disciplinary experiences in research. Thus emerged multi-disciplinarity, in which research questions are studied with the help of more than one discipline. However, in multi-disciplinarity, the different disciplines may cooperate but stay within their own domain. In the interdisciplinary approach, research questions are treated through an exchange between different disciplines. For complex questions this is helpful but still not satisfactory. One more move is necessary to a trans-disciplinary approach. In trans-disciplinarity, scientific disciplines have to engage with multiple knowledges. This means that in addition to scientific knowledge, experiential and tacit knowledge from non-scientific sources also has to be taken seriously. This approach requires the insight that there is also solid and relevant knowledge outside the scientific community. Trans-disciplinarity means that learning becomes interactive co-learning. The creation of knowledge is in fact a communication process that involves both scientific experience and societal experience. The complexity of social problems demands the cooperation between a multitude of stakeholders that are guided by the insight that singular knowledge cannot solve complex social problems. As Klein et al. (2001: 7) observe, "transdisciplinarity is a new form of learning and problem solving involving cooperation between different parts of society and academia in order to meet the complex challenge of society".

Co-learning means that we are all specialists in multiple forms of knowledge about ourselves and the world in which we live. Some of us are specialists with a diploma, others are non-licensed specialists. In order to further multiply knowledges about ourselves and our world, both types of specialists need to cooperate. An obvious obstacle to co-learning is the organization of universities as disciplinary institutions that have no space for trans-disciplinary research. Also, most scientific journals and academic book series are categorized by mono-disciplines. It has to be realistically observed that trans-disciplinary publishing is not particularly helpful for the academic career.

The recent movement towards transdisciplinarity emerged with the discovery that knowledge as a singular entity is not particularly helpful in the multidimensional, multi-polar, complex and chaotic world in which we live. To understand the non-linear structure of our realities – that resemble the complexity of a tropical rainforest – we need multiple knowledges, which include scientific knowledge, narrative knowledge, intuitive knowledge, experiential knowledge, common sense, and indigenous knowl-edge. Moreover, we need to develop a democratic, interactive co-learning process between science and society that is steered by multidimensional interests and values. In the early twenty-first century we may have to consider a further move to extra-disciplinarity.

It is important to see that the disciplines as we know them today are in fact organiza-tional principles for the management of universities, for scientific publications, and for the distribution of research funds. They did not come about as the result of intellectual considerations. They are the result of specific historical and societal challenges, such as the French revolution (the mother of sociology), capitalism and Marxism (the fathers of economy), colonialism (the daughter of imperialism is, according to Lévi-Strauss, anthropology), and the Hobbesian challenge of solving war of all against all which inspired political science.

Communication studies emerged from a variety of disciplinary backgrounds and then developed in a discipline of its own. This discipline "…has lost touch with these other disci-plines, which, in turn, have now largely eliminated media from their research agendas and curricula" (Ekecranz, 2009: 76).

Communication science became a mono-discipline at the time when multi-disciplinarity, inter-disciplinarity, and even trans-disciplinarity were more important due to the difficulty of understanding the complexity of communication in a globaliz-ing word. Communication students became specialists precisely at the moment that communication has become more and more integrated into social, economic, and political systems.

For the study of global communication we have to question the global validity of a sys-tem of social sciences that was born from European realities and that was not the product of Asian, African, or Caribbean realities. It may well be that we have to liberate social (and communication) studies from their narrow origins and study global phenomena from a multitude of realities, experiences, and perspectives. It is obvious that this has wide-ranging institutional and epistemological implications.

Causality

An obstacle to understanding the complexity of global communication is the obsession with causality. The obsessive drive to find causal connections is so strong that scientists often forget that correlations are not proof of causal connections. That A and B occur together does not prove that A causes B, or vice versa. The discovery of causality has a great attraction. It brings academics political popularity, better fund-raising opportunities, and media attention. Media are most interested in science when causal connections are announced: between media violence and aggressive behaviour, between smoking and cancer, between flying and environmental destruction, or between food and health. Causality assumes a simple world of one-to-one linear relations. However, more often than not, scientists can only demonstrate (with grave reservations) a correlation, an association, and then speculate, hypothesize, and guess. The "causality obsession" is fatal for a realistic understanding of the world in which we live. We live in a reality of multiple causalities and it is probably impossible ever to single out one specific causal factor.

The national bias

It is commonly accepted that we live in nation-states. However, this concept poses a serious problem for the study of global communication. It combines a reference to geo-political administrative units with a reference to nations. Nation (the etymological root is the Latin word "*natus*", which translates as he/she is born) is in fact the tribe in which people live; it is the habitat where they share views and sentiments with their tribal community. Nation refers to collectives of people that share common elements, such as ancestry, language, or values. Among today's nations are the Inuits, Zapatistas, Maoris, and Apaches. Actually, all states are multi-nation states, or multi-tribal states. Nation-state wrongly suggests that there is only one tribe in the geo-political unit "state". Most countries have a considerable tribal diversity that states want to massage into the mould of "national" unity through integration policies and strict rules on immigration.

With the creation of the nation-state (through the Peace of Westphalia, 1648) such "nations" were sequestered within the (mostly artificial) borders of centralized administrative units (for governance, surveillance, control of violence through monopoly use, security, and care for infrastructural facilities) that were called "states". States became the decision-makers for nations. The biggest challenge for the nation-state is that it is in fact a multi-nation state with a variety of different and often competing polities (such as urban communities) that may share bonds with polities across national borders. The United Nations should be an association of diverse nations united in global cooperation. This is expressed in the UN Charter that says "We the peoples of this world". The Charter does not say "We the states of this world".

An important question therefore becomes how global communication can indeed be the communication between nations. Although states may aspire towards global perspectives, these will inevitable be bound up with particular interests. Individual states will shape global views "as much as possible in a mold favorable to a given set of national or social interests" (Castells, 2001: 161).

Many studies on global communication are rooted in a framework of national settings. Major research questions are, among others: how do international flows impact on national cultures? How can national autonomy be secured? How does international news flow impact upon national audiences?

Is this approach still useful in the currently changing global communication scape? National controls over international flows continue to be a concern! The role of national legislation and politics is a decisive factor in the shaping of global communication. Global media giants face limits imposed upon them by national governments (China, for example) or by regional political systems (such as the European Union). The basis of the leading theoretical frameworks on propaganda, media and development, and media imperialism was always "inter-nationalism", which provided, for example, the fundamental undergirding of the news flow studies. Such studies described and analyzed message traffic across national borders and between national systems. International news flows were national news flows across borders. Terhi Rantanen (2010) wrote that in these studies the media were primarily conceived of as national media.

Cross-national comparative studies have almost always taken the national society as unit of analysis! In most of these studies, societies were equated with nation-states.

The UN system adopted the nation-state as the key political actor in its aspiration to create world peace. UNESCO singled out the media as crucial actors in the achievement of this aspiration. The emphasis was on the study of the flow of news among nations! Also, studies on media and development have strongly emphasized the role of the nation as central to bringing people into modernity. The creation of nation-ness was essential; the existence of social heterogeneity was seen as an obstacle to modern development.

A promising approach

A way of theorizing that could be very helpful for an understanding of global communication is offered by Nick Couldry (2012). Couldry develops a "socially oriented media theory" (2012: 6) that is concerned "fundamentally with action" (2012: 8) and that concentrates upon the social processes that media constitute and enable. For purposes of studying global communication, the focus may be somewhat limited as "it is concerned with media, that is organized mechanisms and infrastructures for channelling communication rather than 'communication' in some general sense" (2012: 8). The field of global communication will have to address mechanisms and infrastructures and communication processes in a broad sense, like in intercultural communication (Chapter 11) or in diplomatic communication (Chapter 9). For a broader approach, Couldry refers to Klaus Bruhn Jensen (2010). What makes both of these books important for the study of global communication is their emphasis on communicative practice. Future research should address "…at the end of communication ... its intersections with other political, economic, and cultural practices" (Jensen, 2010: 165). This would imply that we conceive global communication as a trans-local communicative practice and study how this practice interacts with economics (Chapter 4), politics (Chapter 7), and culture (Chapter 11).

The "socially oriented media theory" that Couldry (2012: 6) develops is needed to understand how media and the social order interact – as Couldry writes: "to understand better media's contribution to our possibilities for knowledge, agency and ethics" (2012: x). I see very useful prospects for the study of global communication if we take as a starting point the deep embeddedness of media in social space (Couldry, 2012: 29) and undertake to patiently observe how global communication practices may change the way we organize our societies.

Perspectivism

The study of global communication can be guided by:

- The evolutionary perspective
- The complexity perspective
- The egalitarian perspective

Perspectivism is the philosophical position that accepts that knowledge of any phenomenon is inevitably partial and limited by the perspective from which it is viewed. We never understand the totality of anything. Specialists only understand details and even then only partially. Yet we may want to develop a general idea about the phenomenon we study. In this book I propose that we look at global communication as a complex, multilayered manifestation of human behaviour that – in so far as it can be comprehended at all – should be understood from many different and changing ways of looking.

Perspectivism is inevitable. Social phenomena such as global communication can be described from various perspectives. These perspectives do reflect different conceptions of social reality, different ideas of what science is, different notions of what constitute valid interpretations, and even different responses to the question as to what it is that we should understand. There is no universal principle that tells us which perspective is preferable. We have therefore to take a position, and make a choice for a specific viewpoint. Without a viewpoint there is nothing to see. Perspectivism is thus value-laden. Science is possible only from specific valuations that are essentially contestable. The core of science is the challenge to conduct a permanent open and critical dialogue in which the assumptions from where we study phenomena are articulated and thus exposed to contestability. At its core, science is observation and human perception is always guided by subjective preferences, experiences, and values. This biased position is only a problem as long it is obscured and denied.

In teaching global communication, I have found if helpful to adopt an analytical view through which we can begin to understand what global communication is and a normative view through which we can see what global communication could be. The two analytical perspectives that I have selected for the study of global communication are inspired by evolution psychology and complexity theory. We will return to these perspectives in the following chapters when the various dimensions of global communication are discussed.

The selected normative perspective is the democratic-egalitarian ideal. In the following chapters on the economic, political, and cultural dimensions of global communication, essential challenges will be formulated against the yardstick of this normative perspective.

The analytical perspectives help us to understand global communication – its processes, flows, actors, governing institutions, and impacts.

The normative perspective helps us to find a yardstick for judging the role/significance of global communication in human development and to seek guidance for its future direction(s).

The evolutionary perspective

The essential questions here are: What does this perspective tell us? And how does it apply to global communication?

The most general observation in Darwinian biology is that species (and their behaviours) evolve over time through the successful adaptation to their environment. The key to biological evolution is the finding of solutions to adaptive problems.[1] It seems sensible to argue that a similar process occurs in forms of non-biological evolution, such as cultural and psychological evolution. In these forms, human beings find non-genetic solutions to adaptive problems. One such adaptation is human communication: an evolutionary response to problems in our environment. As primates, Neanderthals and the Homo Sapiens began to live in large and complex social groups where they discovered the need for interaction and reciprocity. To meet this critical need, the human species developed adaptations, such as language. According to Pinker (1994), the evolution of language (some 200,000 years ago) represents an exemplary and universal human adaptation. Across time and culture "people know how to talk in more or less the same sense that spiders know how to spin webs ... language is a biological adaptation to communicate information" (Pinker, 1994: 18–19).[2]

Like other living species, human beings communicate largely in non-verbal ways. They use the language of signs, sounds, and gestures. However, in contrast with other species, humans use the tool of the spoken and written language. For some, this represents 10 per cent of their communications. This distinguishes them from the other species as the animal that speaks in words. The tool of verbal language brought about an immensely differentiated communicative capacity. Through its use, human beings were able to develop philosophical reflection, scientific and technological innovation but also to incite fellow humans to commit genocide. The essence of all this is that verbal language systems made abstract thought possible. Human beings discovered the possibility to think about things they had never seen or experienced.

The evolutionary perspective attempts to understand the human mind in terms of the Darwinian evolution proposition. It perceives the mind as an information processing system. Neural circuits in our brain determine how we process information. Our brain's neural circuits generate behaviour that is appropriate to our living circumstances. They help us to adapt to our environment. Just like we have physiological adaptations, so we have psychological adaptations. Adaptations mean that we learn from what worked in the past and from what did not work and in this way they help us to survive and to reproduce. They change over time as our environment changes in time. The basic Darwinian algorithm for successful adaptation is based upon variation, selection, and replication. In the domain of human communication, this can be applied as follows.

Communicative behaviour evolves through variation. A great variety of modalities of communication evolve because of the need to adapt to different and changing environments. This evolution is both non-intentional and intentional, and limited by both genotypical and historical factors. Much of it proceeds (as in the evolution of knowledge in science) by trial and error.

In the evolutionary process the best adaptive solutions are kept. Communication forms that optimally serve human survival and reproduction be retained. Those forms of attention and memory that are designed to notice, store, and retrieve information inputs, and that are useful to solving adaptive problems, will further evolve. Inadequate communicative solutions will disappear.

The most adequate adaptations will be transmitted to future generations.

The primates have learned that the complexity of living in social groups requires them to share the cake. Humans institutionalized the acceptance that some have the cake, eat it, want more, and take more.

The human animal also managed to replace the innate need to cooperate with lethal competition. Most animals know that their survival is determined not by killing each other or by demanding all of the cake for oneself, but by cooperating and sharing (de Waal, 2010: 16).

This is particularly important for animals that live in groups with a high degree of interdependence. Although the theory of evolution gives prominence to the capability to provide mutual assistance, humans have developed highly competitive institutions in fields such as sports, politics, litigation, education, and public communication. Against the natural instinct to cooperate, they promote an all-pervasive competitive strife that may endanger the long-time survival of the species. Since humans are the most destructive animals on the planet, both towards other beings and towards themselves, the question emerges whether this is the first species that destroys itself before nature deems this necessary. Most species disappear after a million years or so, but the human species seems to be so impatient that it cannot wait. This is convincingly demonstrated by human environmental destruction, the grand-scale killing of animals, by genocidal warfare, and by the 33,000 babies that die each day because of avoidable poverty and the resulting misery of hunger and illness.

For the largest part of human history we were hunters and we designed solutions to the adaptive problems of that environment. New adaptive problems come up and it takes time before we find new solutions. The evolutionary process is slow! There has not been enough time to evolve new mechanisms to solve the problems of modernity. The human mind has not substantially evolved since our hunter ancestors. Our modern skulls house stone-age minds.

Changes in our neural circuits can take thousands of years. For the past 10 million years we were hunters and gatherers. We needed the neural circuits for finding mates, hunting, raising kids, finding good living places, and defending against outside aggression. Agriculture came about some 10,000 years ago; and industry only 200 years ago. Global communication has been with us for 100 years: can our neural circuits meet its challenges?

Evolution is about survival. Human survival requires a form of global communication that is based upon cooperation, trust, diversity, and mobility.

- Cooperation – because to survive species have to cooperate (against their inherent drive to compete).
- Altruism – because entirely selfish behaviour does not serve survival.
- Cooperation needs trust – I can expect that you groom me.
- Diversity – because biological organisms that diversify survive better; natural selection favoured organisms that diversified.
- Mobility – survival requires the expansion of horizons; without creativity and curiosity our predecessors might not have walked out of Africa.

This requires us to cope with serious obstacles:

- Take cooperation – it is not so easy in a fiercely competitive environment where all species try to take advantage of the weaker structure of others: thus we end up with winners versus losers.
- Altruism: we are genetically disposed to selfish behaviour (Dawkins).
- Take diversity – it is not so easy as differences can be seen as permanent provocations. Foucault: the fact that you are different from me provokes me; why can't you be like me?; what's wrong with me? Tribalism is deeply engrained in the human psyche (Darwin) and hampers the understanding of others.
- Take creativity – it is not so easy in a world where we seem intent (particularly in education) on killing creativity and curiosity.

Against this, however, there is good news:

- The good news is we can learn altruistic behaviour: we have the power to defy the selfish genes of our birth (as Richard Dawkins wrote).
- The good news is that (as Charles Darwin proposed) we can rise above our origins and can extend positive feelings to all human beings.
- The good news is that entirely selfish behaviour does not serve the survival of species; bullies don't survive long in nature.

- The good news is that evolution is neither pre-determined nor random; there is space between these two and humans, as the greatest social communicators of all species, can use this to shape future survival.

The complexity perspective

Global flows of stories equal the complexity of a tropical rainforest in which everything is related to everything else (interdependence), where small events may have big and unpredictable effects (non-linearity), and where one cannot make reliable forecasts as flows of ideas and opinion may unexpectedly and rapidly change (uncertainty).

A complex system is a collection (universe) of interacting agents that compete for a scarcity of essential resources (like space in traffic or oxygen + glucose in cancer cells). A characteristic of such systems is a mixture of order and disorder. Without a central controller, the emerging disorder (the traffic jam) may resolve as if nothing had happened and without external interference. The traffic jam appears for no reason and then disappears again (Johnson, 2010: 19).

Global communication is both orderly and chaotic. The conduct of its agents is dynamic. To understand this complexity the prevailing scientific preference is for determinism and reductionism as they are not helpful to understand non-linear processes in which unpredictable and surprising phenomena emerge without a central controller. Global communication is a complex system and its student has to accept that such systems can never provide comprehensive information about all its states.

Reductionism proposes that by analyzing and understanding parts of a system (as parts of a clock) we understand the whole system. However, this does not work with complex systems where we have to accept that a great part of our reality is fundamentally unpredictable.

Determinism proposes that it is possible to establish linear causal relations between phenomena in our physical and non-physical environments. Causality assumes a simple world of one-to-one linear relations. More often than not scientists can only demonstrate (with grave reservations) a correlation, an association, and then speculate, hypothesize, and guess. The "causality obsession" is fatal for a realistic understanding of the world in which we live. We live in a reality of multiple causalities and it is probably impossible ever to single out one specific causal factor.

Reductionism and determinism offer an attractive simplicity that suggests we control the phenomena we investigate. This may be psychologically comforting but it does not provide us with reliable knowledge. The acquisition of knowledge requires time. Science needs patience.

The egalitarian perspective

A contemporary theory of politics that does not accept the standard of equal dignity of all humans will not find legitimacy because there is no plausibility in efforts to achieve global agreement on the common destiny of humanity without the premise of equal dignity of all. A normative theory of global communication therefore needs to be based upon the notion of equality. An egalitarian theory of global communication is based upon distributive justice, that is, upon the idea that it is unjust "for some to be worse off than others through no fault of their own" (Temkin, 1986: 100, cf. 1993: 7).

?
Does global communication (for example, in global news or entertainment) treat disabled people with the same respect for their dignity as non-disabled people?

The egalitarian perspective implies an equal entitlement to the conditions of self-empowerment. Among the essential conditions of people's self-empowerment are access to and the use of the resources that enable people to express themselves, to communicate these expressions to others, to exchange ideas with others, to inform themselves about events in the world, to create and control the production of knowledge, and to share the world's sources of knowledge. These resources include technical infrastructures, knowledge and skills, financial means, and natural systems. Their unequal distribution among the world's people obstructs the equal entitlement to the conditions of self-empowerment.

Equality in decision-making about matters of public interest

The egalitarian perspective has important implications for the processes of public choice. If we take the classical democracy literature (for instance, by Schumpeter (1942), Dahl (1956), Pateman (1970) or Dworkin (1985)), and common political practice in democratic states as point of reference, there is a broad consensus about a definition of democracy as a political decision-making procedure that enables all those concerned to participate on the basis of equality. This minimalist definition proposes that the fundamental principle of democracy is political equality.

Although the comfortable consensus may risk falling apart, I think that this basic procedural definition needs considerable qualification if we want to secure the egalitarian nature of democratic arrangements. As Gould (1988) has convincingly argued, conventional conceptions of democracy propose a system of governance that provides a maximum degree of "negative" freedom for the governed while it largely ignores that full human freedom includes "positive" freedom. The latter implies that people should be free to exercise their capacity for self-empowerment (Hamelink, 1994a: 142). Following this, the egalitarian nature of democracy implies that all people are entitled equally to the conditions of self-empowerment.

Political equality is often conceived in a narrow sense which provides no guarantee that a democratic procedure enables the widest possible participation of all people in public decision-making. Actually, in most conceptions of democracy there is a limited interpretation of people's participation. Political equality, however, has meaning only if it goes beyond the right to vote and to be elected, and encompasses civil rights such as freedom of speech, but also extends to institutions through which political equality should be secured. To promote the freedom that is basic to political equality, democratic participation has to extend into areas where ordinary people do not normally participate. For Pateman, who represents, against such "realists" as Schumpeter and Dahl, a normative approach, participation is "a process where each individual member of a decision-making body has equal power to define the outcome of decisions" (Pateman, 1970: 71).

Following this reasoning, we have first to extend the standard of political equality to mean the broadest possible participation of all people in the processes of public decision-making. Secondly, we have to extend democracy as a decision-making procedure beyond the realm of the political. The democratic process should be moved beyond the political sphere and extend the requirement of participatory institutional arrangements to other social domains. Forms of participatory democracy have therefore to be designed for policymaking in the sphere of the production, development, and dissemination of information, culture, and technology.

This raises the question of how to organize democratic decision-making.

There is a strong tendency in most democracies to let a small elite decide on behalf of others. Particularly in large and complex societies, it becomes difficult to avoid forms of delegation of power to politicians, experts, or the forces of the market. There may be nothing wrong with delegating decisions, but those entrusted with deciding for others should provide a full and transparent account to those on whose behalf they are invited to act. This implies that a democratic arrangement should have rules, procedures, and institutional mechanisms to secure public accountability. The principle of accountability logically implies the possibility of remedial action by those whose rights to participation and equality may be violated. Only through effective recourse to remedial measures can fundamental standards be implemented. If those who take decisions engage in harmful acts, those affected should have access to procedures of complaint, arbitration, adjudication, and compensation. The process of establishing the responsibility for decisions taken and demanding compensation for wrongs inflicted, secures the egalitarian nature of the democratic arrangement.

The argument so far assumes a broad consensus about the principle of political equality. On this basis I propose that this principle can only have substance in an egalitarian conception of the democratic ideal. In an egalitarian version, the constitutive dimensions of a democratic social arrangement are the equality of entitlement to the conditions of self-development, the widest possible participation of all in public decision-making, and its extension into all relevant social domains, the establishment of public accountability (for both public and private power holders), and the availability of remedial measures.

The next question to pose is how these dimensions translate into a description of a democratic arrangement of global communication. Within the limits of this chapter, this can be no more than an approximation that demands much more detail in class discussions.

Global communication and the widest possible participation

This principle has two dimensions. It proposes to include all people into decision-making that affects their lives and to extend such participation beyond the political realm. In the arena of global communication, decisions are taken by the bilateral consortium of the most powerful statal and corporate players. In the politics of world communication, ordinary people are excluded (Hamelink, 1994b). This is a reflection of world politics in general where, as Muto writes, "Most of the major decisions which affect the lives of millions of people are made outside their countries, without their knowledge, much less their consent" (Muto, 1993: 156). The current global communication order is highly unrepresentative of the social relations in the world. The present forms of concentration in ownership of communication resources excludes the largest number of people in the world from participating in the control of global communication channels.

In the politics of global communication, democratization requires the establishment a "transborder participatory democracy" which is no longer based upon the states as key constituents, "but the people themselves ... as the chief actors in determining the course of world politics and economics" (Muto, 1993: 156). This will need the establishment of tri-partite arrangements for negotiation and decision-making. The idea of involving more than state players in issues of world politics is not new. The International Labour Organization employs the instrument of trilateral negotiations in formulating its policies. Its decision-making conferences are attended by delegations composed of representatives of governments, employers, and workers.

The principles of maximum participation and extended equality calls for the participation of people in decision-making in former elitist fields such as technology and culture. Especially in the light of the increasing privatization of the production of technical knowledge and cultural expressions, these social spheres should also be subject to democratic control. This requires that affected citizens have a right to participate in decisions about its development and the utilization of technology and culture. This is undoubtedly a complex order, since technology and culture are related to special requirements of expertise, skills, and creativity. It will therefore be necessary to explore introducing forms of democratic control that do not constrain the essential input of individual expertise and creativity. Individual scientists, engineers, and artists may resist the notion of technological and cultural democracy, but it would be fallacious to believe that they are fully autonomous today. They may stand to gain more than they lose, if their creativity is subject to common-good considerations rather than to corporate profit motives.

To sum up the proposed perspectives for the study of global communication:

The evolutionary perspective provides analytical insights for the understanding of the development and organization of global communication.

The complexity perspective provides analytical insights for the understanding of the non-linear nature of the political, economic, and cultural dimensions of global communication.

The egalitarian perspectives can be used as a normative assessment of the rules and practices of global communication. The questions it poses are: is there equality of access to basic resources (such as infrastructures, knowledge, and information-communication literacy) or are people excluded through no fault of their own? Is there equality of participation in public decision-making[3] and public accountability for the representatives to whom people outsource their citizen's rights to participation in public choice? And is there equality in terms of respect for the human dignity of all people?

Notes

1. It should be noted that this is also, among Darwinists, a contested concept. Not all human inventions should be seen as adaptations since they can also be contingent side-effects of human evolution.
2. Although we usually grant the honour of the communication tool *par excellence* to language, it should not be forgotten that more often than not verbal language (with all its varieties) is an obstacle to human communication. To communicate really well we have to speak the same language, which we often do not. It could be that non-verbal language actually is the key communicative tool for the human being.
3. This is based upon a maximalist conception of democracy that strives towards maximum and diversified participation in a broadly defined political domain that goes well beyond institutionalized macro-politics.

Reading spotlight

Egalitarianism

Baker, J., Lynch, K., Cantillon, S. and Walsh, J. (eds) (2004). *Equality. From Theory to Action.* New York: Palgrave MacMillan.

An interdisciplinary examination of political theories of equality. The book addresses a broad range of societal inequalities and provides a meaningful conceptual framework for analysis and social action.

Democracy

Carter, A. and Stokes, G. (eds) (2002). *Democratic Theory Today.* Oxford: Polity Press.

The authors in this edited volume offer discussions on some of the most essential problems and challenges that democracy faces in the contemporary world. In very accessible texts they address such issues as the threats to democracy that are posed by globalization, political apathy and inequality. Authors also explore theoretical reflections on among others deliberative democracy, social democracy and transnational democracy. For the study of global communication in particular the chapters on "Democracy and Citizenship", "Democracy and Inequality", and "Democracy and Nationalism" are good sources.

Gould, C.C. (1988). *Rethinking Democracy: Freedom and Social Cooperation in Politics, Economy, and Aociety*. Cambridge: Cambridge University Press.

> Carol Gould fundamentally rethinks the political theory of democracy with a rigorous argument for extension of democratic decision-making beyond the political arena to economic and social dimensions of public life. This leads her to the critical analysis of democracy in fields such as technology, human rights and international relations. Essential to the book is her argument about the freedom of individuals and their equal rights to the conditions of self-development.

Hackett, R.A. and Carroll, W.K. (2006). *Remaking Media: The Struggle to Democratic Public Communication*. New York: Routledge.

> This is a study on the democratisation of the media based upon the sociology of social movements, critical media studies and democratic theories. The authors depart from the observation of a massive democratic deficit in public communication. The text contains concrete case studies on media activism in different fields ranging from Indymedia to Guerilla media and campaigns for freedom in broadcasting.

Mouffe, C. (2000). *The Democratic Paradox*. New York: Verso.

> In this book Chantal Mouffe offers an incisive analysis of the paradoxical nature of modern liberal democracy. Against those who argue that antagonism has disappeared from today's politics she proposes that the "adversary" is still a crucial actor on democracy. She introduces the concept of "agonistic pluralism" that ultimately implies that deep conflicts cannot be definitely resolved.

Raboy, M. and Bruck, P.A. (eds) (1989). *Communication for and against Democracy*. Montreal: Black Rose Books.

> The authors argue that communication issues have taken on an urgent significance for democratic societies. The authors in this edited volume deal with the media of communication as both instruments of repression and of emancipation. A wide variety of topics are addressed that range from the Canada-US free trade agreement, to alternative media in South Africa and the use of media in promoting social change. As they write in the preface the editors "are concerned with the ways in which communication is related to the realization or thwarting of democracy in its various forms" (p. iv).

Complexity/Epistemology

Johnson, N. (2007). *Simply Complexity*. Oxford: OneWorld.

> The book provides an accessible and lucid introduction to complexity science. It offers the readers analytical tools to understand complex processes. There are numerous concrete illustrations ranging from traffic jams to cancer tumors.

Moser, P.K., Mulder, D.H. and Trout, J.D. (1998). *The Theory of Knowledge: A Thematic Introduction*. Oxford: Oxford University Press.

An accessible introduction to the main problems of contemporary epistemology. The text provides many examples and provides a glossary with essential terms in epistemology and offers suggestions for further reading.

Online resources

Visit the book's companion website at **https://study.sagepub.com/hamelink** to watch the author discussing the theme of this chapter: **Studying Global Communication**

Visit the book's companion website at **https://study.sagepub.com/hamelink** to access the following journal articles free of charge:

Downey, J. and Stanyer, J. (2010). Comparative media analysis: why some fuzzy thinking might help. Applying fuzzy set qualitative comparative analysis to the personalization of mediated political communication. *European Journal of Communication*, 25(4): 331–347.

Downing, J.D.H. (2005). Communication research and political commitment: then, now and next. *Gazette*, 67(6): 535–537.

Lau, R.W.K (2012). Re-theorizing news' construction of reality: a realist-discourse-theoretic approach. *Journalism*, 13(7): 886–902.

Mansell, R. (2007). The problem of internationalizing media and communication research. *Global Media and Communication*, 3(3): 283–288.

Further reading

Asante, M.K. (2011). De-Westernizing communication. In Wang, G. (ed.), *De-Westernizing Communication Research: Altering Questions and Changing Frameworks*. London: Routledge. pp. 21–27.

Carpentier, N. (2011). *Media and Participation: A Site of Ideological-Democratic Struggle*. Bristol: Intellect.

Chomsky, N. (1989). *Necessary Illusions*. Boston, MA: South End Press.

McChesney, R.W. (2000). *Rich Media, Poor Democracy*. New York: The New Press.

McQuail, D. (1983). *Mass Communication Theory: An Introduction*. London: Sage.

Park, D.W. and Pooley, J. (2008). *The History of Media and Communication Research: Contested Memories*. New York: Peter Lang.

Raboy, M. and Bruck, P.A. (1989). *Communication for and against Democracy*. Montreal: Black Rose Books.

Thussu, D.K. (2006). *International Communication: Continuity and Change* (2nd edn). London: Hodder Arnold.

Thussu, D.K. (ed.) (2007). *Media on the Move: Global Flow and Contra-flow*. London: Routledge.

RESEARCH ASSIGNMENT

A way of studying complex phenomena like global communication is to focus on the use of metaphors. A metaphor that could be used to look at global communication is the tropical rainforest. Which characteristics of a tropical rainforest make this a useful metaphor for the study of global communication?

Describe with the help of the relevant literature the essential characteristics of tropical rainforests.

Explore how these characteristics fit into the perspective of complexity theory.

Investigate – in a critical way – why or why not the tropical rainforest metaphor is a useful tool for the study of global communication.

THE HISTORY OF LONG-DISTANCE COMMUNICATION

Few scholars had such illuminating insights into the imperial function of communication throughout human history as Harold Innis.

Harold Innis (1894–1952)

Innis was professor of political economy at the University of Toronto and author of essential books on media and communication theory. He investigated the role of media and their various formats (such as oral and written) in the processes of civilization. He took the independence of universities very seriously and warned against the political and economic pressures that undermined them as centres of critical thinking.

His major publication for the study of global communication is *Empire and Communication* (1950).

For the study of global communication, Harold Innis taught us to critically reflect on the imperial nature of human communication.

Having addressed the field of study, its contemporary context, and the perspectives from where to study global communication, we should now take a closer look at the historical development of communication across long distances.

We will look at:

- Manual carriers for flows of stories
- Electric carriers for flows of stories
- Electronic carriers for flows of stories
- Digital carriers for flows of stories

Communicating across distances

Throughout history people have always moved across borders as they traded, battled, explored new lands, conquered foreign soils and minds. Although most people stayed home in the village, since the dawn of history human beings have communicated across long distances. Most of these communications took place within the borders of vast empires and were intended to serve their control, coordination, and expansion. The carriers that were used to transport messages had serious limits in terms of distance, volume, speed, and reliability. In the first phase of long-distance communication human "interaction capacity" was hampered by its largely manual-mechanical means of transport technology.

Based upon relays of men and horses along imperial highways, messages could reach the most distant corners of the Egyptian, Persian, Greek, Chinese, and Roman territories. The imperial courier systems – predecessors of today's mail services – operated through word of mouth or writing. These oral or written messages were carried by runners or horsemen. An example of such an ancient telecommunication system was the network developed by the Persian emperor Cyrus (6 BC) who had a specially appointed post-master who controlled a stable with horses and a system of couriers. When the post-master received a letter from one of the courier posts in the empire, he would arrange for a fresh horse and a courier to deliver the message.

Exceptionally, one also finds a reference to the use of fire signals for long-distance communications. The news about Troy, for example, travelled in one night with fire signals over a distance of some 500 kilometres, as Aischylos reports in his book *Agamemnon*. There are also records of the use of carrier pigeons by the Egyptians. The early postal systems were established exclusively for governments and they provided essential support to the empire.

The Egyptian postal service that was established under Amenophis III in the thirteenth century BC provided a service that extended between the capital and all the cities of the empire. For a long time the written transmission was impaired by its medium, the clay tablet. This changed when papyrus became the new medium to facilitate the transport of messages. Alexander the Great appears to have used written messages and an elaborate system of messengers to keep in touch with the events in his empire. Given the primitive state of the roads and the hazards of sea traffic, communications in his vast empire must have been wanting and were probably a contributory factor to its demise.

Extensive long-distance communications are also reported from the Chinese empire during the Han dynasty (206 BC–219 AD). The imperial court had established a postal system through which news on events in the empire was collected and transmitted along specified routes in the form of handwritten newsletters.

The Roman empire developed long-distance message traffic with the written medium. Over a period of almost three centuries there appears to have been regular communications across the empire of the "acta senatus" and the "acta diurnal". The messages travelled across sea routes and the 49,000 miles of road network the Roman empire had constructed.

Although most of these early long-distance communications were probably fairly limited to regional traffic, there were also early exchanges across the world through trade, diplomacy, and religion. Illustrative cases are the encounters between the Chinese and the Indian civilizations. "Historically, there were few military or diplomatic relations between them; rather, their communications with one another were filtered through middlemen and intermediate cultures; their encounter was pacific – the movement of ideas, words, books, things – rather than invasion, infiltration or conquest; the flow was mainly one way, from India to China" (Wright, 1979: 205). In this cross-cultural encounter Buddhism was brought from India to China through the travels of the Chinese monk Fa Hsien (399–414 AD).

Much in advance of the formal diplomacy that originated with the European society of states (after the 1648 Peace of Westphalia), there have been international diplomatic exchanges. The early Egyptian, Hellenic, Greek, Chinese, and Byzantine state systems had developed sophisticated forms of international diplomacy. There is evidence that Egyptian diplomacy began under the eighteenth dynasty (1580–1350 BC). "The Pharaoh sent his representatives to neighbors in the Mediterranean by Phoenician-made oared boats or by Egyptian ships known by such names as 'Appearing in Memphis' or the 'Sun-Disk Lightens'" (Tran Van Dinh, 1987: 12). The Greeks had roving ambassadors and regularly hosted diplomatic emissaries from abroad. China under the Han dynasty and later under the Tang dynasty (618–906 AD) maintained extensive diplomatic contacts with other territories. Among them were the Syrians, Persians, Koreans, Japanese, Tibetans, and Vietnamese. As ambassadors of their faith, the early Christian apostles travelled great distances throughout Asia Minor, Greece, and the Roman empire. By the year 200 AD missionaries had also gone to Egypt and Africa. In the middle of the third century Christians could be found in Western Europe, the Armenian Kingdom, Arab countries, Mesopotamia, and India.

There have also been early forms of international public relations as attempts to cultivate images in the service of foreign policy. The use of propaganda messages in international relations was well known in antiquity. Alexander the Great had what amounted to a PR unit. "Reports written to serve his ends were sent to the Macedonian court, multiplied there and disseminated with propagandistic intent" (Kunczik, 1990: 73).

Early trading also provided important carriers for the exchange of information and culture. Trade and information routes connected Asia, the Mediterranean, Africa, and the Pacific. The spice and silk routes linked Mesopotamia and Iran with India and China. Gold was extracted in West Africa and transported across the Sahara to North Africa and the Middle East. Before Vasco da Gama's travels from Portugal in the fifteenth century, trading took place between what is today Zimbabwe and China (for Chinese pottery) and India (for gold and ivory). Before Captain Cook travelled to the South Seas, Melanesian and Polynesian seafarers had sufficient geographical information to make very long sea voyages. The early courier systems expanded throughout the Middle Ages and from the twelfth century on an organized information traffic emerged in Europe. Although it is likely that most people did not travel, there was a growing number of travellers to far destinations. They included crusaders, missionaries, artists, traders, and pilgrims.

New cultural centres emerged in Europe and they began to communicate with each other. From the twelfth century some European universities, notably the University of Paris (Sorbonne), and several monasteries developed their own systems of couriers. These couriers became professionals with special rules on payments, working-time and sanctions in case of malpractice. In the fourteenth century the Hanseatic League developed a communication network for its commercial purposes.

Oral media of transmission remained important carriers of foreign news in the thirteenth century. For example, town criers reported the news about the taking of Milan or the treaty with Pope Clement VII in Paris (Stephens, 1988: 40).

Towards the late Middle Ages networks of correspondents and intelligence agents had begun to operate as professional carriers of political, military, or ecclesiastical information along well-organized traffic routes. Usually the towns that had become key trading centres were also the chief news centres. "Through Vienna came dispatches from the Balkans; Augsburg processed news from Italy, Switzerland, southern Germany and the East (via Venice); in Cologne messages from France and the Netherlands converged with news from Britain, which came by way of Antwerp. Material from Russia and surrounding countries passed through Danzig and Breslau, while Hamburg was the arrival point for news from Scandinavia and the whole of northern Europe. By 1600 the demand for such information had reached the level at which it had become economic to find printed means for distributing it" (Smith, 1979: 19).

In the sixteenth century the first postal system covering several European countries was initiated by Franz von Taxis. On March 1, 1500, King Philip I appointed Von Taxis "captaine et maître de nos postes". Against an annual salary he was to maintain postal traffic between the Low Countries, Germany, France, and Spain. In 1516 Von Taxis was appointed Chief Postmaster by the emperor Maximilian I and was given the sole privilege of operating the postal system in the Low Countries.

In the sixteenth century, authorities in Spain and Germany permitted private mail services. In England the post was established as a national system (sixteenth century) and the postmaster primarily delivered for the King, who had monopoly control. The service was not in the first place public, although messages for private clients were also delivered since they brought in profits.

Gradually, the European postal services expanded and developed on a large scale during the Renaissance as more and more governments set up postal services for public use. Rulers such as Frederick III of the Holy Roman Empire, Louis XI of France, and Edward IV of England were committed to more efficient postal services. In this historical process the postal services and the news services became distinct entities.

It can be argued that the fifteenth century saw the first organized deliberate distribution of information to other nations. This was initiated by the political community wanting to spread knowledge about itself and to gather intelligence about foreign countries. Most monarchs had their private networks of foreign correspondents and international spies.

There was, for instance, extensive knowledge about Italy in England through a vast network of diplomats and agents. This was also the beginning of the deliberate distribution of information to other nations. In the fifteenth century, handwritten newsletters began to spread news among the countries of Europe. The newsletter about Edward IV reclaiming his crown in 1471 was published in English and French and was distributed with enormous time delays. In 1483, for example, in Flanders, a copy was made for Edward, Prince of Wales, of a newsletter sent by an Italian in Constantinople in 1481 at the time of the death of Sultan Mohammed II.

In the sixteenth century, Europe's trading community began to develop cosmopolitan interests and consequently a strong need for information from abroad emerged. For the Venetian merchants, information about safe arrivals of ships or their losses was crucial to market prices. Prices of wheat were also determined by military news, for example about the movements of the Turkish fleet.

Members of the trading community created their own information systems, and in 1536 the first trader's news agency was established in Venice. The financier Philip Eduard Fugger created the Fugger letters between 1568 and 1604. These handwritten letters were spreading international information of general and financial interest (Stephens, 1988: 75).

In the sixteenth and seventeenth centuries the first European newspapers were created and they in their own way furthered cross-border communications. The Venetian gazette travelled to London in the mid-sixteenth century and contained foreign news, for example information from Vienna about the advance of the Turks by sea and in Hungary (Stephens, 1988: 153). Much of the international messages were about politics or the military. By 1566, weekly handwritten news sheets were produced in Venice but the scope of their distribution is unclear.

There is some evidence that information about Italy circulated in Germany through handwritten news sheets by the late sixteenth century. The oldest printed newspapers, for instance the *Courante uyt Italien, Duytslandt, &c.*, published at Amsterdam, contained foreign reports. By the mid-seventeenth century there were some eight weekly or bi-weekly printed publications in Amsterdam that provided the cosmopolitan trading community with foreign news of special interest to them, not only about Italy and Germany, but also about America, Africa, and Asia.

In the seventeenth century also, the Reformation and the Counter-Reformation, using the new technology of movable-type printing, pushed cross-border communications further. The messages of Reformation preachers spread across Europe and the Catholic Church began to expand its mission to other continents, such as Latin America and China. When Pope Gregory XV in 1622 founded the Sacra Congregatio de Propaganda Fide, the congregation received among its briefs to propagate the catholic faith to the New World. In 1627 Pope Urban VII established a special training centre, the "Collegium Urbanum de Propaganda Fide" where catholic propagandists received their training before spreading their religious ideas across the world.

In the seventeenth century a cosmopolitan academic community emerged and information about scientific discoveries began to travel across borders through newspapers, books, and journals. Scientists began to organize themselves in groups, such as the Royal Society in England. The mail was the most common vehicle for cross-border communications but was of course highly inadequate to keep the expanding scientific community informed.

In the second half of the seventeenth century scientific periodical publications arrived, such as the *Journal des Savants* in France (1665) and the *Philosophical Transactions in England* (1665). Isaac Newton's *Principia Mathematica* (1687) was reviewed in the *Journal des Savants*, in the *Bibliothèque Universelle* (published in Holland), and in the *Acta Eriditorum* (published in Leipzig).

Throughout the eighteenth century into the early nineteenth century newspapers did attempt to bring foreign news but continued to be hampered by the wars and the adverse weather conditions of the time, which caused enormous delays and inaccuracies in reporting.

Long-distance communications moved at a very slow pace. Letters from Europe to India would take routinely almost eight months, and sending and receiving a reply could take as much as two years. Particularly with regard to people and events in faraway places, the information would tend to be distorted and often focus on the exotic and bizarre. French news sources would, into the early nineteenth century, refer to the population of distant countries as "savages" (Stephens, 1988: 219).

The eighteenth century saw the performance of one of history's greatest propagandists, Napoleon. "He engaged in a veritable propaganda battle with the rest of Europe, a battle of big words. Against Britain, which was waging a caricature campaign against Napoleon, a battle was fought in the press in which Napoleon, however, reached mainly the French people and the inhabitants of areas occupied by France. Napoleon's press policy in the occupied areas showed itself, for example, in press guidelines being decreed in the German kingdom of Saxony after Napoleon's victory under which anything 'which might be objectionable to the French imperial court must be avoided with the greatest care'. ... But Napoleon also communicated selectively with foreign countries. His open appeal to the civilian population was something fundamentally new. Thus in 1796 he directed a manifesto to the Tiroleans to give up 'the hopeless cause of their emperor'" (Kunzcik, 1990: 75).

Only in the nineteenth century did the collection and distribution of international news become a large-scale operation. The British post office sold summaries of articles in the foreign press to the newspapers in London. In 1832 the first private international news agency was established by Charles Havas in France, using carrier pigeons and the semaphore telegraph (Stephens, 1988: 259). In 1848 the New York newspapers (Associated Press) agreed to share expenses for the collection and distribution of foreign news through a chartered steamer (that would meet ships from Europe at Halifax) and the telegraphic traffic of information from Boston (where the steamer would arrive) to New York. By 1855 Bernard Wolff began his service in Berlin and in 1858 Paul Julius Reuter started a service for the London papers. In the mid-nineteenth-century Reuter, who founded the Reuters News Agency, deployed dozens of pigeons to have messages about stock market prices transported from Brussels to Aachen.

Lifting the limits

The essential limits to communicating across distances in this first phase of global communication began to be lifted when manual-mechanical means of transport were exchanged for electrical carriers. The manual-mechanical tools for long-distance communication, such as couriers, fires (the Greeks announcing the fall of Troy), pigeons, and semaphor (non-electric) telegraphs,[1] had serious limitations in terms of distance, speed, and volume.

A crucial technological breakthrough came with the invention of the telegraph by Samuel Morse in 1830. Morse sent the first electrical telegraphic message in 1838 with the text "What has God wrought?" In 1861 the first telephone conversation took place in Germany with a contraption made by Johann Philip and the message was "Das Pferd frischt keinen Gurken Salat". The first underseas cable was operated in 1866 between Valencia and Newfoundland. The first telecommunication connection using the human voice was on January 25, 1878, in New Haven. Around the turn of the century there were some two million telephone connections operational across the world. Before the end of the nineteenth century the possibility of wireless transmission was also explored by Alexander Stepanowitsch Popow and Guglielmo Marconi, who used knowledge generated by Heinrich Hertz. In 1901 Marconi could send radio signals over a distance of 3,540 kilometres between England and the United States. Around 1906 the first human voice was transmitted through radio broadcast. The business community was quick to make use of this new technology. The speed and reliability of telegraphy were seen to offer opportunities for profit and international expansion (Headrick, 1991). According to the International Telegraph Union, the number of telegraphic transmissions in the world shot from 29 million in 1868 to 329 million in the early 20th century. According to Daya Thussu (2006: 9): "The newspaper industry played a significant role in the development of international telegraph networks, to be able to exploit the rapid increase in demand for news, especially the financial information required to conduct international commerce. … The establishment of the news agency was the most important development in the newspaper industry of the nineteenth century, altering the process of news dissemination, nationally and internationally. The increasing demand among business clients for commercial information – on businesses, stocks, currencies, commodities, harvests – ensured that news agencies grew in power and reach". Important early applications of electric transmission were film, gramophone record, and radio.

In the course of the nineteenth century international diplomacy began to use the mass media as instruments of foreign politics. This was part of a change from the conventional form of secret diplomacy to a new type of more open diplomatic negotiation. The newspapers played an important role in this change, but it was particularly the development of wireless radio which significantly increased the potential for this new form of diplomacy. More and more diplomats shifted from traditional forms of silent diplomacy to a public diplomacy in which the constituencies of other states were directly addressed.

Ever since the advent of the medium of radio, its use for propaganda was an integral part of its development, with its power to influence values, beliefs, and attitudes (Taylor, 1997). During the First World War, the power of radio was quickly recognized as vital both to the management of public opinion at home and propaganda abroad, directed at allies and enemies alike. The Second World War saw an explosion in international broadcasting as a propaganda tool on both the Nazi and Allied sides.

After the Second World War the third phase in the history of global communication switched from electrical to electronic means of transport. This began in 1946 with the invention of the computer. The development of micro-electronics (silicon transistors, semi-conductors), integrated circuits (chips), satellite communication and network designs (Arpanet, the US military predecessor of the Internet) enormously expanded the reach of cross-border message flows.

In the course of the 1950s telecommunication technology and electronic data processing became integrated. Computer-communication networks were created that consisted of computers with communication channels attached to them that could link computers to other computers. The networks were constructed as centralized systems in which data were transported for processing, storing or forwarding to central computers. They were also built as distributed systems with data traffic between decentralized computers or terminals. Transmission through such networks commenced with the first circuits for defence systems and airline reservations. During the 1960s and 1970s they were increasingly applied to international banking, credit control, databanks, and databases, and intergovernmental cooperation.

An important development for the emerging networks was also the introduction of a non-terrestrial mode of data traffic through communication satellites. Transnational commercial satellite transmission began in 1965, when the International Telecommunications Satellite Organisation (INTELSAT) launched its first satellite "the Early Bird" on April 6. "Early Bird" or INTELSAT I became operational from June 28, 1965. This satellite had a capacity of 240 two-way audio-circuits or one television channel. Three years later in 1968 a series of INTELSAT II satellites became operational with each having a capacity of 1,500 two-way audio-circuits or four TV channels. With the INTELSAT IV series the capacity became, between 1971 and 1975, 3,750 circuits plus two TV channels.

Data networks also became more attractive through the developments in computer hardware and software. Micro-electronics, which since the early 1970s has produced the microprocessor, made it possible to apply computer capacity very broadly and cheaply. As a matter of fact, small computers became vital to data communication networks, both for communications and for data-processing facilities.

Together with these developments in hardware, there were considerable advances in the accompanying software and peripheral equipment. New programming languages were developed in order to improve the machine–user relationship and to design a mode of instructing the machine that would be close to the user's language.

Developments in hardware, software, and peripheral equipment largely contributed to the rapid growth of the utilization of computers and to the convergence of tele-communication and data processing into "telematics". An important application of "telematics" was the collection from outer space of data about natural resources, and the transmission and processing of such data. Since 1972 remote resource sensing was mainly done by NASA's Landsat satellites to explore iron formations, to measure sugar cane and rice crops, to map river sediments and forests, and for purposes of oceanography and demographic mapping.

The 1980s and beyond

Then, in the 1980s, the phase of digital transport began with the transfer from analogue to digital information processing. Messages were encoded in binary form and are thus represented in "yes/no" or "on/off" signals. The digitizing of all message traffic made recording, storing, and transmission much easier and faster, and the earlier restrictions of distance, speed, volume, and reliability were lifted in unprecedented ways. Digitization also allows for new forms of manipulation of images and sounds. Technologies for the processing and transmission of messages began to use the same language. This facilitated the convergence of telecommunications, computers, office technologies, and assorted audio-visual consumer electronics. This integration offered speed, flexibility, reliability, and lower costs. Digital technologies created multi-media interactive systems with a great variety of applications that ranged from virtual (i.e. electronic) shopping in the world's largest department stores to instant audio, visual, text, and data communications between scientists in distant locations.

Digitization provided the technical infrastructure for the much heralded "global information superhighway". This project was strongly promoted by the Clinton–Gore administration in the USA where, in 1993, an action plan for a National Information Infrastructure was adopted. According to Al Gore (in a speech on March 21, 1991 to the International Telecommunication Union in Buenos Aires), "The President of the United States and I believe that an essential prerequisite to sustainable development, for all members of the human family, is the creation of a Global Information Infrastructure. This GII will circle the globe with information superhighways on which all people can travel."

This global information structure became, in the late twentieth century, the Internet-based world wide web. For global communication, the rapid proliferation of web-users (often also web-producers) seemed to herald the promise of a veritable four-dimensional revolution. A global network society was in the making that was characterized by decentralization (horizontal communication links replacing the conventional hierarchical structures), de-institutionalization (flexible and open forms of production and governance), de-professionalization (the citizen as journalist), and democratization (more access for more people, thus contributing to a better informed polity and more participation in policy processes).

One of the burning questions of the early twentieth century is whether indeed such a revolution has taken place. Evgeny Morozov (2011) has warned in his book, *The Net Delusion*, of the serious risks of censorship, surveillance, manipulation, and the stifling of dissent in the network society.

?

Will the risks of the Internet, as Morozov (2011) describes them in *The Net Delusion*, dominate, or will its promising possibilities for equality prevail? What is your expectation?

The limitations of distance, time, volume, and reliability have now been lifted.

As Daya Thussu (2006) has aptly put it, global communication is characterized by continuity and change. Continuity means that although the carriers have become more sophisticated, they continue to do what they always did: transporting stories (in words and images) across large distances that provided people with (more and less reliable) maps of the globe. Discontinuity means that through its historical development global communication has fundamentally changed our conceptions of time and space.

Note

1. The semaphore or optical telegraph was very popular in the late eighteenth and early nineteenth centuries. The semaphore system used towers and pivoting shutters. The position of the shutters represented symbols through which messages could be relayed. The first system was designed by the Chappe brothers in France in 1790.

Reading spotlight

History General

Fortner, R. (1979) *International Communication*. Belmont: Wadsworth Publishing Company. (See Chapter 1).

Lasswell, H.D., Lerner, D. and Speier, H. (eds) (1979). *Propaganda and Communication in World History*. Honolulu: The University of Hawaii Press.

In three volumes the history of communication is presented. Volume I entitled: "The Symbolic Instrument in Early Times" ranges from early Mesopotamia to the Western Middle Ages. Volume II "Emergence of Public Opinion in the West" treats the Renaissance and Reformation Era, the Enlightenment, Communism, Global development and Security and Nuclear power. The third Volume "A Pluralizing World in Formation" analyzes the development of global communication in contemporary contexts and concludes with an essay on the future of world communication and propaganda.

Williams, R. (ed.) (1981). *Contact: Human Communication and Its History*. London and New York: Thames and Hudson.

The history of human communication through a series of contributions on language, symbols, non-verbal communication, writing, printing, sounds, images and technologies. Concludes with a chapter on the future of the media. Richly illustrated.

History of the News

Smith, A. (1979). *The Newspaper: An International Historty*. London: Thames and Hudson.

An indepth view of global development of the newspaper. Smith traces technical developments, portrays significant characters in journalism, and analyses the politics of journalism. There is a chapter on the "demon of sensationalism". In the concluding paragraph the author discusses the contextual influences that are always at work in the daily operation of the newspaper. There is a useful reading list and many illustrations.

Stephens, M. (1988). *A History of News: From the Drum to the Satellite*. London: Penguin Books.

This is a comprehensive historical account of the gathering and dissemination of news. The book deals with the history of journalistic styles. The study ranges from the spoken news by messengers and criers and the role of seventeenth-century coffeehouses, via written and printed news to modern electronic news.

Online resources

Visit the book's companion website at **https://study.sagepub.com/hamelink** to watch the author discussing the theme of this chapter: **Global Communication: History & Rules**

Visit the book's companion website at **https://study.sagepub.com/hamelink** to access the following journal articles free of charge:

Adolf, M. (2011). Review of *Refiguring Mass Communication: A History*, by Peter Simonson. Champaign, IL: University of Illinois Press (2010). *Contemporary Sociology: A Journal of Reviews*, 40(4): 489–491.

Peters, B. (2011). Review of Marshall T. Poe, *A History of Communications: Media and Society from the Evolution of Speech to the Internet*. Cambridge: Cambridge University Press. *New Media & Society*, 14(2): 356–359.

Tunstall, J. (2003). Review of Asa Briggs and Peter Burke (2002). *A Social History of the Media: From Gutenberg to the Internet*, Cambridge: Polity Press. *Journalism*, 4(1): 132–136.

Wei, R. (2013). Mobile media: Coming of age with a big splash. *Mobile Media & Communication*, 1(1): 50–56.

Further reading

Franco, G.L. (editor and publisher in collaboration with the International Telecommunication Union) (1987). *World Communications: Ways and Means to Global Integration.* Uxbridge: Novy Eddison & Partners.

Hauser, M.D. (1997). *The Evolution of Communication.* Cambridge, MA: The MIT Press.

Huurdeman, A.A. (2005). *The Worldwide History of Telecommunication.* New York: John Wiley & Sons.

Poe, M. (2011). *A History of Media and Society: From the Evolution of Speech to the Internet.* Cambridge: Cambridge University Press.

Williams, R. (ed.) (1981). *Human Communication and its History.* London: Thames & Hudson.

Winseck, D.R. and Pile, R.M. (2007). *Communication and Empire: Media, Markets, and Globalization, 1860–1930.* Durham, NC: Duke University Press.

RESEARCH ASSIGNMENT

How would international politics function if a time machine transported us back into the first phase of communicating across distances?

How would you research this question? What method(s) would you use? Would there be a theoretical angle that would be helpful?

How would you write your final report?

THE ECONOMY OF GLOBAL COMMUNICATION

Herb Schiller was a special friend for many years and his transparent and deep critique of the economic driving forces behind the development of global communication was, for me, an essential inspirational source.

Herbert I. Schiller (1919–2000)

Schiller studied and earned his PhD in 1960 from New York University. He was professor of communication at the University of California at San Diego. He was a central figure in the critical political economy analysis of the media both in the USA and worldwide. The focus of much of his writing and (highly inspiring) lecturing was on the privatization of public space and the global control of US corporate interests over cultural expressions.

Among his many books, the student of global communication will certainly benefit from reading his memoir-type reflections on American empire in *Living in the Number One Country* (2000). The key argument is that the core of the US economy, which is the communication industry, is the most critical pillar of the maintenance of the capitalist system.

Other important readings include: *The Mind Managers* (1973); *Who Knows: Information in the Age of the Fortune 500* (1981); *Information and the Crisis Economy* (1984); and *Culture Inc.: The Corporate Takeover of Public Expression* (1989).

For the study of global communication, Herbert Schiller taught us to critically reflect on the essential role that transnational corporate capital plays in global communication.

This chapter introduces you to the economic dimension of global communication. The three economic key sectors of global communication are analyzed:

- Infrastructure
- Services
- Content

The concluding paragraphs discuss how the economy of global communication can be studied and how the analytical and normative perspectives can be guides for your study.

Development of a global communication industry

In the second half of the twentieth century a global communication industry began to develop that would become in the early twenty-first century an essential segment of the world economy.

In the early 1950s Western industrial production began to move towards the countries of the South in search of cheap labour and new markets. With the combination of rising labour costs and the development of such technologies as containerization and satellite communication, this transnationalization of industry became both a necessity and a possibility.

The proliferation of industrial investment required the coordination of widely dispersed units of transnational corporations. In order to coordinate the globally dispersed affiliates and markets of large transnational corporations, modern telecommunications became an indispensable instrument.

On average, a large corporation with sales of US$1 billion would spend some US$14 million annually on telecommunication bills alone. This was corroborated by the worldwide establishment of production centres and markets: the "global shopping centre" emerged, and with it the worldwide proliferation of advertising and marketing. During the 1970s many of the major transnational corporations began to organize their own information provision to support their worldwide marketing, advertising, and public relations needs. The largest transnational corporations (the so-called "Fortune 500" [1]) established an in-house capacity for the production of film, TV, and video presentations that could easily compete with major international audio-visual networks. Responding to the emerging wave of critical questions directed at the legitimacy of modern corporate business, the latest technical innovations for international "image-cultivation" were employed. Between 1975 and 1984 US corporations increased their budgets for corporate advertising from US$305 million to over US$1 billion (Pavlik, 1987: 49). By 1985, over three-quarters of major US corporations used the services of international PR firms, mainly for marketing purposes (Wilcox et al., 1989: 397).

The international expansion of industrial production since the early 1950s also brought an export of related services such as travel, finance, marketing, and advertising. In addition, the transnationalization of banking drastically increased the need for international information networks. Actually, an essential feature of the post-Second World War global economic development became the emergence of an expanding services sector. This sector grew in the national economies of most Western industrial countries and also came to account for a significant portion of world trade. This implicitly caused a growth of cross-border information traffic, as so many activities in the services sector are based upon the trading of information or are facilitated by information technology. By 1980, the total world trade in services amounted to some US$400 billion, which represented over 20 per cent of overall world trade. The economic development in the affluent part of the world also meant the increase of private consumer expenditures and together with the proliferation of demands for education and entertainment this contributed to a significant expansion of information handling across borders.

Related to the overall economic expansion, a global communication industry developed and began its proliferation across the world.

In 1980, the world market for telecommunication equipment and related services amounted to some $80 billion. If one added to this figure the sales of electronic components and consumer electronics, the total global communication market could be estimated at some $350 million, which represented some 18 per cent of total global trade (Hamelink, 1984: 23). This industry adopted several striking features, such as strong alliances within the industry and between the industry and such sectors as the defence establishments of major industrial countries, the need of large volumes of finance capital, the role of tycoons, and the development of consolidated mega-conglomerates.

Interlocking interests

Throughout the 1970s the communication industry became largely controlled by a network of some 80 very large transnational corporations with strong interlocking interests. On the surface it looked as if the international production and distribution of communication goods and services was carried out by a small, but competitive, group of contending parties with diverse interests. Closer analysis, however, revealed that the information industry was characterized by an intricate web of interlocking connections. This had various dimensions. Between the major communication corporations there were direct connections in the form of joint ventures, joint ownership of subsidiaries (such as between Philips and Siemens with Polygram, between NCR, Control Data, and ICL with CPI, between Honeywell and Control Data with MPI), stockholdings (such as in the case of General Electric holding 11 per cent of the stock in Toshiba, Philips holding 24.5 per cent of the Grundig stock), licensing, supply, sales, or production agreements (such as between Fujitsu and Siemens, Honeywell and Nippon Electric, Xerox and Mitsubishi, Olivetti and Hitachi, AEG/Telefunken and Thomson/Brandt), joint directorates (such as between IBM and Time, Honeywell and GE, Interpublic and CBS, McGraw-Hill and Sperry Rand, ICL and Plessey). In addition to these direct alliances, there were important indirect connections, mainly through directorates. Such connections implied that directors of corporation A would meet directors of corporation B across the boardroom tables of X other corporations.

This meant that what seemed to be major competitors in the information industry, such as IBM and AT&T, had 22 indirect routes through which they could "supply convenient conduits for possible private solutions of the public debate between monopoly and competition in the telecommunications industry", according to the report of a US Senate Subcommittee (Hamelink, 1983b: 24). The indirect interlocking interests provided, as the report commented, "substantial opportunity for direct policy discussions and potential understandings among these major competitors" (Hamelink, 1983b: 24). Such discussion and understanding reduced genuine competition to what was termed "courteous competition". No genuine free market developed and very little space was made for newcomers.

A particular development was the combination of interests in the hardware and software sectors. The industry counted a number of corporations that were active in both areas. Illustrations were: the US firms RCA, Xerox, IT&T, Litton, Singer, Lockheed; the UK firms EMI, Rank, Decca; the German firm Siemens; and the Dutch firm Philips.

There were also direct and indirect links between the leading firms in the hardware sectors and the same firms in the software sectors. Significant firms were: IBM interlocking with Time, CBS, ABC, the New York Times, McGraw-Hill, the Washington Post, Interpublic, and MCA; General Electric interlocking with Time, CBS, ABC, the New York Times, and McGraw-Hill; RCA interlocking with CBS, ABC, Time, Interpublic, and Disney Productions; EMI interlocking with Thomson, Pearson, Reed, and ATV/ACC; Philips interlocking with MCA and Polygram; Siemens interlocking with Polygram and Bertelsmann.

In terms of the essential external interconnections of the industry, those with the military deserve some detail. The military leadership had a more than passing interest in the type of information technology which was to be developed. In most of the recent communication innovations, military inputs have played an important role. One can observe this in the development of the electronic computer, the integrated circuit, radar, lasers, computer software (the language COBOL), the integration of optical and electronic systems (for the development of an extremely rapid operating computer using light instead of electrons), and the so-called "superchip". Regarding the latter: in 1984, the US Defense Department paid $170.2 million to IBM, TRC, and Honeywell for the development (by 1989) of a chip of 0.5 micron size for deployment in weapons systems. In some cases the military took the initiative and proposed to industry the development of a specific technique. In other cases, research already under way was subsidized through considerable funding in order to reduce the time span between commercial availability and military application. This has led to a mutual dependency between the military leadership and large contractors for military projects.

Among the latter were several of the leading international communication companies. In the fiscal year 1982, the US Ministry of Defense spent a total of $125,000 million on civilian contracts for military products. Some $14,000 million were allocated for electronics and communication systems. An amount of approximately $14,000 million was spent in 1982 on research and development. Out of this expenditure, $2,800 million was utilized for electronics and communication systems. Among the 100 largest US defence contractors (providing over two-thirds of all military equipment), the communication companies in 1982 accounted for over 50 per cent of the defence contracts. Among the 100 transnational communication industries that control most of the world's information production and distribution, at least 30 have close links with military interests. They are among the largest contractors for both equipment and research.

These military purchaser–industrial supplier interconnections had a number of consequences. Among them were:

- The choice of techniques to be developed became largely defined by military interests. The research and development (R&D) effort needed for technological innovation is highly capital-intensive and makes the industrial manufacturers of technical products largely dependent upon external funding. The military have been very generous in providing such funds, evidently with an indication of the type of equipment they need. During the First World War the US military needed transmitters, receivers, and detectors. The electronics industry provided them and consequently boomed as a result of large defence contracts.
- The funding of R&D through selected industrial corporations strengthened the degree of industrial concentration. The availability of funds to a limited number of large firms created an important advantage for these companies over other contenders in the market. As a result, markets were increasingly dominated by ever fewer firms.
- The invention of useful civilian "spin-offs" from military R&D (for example, ceramic ovenware resulting from space research) usually fulfilled the function of partial legitimation of excessive defence spending. The fact that all such spin-offs could have been developed at far less expense without military research was more often than not conveniently ignored.

Capital intensity

In the telecommunication sector of the communication industry, labour intensity has largely been exchanged for capital intensity. This sector used to employ large volumes of factory workers, maintenance crews, and systems operators. Increasingly, new technologies made them redundant. Electronic exchanges in the telephone system, for example, could be manufactured, maintained, and operated by a few people with specialized computer technique skills. Between 1974 and 1977 large telecommunications equipment manufacturers, such as Philips, Siemens, and Western Electric, reduced employment by 5–25 per cent.

A crucial factor in the increasing capital needs in this sector was the costs of research and development (R&D), similar to those in the data-processing sector and the electronic components industry. High expenditures were made for the exploration and implementation of such techniques as optical fibres, lasers, and microprocessors. In 1977, the combined average percentage of sales spent on R&D for US aerospace, data processing, and electronics was 4.1 per cent, as compared to 2.5 per cent in another R&D-intensive industry, the chemical industry. In 1979, R&D expenditures in the US data-processing sector were considerably greater than in all manufacturing. In the Federal Republic of Germany, the electrical/electronics industry spent 6.4 per cent of sales on R&D in 1978, which compares with 4.7 per cent in chemicals, 5.7 per cent in automotive, and 3 per cent in engineering and mining. Some of the leading FRG firms spent more, like Siemens with 10 per cent and AEG/Telefunken with 7 per cent of total turnovers.

On a world scale, it could be estimated that R&D expenditure for information technology amounted to some 30 per cent of the world research and development budget. This demanded large funds and attracted large investments, both from private and governmental sources. Among large investors there was an increasing interest in corporations' R&D figures.

In the communication industry, the more traditional mass media sectors also became capital intensive and in need of increasing investments for their fixed costs. Large fixed capital was needed in the publishing industry, i.e. for the costs of paper and printing ink. Over the last decade, prices for the paper used for most magazines had doubled and prices for printing inks increased by some 40 per cent. Some companies could not comply with this demand and were forced out of the business. Illustrative of this market expulsion was the case of United Press International. Already in the 1980s UPI made increasing losses (up to some US$7 million) and its owner, E.W. Scripps Co., was forced to seek a buyer. After a series of tumultuous years, UPI was finally declared bankrupt and auctioned. In 1992 the agency was bought by the Middle East Broadcasting Co.

Product promotion became a major expenditure in the sector for recorded music, where promotion budgets for top-selling categories such as rock music increased three times over the 1970s. Another aspect of capital intensity in the record industry was the rapidly increasing front investment which, for example, in a rock music LP album rose from $100,000 to $250,000 during the late 1970s. This was caused by the costs of sophisticated recording equipment and the high royalties for musicians and fees for producers. MCA, for example, paid Elton John $8 million for a five-year contract in the mid-1970s. Warner Brothers guaranteed Paul Simon $13 million in 1978 for his transfer from CBS. CBS signed an $8 million contract with Paul McCartney in 1979 for three albums. Top performers like Prince or Madonna asked and got astronomical fees for their recordings.

Capital investment for production was also on the increase in the film sector. With the increasing volume of fixed capital, the risks for capital to be invested in film production became greater. This, in turn, caused greater control by financiers and less likelihood for small, independent producers to get credit. In the 1980s the costs of the average feature film production began to exceed the $15 million mark. The increasing costs of production were due to the considerable expansion of fixed capital in the industry, i.e. capital to be invested in the means of production, such as studios, technical equipment, and special effects. There were also rising costs for marketing, the employment of "stars", and distribution. The latter was possible only through very expensive international networks. Exhibition became more capital intensive with the emergence of luxurious cinemas. Production costs in Hollywood continued to soar. In 1990 the average feature film costs some $30 million. Star performers were also increasingly expensive: Stallone, for example, received $20 million for *Rocky V*.

The communication industry developed as a growth sector, a capital-intensive industry, and as a very profitable enterprise. This profitability of the industry attracted new investors: large companies that formerly had little or no operations in the information field. Examples include Boeing, McDonnell Douglas, Fiat, Coca-Cola, Exxon, and Matra. As the information producers became integrated into large industrial conglomerates, their industrial policies were predominantly guided by economic concerns.

Ownership structures

In the communication industry, as in other industrial sectors, the institutional investors became the key players. These are such institutions as pension funds, insurance companies, or banks. In the past decades institutional investors have become increasingly active in the management of companies through their stock ownership and through their participation on boards of directors. In many of the largest communication companies over half of the stock is controlled by these institutional investors. Among them, the international banks are most prominently present. It is obvious that institutional investors are primarily interested in a maximum return for the interests they represent.

A characteristic element of the communication industry is the considerable number of cases in which one individual or one family group, often identical or strongly related to the original founder, has much of the voting stock. Significant owner control exists in those corporations in which one individual or one family group holds over 10 per cent of the voting stock, and no other stockholder owns a similar proportion. This type of control occurs in almost a quarter of the 100 largest communication corporations. Well-known examples of "tycoons" or "media-moguls" are the late Robert Maxwell, Rupert Murdoch, Robert Hersant, Leo Kirch, Silvio Berlusconi, or Sumner Redstone.

A characteristic of this type of control is the direct involvement of individual owners in the daily operations of their media. There are, however, many indications that point to serious difficulties for the survival of the "tycoons". In order to operate on today's world market in a competitive way there is the need for enormous investments that come with considerable financial risks. As a matter of fact, many of the large companies are heavily in debt and they may only escape bankruptcy if they merge with other companies. In sheer economic terms, the survival chances of information companies that become part of larger industrial conglomerates are better. It needs to be pointed out, however, that the expected "synergy" does not always materialize. The Japanese companies Sony and Matsushita, for example, which added vast software interests to their hardware manufacturing, have so

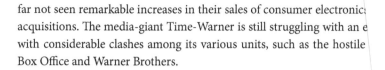

far not seen remarkable increases in their sales of consumer electronic acquisitions. The media-giant Time-Warner is still struggling with an e with considerable clashes among its various units, such as the hostile Box Office and Warner Brothers.

Concentration

A characteristic of the development of the global communication industry has been a high level of concentration in all its sectors. In most sectors this was already the case in their early history. Between the two world wars international advertising was already largely in the hands of two agencies: J. Walter Thompson and McCann. The film industry has had a strong degree of concentration since the 1920s, when eight major companies practically controlled production, distribution, and exhibition (Paramount, Warner Bros., 20th Century Fox, Loew's Inc., United Artists, Universal Pictures, RKO, and Columbia). From the outset, the development of the film industry was determined by a tendency towards decisive influence upon the market for maintaining and expanding profits.

> This oligopolistic structure not only controlled the U.S. industry, it also already dominated the world industry and drew a significant proportion of its revenues and profits from the non-U.S. market. (Hamelink, 1983b: 34)

For the record industry, Chapple and Garofalo gave the following account:

> The industry did not begin with a number of small companies gradually coming to be monopolized by a few powerful firms. From the beginning a few, two or three, large firms have accounted for a majority of industry volume. The major reason for this is that the two biggest record companies have since 1900 been linked to phonograph firms and since the thirties to large broadcasting and electronics corporations. (Chapple and Garofalo, 1977: 92)

The international production and distribution of news has been dominated by four large agencies since the late nineteenth century.

The beginning of concentration in the data-processing sector is of more recent date. In the early 1950s the US industry supplied more than 95 per cent of the world market. Among these US firms one company had the uncontested leader position: IBM. During the 1960s its market share was estimated to vary between 66 per cent and 72 per cent. In 1978, 13 telecommunication manufacturers dominated some 90 per cent of the world market for telecommunication equipment. This market was estimated at US$34 billion and three US corporations (Western Electric, ITT, and GT&E) accounted for over 52 per cent (Hamelink, 1984: 36). The market control by a few companies was reinforced by the wave of mergers in the 1970s, then further strengthened by the development of conglomerates throughout the 1980s, and then consolidated in the global markets of the 1990s.

During the 1980s many companies in the communication industry became either part of larger industrial conglomerates, or became communication conglomerates themselves. Examples of such communication conglomerates are companies like Bertelsmann (with books, records, TV, video, and printing), Rupert Murdoch's News Corporation Ltd (with newspapers, magazines, TV, and film), and Time/Warner Inc. (with magazines, books, records, cable TV, and film). Examples of industrial conglomerates with considerable interests in communication investments are companies like General Electric (manufacturing washing machines, light bulbs, ceramics, components for weapons systems, computers, telecommunications, and running the TV network NBC), and Silvio Belusconi's Finivest (real estate, insurance, department stores, TV networks, advertising, and newspapers).

The United States emerged through its entertainment industry as the leading global exporter of cultural products. UNESCO's 2005 report, *International Flows of Selected Goods and Services*, estimated that the global market value of the cultural and creative industries was $1.3 trillion and was rapidly expanding. According to the report, between 1994 and 2002 international trade in cultural goods increased from $38 billion to $60 billion (UNESCO, 2005). For the US export of media products, the European region developed as the largest market.

? Does concentration in the industry promote or hamper a diversity of products and/or services?

Three sectors

The global communication industry developed in three separate but related sectors: the manufacturing of infrastructures, the provision of connectivity and information services, and the production and distribution of content.

- The infrastructure sector: manufacturing the global infrastructure
- The services sector: servicing global communication
- The content sector: creating global contents

The infrastructure sector consists of the manufacturers of all the technical equipment necessary for global communication. This includes maritime cables, satellites, computer networks, and consumer electronics. A rapidly growing sector in providing the global infrastructure is wireless broadband communications, through the proliferation of smart phones and tablet PCs. By the end of 2010 wireless broadband subscriptions in OECD countries exceeded half a billion, according to OECD statistics. (OECD, 2011). The services sector encompasses all those companies that provide connectivity, such as telecommunication operators, and that facilitate access to sources of information. The content sector consists of all the firms that produce and distribute global news, entertainment, and advertising. These sectors will be discussed in the following paragraphs.

The infrastructure sector

The first infrastructure for global communication was based upon long-distance cables for telegraphic traffic. The telegraph was invented in 1837 by Samuel F.B. Morse and major manufacturing companies were Siemens and Slaby-Arco, the later Telefunken (Germany), Thomson in France, Western Union, AT&T, United Wireless in the USA, Philips of the Netherlands, and later Cable and Wireless in the UK, plus GE and RCA in the USA. The first undersea cable (to connect telegraphs between Dover and Calais in 1851) was laid by the British Electric Telegraph Company and the Magnetic Telegraph Company. In 1852 the Electric Telegraph Company had cables between London, Amsterdam, and Rotterdam. The first cross-Atlantic cable went into operation in 1866. In the USA, the driving forces were Western Union and the American Telegraph Company (1854). The wireless telegraph was invented by Guglielmo Marconi in 1899. With the manufacturing of telephones and telex machines in the nineteenth century, a global communication hardware industry emerged. In the first decade of the twentieth century two companies became the giants of wireless communications: the Marconi Wireless Telegraph Company (1897 in the UK and in 1899 in the USA) (support from the UK Post Office and Lloyd's Marine Insurance) and Telefunken (in 1903), by arrangement between Siemens and Allgemeine Elektrizitäts Gesellschaft (AEG) (with support from the German government).

For almost 80 years telecommunication technology generated and upgraded techniques for transmissions between people-centred "transducers", such as telephones, facsimile machines, and TV systems. In its development, it added to transmission and transducers the technique of switching, which made networking possible. When electronic data processing became available it was applied to telecommunications for the enhancement of its efficiency, particularly in switching systems.

In the course of the 1950s the two technologies became integrated: machine-centred transducers were linked with each other and with people. Transmission through such networks commenced with applications to defence systems and airline reservations and were in the 1960s and 1970s increasingly applied to international banking, credit control, databanks and databases, and intergovernmental cooperation.

The widening application of computer-communication networks has been made possible by a number of technological developments which have considerably increased the performance capacity, the accessibility, and the compatibility of computing and telecommunication facilities. The traditional telephone networks greatly enlarged their capacity for data traffic through such techniques as modems and multiplexors. The development of optical fibres further increased the data transmission capacity of the telephone network. They made it possible to transport digital signals through light over glass-fibre cables.

An important development has also been the introduction of a non-terrestrial mode of data traffic through communication satellites. In the 1950s global telecommunications expanded significantly through the advent of satellite technology. In 1957 the first satellite (Sputnik) was launched by the Soviet Union and in 1965 the first geostationary satellite was launched into space by INTELSAT (International Telecommunication Satellite Organization), which was established in 1964.

In 1969 the first global network, linking computers through telecommunications, emerged as the Arpanet (Advanced Research Projects Agency network), which was operated by the US Defense Department that was the fore-runner of the Internet. Data networks became more attractive through the developments in computer hardware and software. Micro-electronics which, since the early 1970s, produced the microprocessor, made it possible to apply computer capacity very broadly and cheaply. Between 1960 and 1988 the world's computer population grew from 9,000 to 1,750,000 (Hamelink, 1984).

From 2005 onwards mobile phone networks began to take over from fixed landlines.

One of the characteristics of the infrastructure sector has been its strong interlocking interests with the worlds of banking and defence contracting. These connections have been documented by Hamelink (1983b, 1986).

Current data on the trade in products for the global communication infrastructure can be found in OECD publications, such as *Communications Outlook 2011*. Here it is documented that the largest exporter of communication equipment in 2009 was China (with US$87 billion) followed by Korea, Mexico, the Netherlands, and the USA (some US$22 billion). It is interesting that the historically largest exporters, such as Canada, Finland, France, and Germany, saw a noticeable decline of exports in the early twenty-first century. The countries that did best in terms of trade balances were Hungary, Korea, and Mexico, each of which had a high trade surplus. The equipment that accounts for the highest volumes of export (72 per cent of all telecom equipment exports) are devices for the transmission and reception of voice, images, and data, such as cell phone handsets.

Total global trade in communication equipment in 2009 amounted to US$589,012 million. Over the past 10 years the largest manufacturers and operators of global communications have represented 20 per cent of the world's largest (Fortune 500) companies.

The services sector

Communication services refer to telecommunications services and postal courier services. The leading exporters were in 2009 the USA, the UK, Germany, France, and the Netherlands. They were also the largest importers of services. Interestingly, Luxembourg – a relatively small country – ranked very high on the trade balance for services, probably partly due to the presence of Skype in this country. In particular, the so-called BRIC countries (Brazil, Russia, India and China) saw a rapid growth of their trade in communication and telecommunication services (OECD, 2011: 372) (see Table 4.1).

The largest growth in communication services is presently found in mobile services. Revenues for these services in 2009 reached US$527 billion, which amounted to a share of 45 per cent of total global communications revenues (OECD, 2011: 100).

Table 4.1 The rapid growth of trade in communication and telecommunication services in the BRIC countries

	2000 in US$ millions	2008 in US$ millions
Brazil	36	466
Russia	385	1,493
India	599	2,423
China	1,345	1,570

? What could be the roles of closed user networks such as SITA (for airlines) or SWIFT (for banks), or courier services such as DHL, and social networks such as Facebook in the global communication services industry?

The content sector

This sector produces and distributes on a global scale news, music, film, television, and advertising. The content of global communication are the stories that the cultural industries produce and distribute worldwide through news, entertainment, and advertising.

The cultural industries "are involved in the making and circulating of products – that is texts – that have an influence on our understanding of the world" (Hesmondhalgh, 2007: 3). They contribute to our sense making of the world and thus are important forces in the daily experiences of people around the globe. Important factors in the growth of this sector have been the smart use of new technological options (by Rupert Murdoch, for example: time lease on the Astra satellite), the digitizing of content, and the application of interactive television. The great success formula for content was, and is, usually the triple S combination of scandal, sports, and sex.

Corporate expansion in the content sector has largely developed through vertical integration, which made around-the-clock and around-the-world operations possible. A crucial additional effect on the growth of this sector has been deregulatory politics.

? Can you identify the largest companies in each of the three sectors?

How to study the economic dimension of global communication

Most characteristic of approaches to the economy of global communication have been studies in the political economy of communication.

Political economy

In a very general way this can be described as the study of the relations between economic factors (such as ownership) and political factors (such the exercise of political power). In his book *The Political Economy of Communication*, Vincent Mosco defines political economy as "study of social relations, particularly the power relations, that mutually constitute the production, distribution, and consumption of resources, including communication resources" (Mosco, 2009: 2). A crucial notion in the political economy approach is power, and particularly the relationship between power and wealth.

Political economy as a field of economic studies emerges in the late eighteenth and early nineteenth centuries with the first professorial chair at the University of Vienna (1763), and in 1805 in Britain's East India Company College. Important representatives were Adam Smith, David Ricardo, and Karl Marx. The notion "political economy" generally refers to the study of the economic behaviour of such political entities as national states. Its students are interested in the analysis of the structural relationships between economic and political behaviour.

In the field of communication, a political economy approach emerged with Harold Innis's study, *Empire and Communication*, in 1950. The book "examines the evolution of communications media from stone tablets to printing presses, and the direct impact of various media on the duration and prosperity of the empires of Egypt, Greece, Babylon, Europe and America" (1950). Innis explored the impact of the monopoly access to knowledge by privileged groups on their societies. Other early exponents of the political economy approach were Horkheimer and Adorno with their work on "cultural industries". Among later scholars who used the political economy approach in their work are Smythe, Schiller, Garnham, Murdock, Golding, Silverstone, Mansell, Mosco, and Wasko (see selected key texts and further reading at the end of this chapter). Many of the political economy studies addressed the ownership structures in media industries.

For global communication, a political economy approach implies the attempt to understand the structural relationship between the economic and the political significance of trans-local flows of stories. This can be further explained by looking at economic and political behaviour of the participants in global communication. Economic behaviour produces and distributes goods and services that represent values: use values (e.g. information, knowledge, and entertainment) and exchange values (monetary rewards, profits). Political behaviour deals with the exercise and the distribution of power: who gets what. Political economy studies how value and power are structurally (i.e. non-accidentally) related. For example, if people often behave on the basis of ideas about reality, where do they get these ideas from? Who produces and distributes them, and with what interests?

The political economy analysis tries to uncover the way in which economic processes are managed and organized in the communication industry – the politics of the economy! It tries to understand how industrial concentration develops and who profits from this. How the corporate system transforms use values (being informed, being entertained, feeling good, escaping the unbearable harshness of daily life) into exchange values, i.e. into commodities that bring profits (Mosco, 1996: 143–144).

? How would you analyse, both from a political economy and a cultural studies approach, the "Easternization" of globalization. China is rapidly becoming the largest exporter of IT products and India is expanding its IT industry. Both countries have enormous consumer markets. How successful can their exports be: economically and culturally?

The perspectives

The evolutionary perspective

In the understanding of the economy of global communication the evolutionary perspective may be a helpful tool. The prevailing economic models that are inspired by neo-classical theory tend to propose that the maximization of wealth is largely steered by rational and well-informed processes of decision-making. They tend to ignore the dynamic complexities of institutional and individual economics which are not helpful in understanding the real conduct of parties on markets. As Wikström argues, "societal and economic systems are often not in equilibrium, and socio-economic structures do change, sometimes even rather dramatically. Also, individuals and organizations are often unable to make well-informed decisions. And, often, these decisions are biased and irrational, contrary to neoclassical economic theory" (Wikström, (2009: 36). Analyzing the economies of global communication from an evolutionary perspective focuses upon structural change and development whereas a neo-classical approach emphasizes linear economic growth. The economic dimension of global communication can best be understood if we see economic development as a process of adaptation that is characterized by complexity, chaos, and self-organization. March and Simon (1958) and Cyert and March (1992) offered a useful evolutionary approach when they developed the behavioural theory of the firm (Wikström, 2009: 37). They explained intra-organizational decision-making by using the concept of bounded rationality. This means that decision-makers may not be well-informed and rational. Actually, their choices may even be irrational. The evolutionary perspective helps us to better understand the economic behaviour of communication organizations.

The complexity perspective

Cultural industries are a complex and at times contradictory business. They are, as with all other businesses, intent on making profits but their products may serve more than commercial interests and may sometimes not be supportive of those interests. The characteristics of cultural industries are high risk and volatility, high production costs versus low reproduction costs. According to Nicholas Garnham, "The problem with cultural and informational goods is that, because their use value is almost limitless (they cannot be destroyed or consumed by use) it is extremely difficult to attach an exchange value to them. They are classic public goods" (Garnham, 1990: 38). A peculiar economic problem with information is that, contrary to tangible goods, the same product can be used by many users. This begins already with the invention of movable print, the book. To create revenues there has to be a (temporary) monopoly through copyright legislation. In the digital world, scarcity was replaced by abundance and all content could be free to all at no cost. The corporate answer was copyright enforcement and limitations to the functions of digital devices, plus advertising. What initially looked like an enormous contribution to collective well-being turned into the growth of private riches. The Internet represents an abundance that poses a threat to private gain.

The egalitarian perspective

> The way the cultural industries organise and circulate symbolic creativity reflects the extreme inequalities and injustices (along class, gender, ethnic and other lines) apparent in contemporary capitalist societies. There are vast inequalities in access to cultural industries. Those who do gain access are often treated shabbily and many people who want to create texts struggle to earn a living. (Hesmondhalgh, 2007: 6)

The democratic perspective is helpful in identifying inequalities in participation in public decision-making in the domains of communication infrastructures and communication contents. Its egalitarian dimension suggests the need for exploring the extension of democracy to all aspects of social life, including communications and thus encourages research into issues of control and power.

? What are the major challenges relating to the economic dimension of global communication?

Note

1. *Fortune* is a business magazine published monthly by Time Incorporated. Each year it presents its list of the world's largest corporations, the Fortune 500.

Reading spotlight

Political Economy

Garnham, N. (1990). *Capitalism and Communication. Global Culture and the Economics of Information*. London: Sage.

> Garnham presents in this book an essential challenge to postmodernist and information society theories. Through theoretical reflection and empirical cases he explores the role of communication institutions in capitalist societies. There is special attention for global ecomonic restructuring and the related proliferation of telecommunication technologies.

Mosco, V. (2010). *The Political Economy of Communication*. London: Sage.

> The book offers a comprehensive introduction to the field that presents the different schools of thought and the historical emergence of political economy in communication research. Mosco makes complex key notions such as commodification, spatialization and structuration accessible to students of global communication.

Smythe, D.W. (1981). *Dependency Road: Communications, Capitalism, Consciousness, and Canada*. Norwood: Ablex Publishing.

> Although the book focusses on Canada Smythe's analysis of the consciousness industry as a central agent in monopoly capitalism has global relevance. Crucial among his observations is that the survival of capitalism "depends upon its ability to produce people ideologically willing to support it in the long run" (p. xi). In this process the mass media as inventions of the capitalist system and operated by a small number of giant corporations set a "daily agenda of issues, problems, values and policies for the guidance of other institutions and the whole population. They mass produce audiences and sell them to advertisers" (p. xii). As Herbert Schiller writes in the Preface, this book will "help students, teachers and general readers better understand the multiple crises of advanced capitalism, as they work their way into everyday life" (p. xx).

Wasko, J., Murdock, G. and Sousa, H. (eds) (2011). *The Handbook of Political Economy of Communications*. Oxford: Blackwell Publishing.

> This handbook covers the field of the political economy of communication through overviews, case studies, and theoretical reflections. It introduces the most important debates on the political economy of communications, addresses issues such as ownership, creativity, consumption, and concludes with newly emerging topics. Very useful as a key source book for the understanding of the political and economic power upon which the media's role on modern societies is based.

Industries

Hesmondhalgh, D. (2007). *The Cultural Industries*. London: Sage.

> This study provides – beyond political economy and cultural studies approaches – an insightful analysis of changes in the cultural industries. It places transformation in a broad political, economic and cultural context. Its offers useful material on issues of copyright, celebrity power and the digital distribution of music.

Herman, E.S. and McChesney, R.W. (1997). *The Global Media: The Missionaries of Global Capitalism*. London: Cassell.

> This book offers a survey of the global communication industry. The authors describe and analyse how the industry grew and became a network of large transnational conglomerates. They argue that the processes of consolidation and concentration in this industry largely have eroded the "public sphere". The book is concluded with a discussion on local and national resistance against current globalization processes.

Schiller, H.I. (1989). *Culture Inc.: The Corporate Takeover of Public Expression*. Oxford: Oxford University Press.

> Schiller offers a deeply disturbing analysis of the increasingly powerful role of the private sector (in the US and abroad) over cultural domains such as museums, theatres and public broadcasting. He demonstrates how private control transforms once inexpensive information into a profitable commodity and public meeting places (markets) into selling machines (shopping malls). Schiller also discusses this process threatens the accessibility and diversity of cultural production.

Online resources

 Visit the book's companion website at **https://study.sagepub.com/hamelink** to watch the author discussing the theme of this chapter: **The Global Communication Industry**

Visit the book's companion website at **https://study.sagepub.com/hamelink** to access the following journal articles free of charge:

Boyd-Barrett, O. and Rantanen, T. (2000). European national news agencies: the end of an era or a new beginning? *Journalism*, 1(1): 86–105.

Chalaby, J.K. (2012). At the origin of a global industry: the TV format trade as an Anglo-American invention. *Media, Culture & Society*, 34(1): 36–52.

Hesmondhalgh, D. (2006). Bourdieu, the media and cultural production. *Media, Culture & Society*, 28(2): 211–231.

Leyshon, A., Webb, P., French, S., Thrift, N. and Crewe, L. (2005). On the reproduction of the musical economy after the Internet. *Media, Culture & Society*, 27(2): 177–209.

Marshall, L. (2004). The effects of piracy upon the music industry: a case study of bootlegging. *Media, Culture & Society*, 26(2): 163–181.

Further reading

Anderton, C., Dubber, A. and James, M. (2012) *Understanding the Music Industries*. London: Sage.

Bagdikian, Ben H. (2004). *The New Media Monopoly*. Boston, MA: Beacon Press.

Boyd-Barrett, O. and Rantanen, T. (eds) (1998). *The Globalization of News*. London: Sage.

Gershon, R.A. (1997). *The Transnational Media Corporation: Global Messages and Free Market Competition*. Mahwah, NJ: Lawrence Erlbaum Associates.

Golding, P. and Murdock, G. (2005). Culture, communications and political economy. In Curran, J. and Gurevitch, M. (eds), *Mass Media and Society* (4th edn). London: Arnold. pp. 60–83.

Hesmondhalgh, D. (2007). *The Cultural Industries*. London: Sage.

Murdock, G. (1982). Large corporations and the control of the communications industry. In Gurevitch, M., Bennett, T., Curran, J. and Wollacott. J. (eds), *Culture, Society and the Media*. London: Methuen. pp. 118–150.

Murdock, G. (1990). Re-drawing the map of the communications industries: concentration and ownership in the era of privatization. In Ferguson, M. (ed.), *Public Communication: The New Imperatives*. London: Sage. pp. 1–15.

McPhail, T. (2002). *Global Communication*. London: Allyn and Bacon.

Wall, T. (2012). *Studying Popular Music Culture*. London: Sage.

RESEARCH ASSIGNMENT

Analyze the significance of the global communication industry as part of the world's total industrial activity.

Collect data on the scope of the global communication industry (figures on sales and revenues) from various industry and trade sources.

Collect data on the scope of the world's total industrial activity.

Establish what part of the world's total industrial activity is made up by the communication industry.

FLOWS OF GLOBAL CONTENT

5

For this chapter, I learned much from George Gerbner – during many meetings at global conferences. His long-standing research on the cultivation impact of the flows of television images continues to inspire thinking about global flows of stories that audiences share worldwide.

George Gerbner (1919–2005)

Gerbner was Dean and Director of the Cultural Indicators research project at the University City Science Center in Philadelphia (USA). From 1964 to 1989 he was Professor and Dean of The Annenberg School for Communication at the University of Philadelphia. After leaving the Annenberg School he became, in 1997, Bell Atlantic Professor of Telecommunication at Temple University, Philadelphia. In 1990, he founded the Cultural Environment Movement to promote the diversity of content in public communication media.

For the study of global communication, his important publications are: *Communications Technology and Social Policy: Cultural Indicators - The Third Voice* (edited with L.P. Gross and W. Melody) (1973); *World Communications: A Handbook* (edited with M. Siefert) (1984); *Triumph of the Image: The Media's War in the Persian Gulf - A Global Perspective* (edited with H. Mowlana and H.I. Schiller) (1992); and *The Global Media Debate: Its Rise, Fall and Renewal* (edited with H. Mowlana and K. Nordenstreng) (1993).

For the study of global communication, George Gerbner has taught us to critically reflect on the mediated representations of reality and their impact on our daily lives.

To continue, I would like you to investigate the content of global communication. You can do this by focusing on three dominant global flows of stories:

- Global news
- Global entertainment
- Global advertising

The global news providers

A prominent product of the global communication industry is the daily provision of news stories about the state of the globe. The understanding of global news provision needs some historical background.

In the sixteenth century, Europe's trading community began to develop cosmopolitan interests and the trading community created its own information systems. In the sixteenth and seventeenth century the first European newspapers were created and they in their own way furthered cross-border communications. Throughout the eighteenth century into the early nineteenth century newspapers did attempt to bring foreign news but continued to be hampered by wars and the weather conditions of the time, which caused enormous delays and inaccuracies in reporting. Only in the nineteenth century did the collection and distribution of international news become a large-scale operation.

Developments in the twentieth century

At the beginning of the twenty-first century global news is a very competitive business. The major global agencies are Associated Press (USA), Reuters (UK), and AFP (France). The big three are likely to provide some 80 per cent of the world's news worldwide. Reuters and APTV, in particular, provide most of the global television news. Associated Press (AP), "the essential global news network", is the largest producer and distributor of text, audio, photo, and video, reaching out to more than 1 billion people daily. Other important video news providers are the BBC World and CNN (see Box). Detailed information about the leading news agencies can be retrieved from the company websites.[1]

The political significance of global news is related to the fact that around the world people share experiences of events "through their shared exposure to narrations of those events" (Appiah, 2002: 7). Today's world citizens are "participants in a common story" (ibid.). CNN has been described as the sixteenth member of the UN Security Council (by the former United Nations Secretary-General, Boutros Boutros-Ghali) and its effect upon global politics has been analyzed as a direct effect on political actions (as in the case of the 1992 US intervention in Somalia), as some effect but no real impact on decision-making (as in the non-intervention in the Bosnian conflict in 1991–92; Gowing, 1994), or as agenda-setting without directly impacting decision-making (Jakobsen, 1996).

The case for the influence of CNN is often suggested by those politicians who never gave up the myth that TV coverage caused the defeat in Vietnam. The "manufacturing consent" theory proposed by Chomsky and Herman (1988) actually points to the support that media usually give to government positions. They reflect official policy rather than control such policies. The "CNN effect" theory proposes that global TV has become a controlling factor in foreign policy decisions.

Real-time 24/7 news coverage

Evidently, political leaders have always used the media of their times as sources of information on other countries. Global television news has changed the pace of this collection of information – it now arrives in real time and in dramatic presentations. As George Bush (senior) commented during the Gulf crisis of 1990–1991, "I learn more from CNN than from the CIA" (Friedland, 1992: 7–8).

CNN

Cable News Network (CCN) was established in June 1980 by Ted Turner. As McPhail (2002: 118) writes: "Without a doubt, CNN is the godfather of global television news reporting to audiences around the world. The twenty-four-hour all-news format is now seen by millions in over two hundred nations. Historically, the markets for Britain's *The Economist* or the *International Herald Tribune* were early indications that there was a niche market for the international news sector. What CNN managed to do was to make the development of the niche television news market a global phenomenon." And as Thussu reports (2000: 136–137): "CNN's on-the-spot reporting of global events gave it unparalleled power to mould international public opinion and even contributed to influencing the actions of people involved in the events it was covering. Chinese students protesting against authorities in Beijing's Tiananmen Square in 1989 were aware that the world was watching the unfolding events through CNN – the Chinese government pulled the plug on the CNN transmission before its crackdown on protesting students."

Although CNN is watched by a relatively small proportion of viewers, they fall into the category of what CNN calls "influential", that is government ministers, top bureaucrats, company chief executives, military chiefs, and religious and academic elites (Flournoy and Stewart, 1997). Perhaps more importantly, CNN is constantly being monitored by journalists and news organizations worldwide for any breaking news stories. By virtue of the AOL-Time-Warner merger of 2000, CNN became part of the world's biggest media and entertainment conglomerate, whose significance in international communications is likely to grow. Its version of world events – more often than not an American one, which might even be delivered in local languages – is likely to define the worldview of millions of viewers around the globe. (For ratings on CNN, see the study by the Pew Research Centre at http://stateofthemedia.org/2012/cable-cnn-ends-its ratings-slide-fox-falls-again/cable-by-the-numbers.)

Among the leading global news providers there are such global radio news stations as BBC World Service, Voice of America, Radio France International, and the Deutsche Welle. Their websites give detailed information about their operations. For the provision of global financial news, the key agencies are: Associated Press-Dow Jones, Agence France Press, Financial Times, Bloomberg News, and CNBC. Since the late 1960s an alternative format for global news has been offered by the Rome-based Inter Press Service (IPS) (see Box).

IPS

The IPS International Association is a non-profit, non-governmental organization with headquarters in Rome and bureaux in 41 countries. Professional journalists and others in the field of communications, whether staff or friends of IPS, are entitled to join the association. In 1997, IPS's articles of association stipulated that its main object is to contribute to development by "promoting free communication and a professional flow of information to reinforce technical and economic cooperation among developing countries" (Inter Press Service, 1997).

IPS offers a range of services that go beyond the traditional functions of a news agency. Its products can be divided into three broad categories. IPS News Service, an independent global news wire, facilitates information flow among developing countries and distributes news about those nations to clients in the industrialized nations. IPS Projects designs and manages programmes for training, information exchange, and increasing public awareness of global issues. IPS Telecommunications offers technical expertise in opening up communication channels for regions and people usually overlooked by mainstream media.

Arguably the most important alternative in global news provision is Al-Jazeera and, more especially, its English language service (see Box).

AL-JAZEERA

Al-Jazeera is an Arab media service with a global orientation. With its motto "the opinion and the other opinion", it acts as a forum for plurality, seeking the truth while observing the principles of professionalism within an institutional framework. While endeavouring to promote public awareness of issues of local and global concern, Al-Jazeera aspires to be a bridge between peoples and cultures to support the right of the individual to acquire information and strengthen the values of tolerance, democracy, and respect of liberties and human rights (Al-Jazeera, 2004).

? What would you see as the differences and similarities of global news production between CNN and Al-Jazeera?

The global entertainers

- Music
- Television entertainment
- Film
- Children's television

The global entertainment industry encompasses the production and distribution of films for cinema, books, recorded music, TV programmes, Internet entertainment, the buying and selling of TV programme formats, and computer games. Using various sources (editions of *Fortune*, *International Advertising Age*, the Motion Picture Export Association, company websites, annual reports of companies, *Screen Digest*, European Audiovisual Laboratory, *Variety*) it can be estimated that the content industry reached, in 2010, the US$1.2 billion sales mark.

As a suggestion for ways of studying the global entertainment sector, some of its products will be investigated below.

Music

The characteristics of the music industry are a high level of uncertainty and volatility (Wikström, 2009: 22, 23). In the music industry, it is very difficult, if not impossible, to predict which products will be successful, and what new types of music consumers will like and pay for. This is always difficult but with copyright products there is the additional problem: as Wikström writes, a copyright product can only be evaluated by the consumer after "the first copy" has been produced. Only then (maybe) is market research of any relevance. In addition, the consumption of copyright products is highly volatile and unpredictable (Picard, 2002: 7). Decision-makers in copyright firms often have to make decisions about how to spend their investment monies based on intuition and gut feeling (Hesmondhalgh, 2002: 23). One common way of dealing with such a high exposure to risk is to use the principles of portfolio theory (Picard, 2002: 200 *et seq.*; Reca, 2006). Risk is reduced by investing in several diverse markets and products, in the hope that aggregate return from these investments will at least attain some degree of stability. Hesmondhalgh (2002: 23) refers to this strategy as "throwing mud" in order to see what sticks.

Wikström (2009: 49) has defined the industry as follows: "The music industry consists of those companies concerned with developing musical content and personalities which can be communicated across multiple media."

The three parts of the industry are: recording, music publishing, and live performance. The latter segment is the oldest. For centuries musicians have managed to make money with their performances, albeit usually in modest amounts and certainly not in an industrial fashion. Music publishing began with the development of printing and became a sort of business in the late nineteenth century. Sound-recording emerged at the end of the nineteenth century (Edison, Columbia, and Victor). The recording companies "chose to include the task of finding and developing new personalities, as well as the manufacturing, marketing and distribution of the physical products as parts of their businesses. The music publishers, which previously had been such important actors in the music industry, were reduced to administering copyrights of composers and lyricists and to collecting royalties from the sales of records and other kinds of music licensing" (Wikström, 2009: 63).

The 1990s saw the development of digital technology, which led to the unprecedented growth of the recording industry. Sales in music worldwide peaked in 1998 (Wikström, 2009: 64). However, the early twenty-first century saw the decline of sales of the CD (which had only emerged in 1982) and the rise of digital technology, in particular the widespread use of the Internet. To date, the mix of digital technology and the Internet has proven to be more of a challenge than an opportunity to the music industry.

Another important factor has been the emergence of piracy on a massive scale in the form of unauthorized peer-to-peer sharing.

Sales of recorded music declined from US$26 billion in 2000 to US$17 billion in 2009. Whereas physical sales were plummeting, digital sales went up and companies began to invest more in online, subscription-based services. Examples are Apple's iTunes or mobile phone manufacturer Nokia's Comes with Music, or PlayNow Plus by Sony and Ericsson, offered by T-Mobile. Television became increasingly important for record companies. A good illustration is the case of Susan Boyle who was the great surprise in 2009 in Simon Cowell's TV show *Britain's Got Talent* when she sang "I Dreamed a Dream". Sony Music issued her first album and it sold 8.4 million copies worldwide.

The global music market was, by 2010, exceeding revenues of US$18 billion. Almost 80 per cent of this revenue was made by the five largest firms in recorded music: the Universal Music Group owned by Vivendi in France, Sony Music Entertainment owned by Sony Corporation of Japan, the Warner Music Group, USA, the EMI Group in the UK, owned by Terra Firma Capital Partners, and BMG Entertainment, which is a division of Bertelsmann in Germany. (For detailed and updated information visit the company websites. Useful sources are also available at www.musicinthecloud.net and BillBoard Soundscandata.)

MTV

The most successful combination of recorded music and television are Viacom's Music Television (MTV) channels, which reach out to over 500 million households and (especially young) people in over 160 countries. Launched in 1981, MTV became the largest 24/7 promotional campaign for a consumerist lifestyle

(Continued)

(Continued)

and for many artists the decisive factor in their success or marginaliza-tion. As McPhail (2002: 113) writes: "You are a musician who is part of it, you reach a global audience and become rich and world famous virtually overnight, but if you are not part of MTV, your chances of succeeding as a music video artist in any significant way are reduced substantially". MTV was the first twenty-four-hour, seven-day-a-week music video network. It is supported by advertising and constitutes a basic service on most cable networks. Targeted at the twelve- to thirty-four-year-old age group, MTV's international satellite-delivered music programming reaches over 71 million subscribers through over nine thousand affiliates around the globe. The biggest market is in Asia and the second biggest is in Europe. In particu-lar, its catering for local music tastes has made MTV very attractive for advertisers, such as Coca-Cola. It is also a major promotional medium for recording companies and Hollywood film companies. Because music tastes are highly localized, over 90 per cent of MTV's airtime is filled with locally produced programming. Despite this fact, teens round the world are basically listening to and viewing the same music videos. MTV worldwide is one large, continuous commercial advertising network. Not only are the music videos 'commercials' designed to enhance the sale of albums, but they are also sur-rounded by advertising for other products, and many artists openly promote commercial products within the music videos themselves.

Sources

McPhail, Th. (2002). *Global Communication*. London: Allyn and Bacon.

Sirois, A. and Wasko, J. (2011). The political economy of the recorded music industry. In Wasko, J., Murdock, G. and Sousa, H. (eds), *The Handbook of Political Economy of Communications*. Oxford: Blackwell Publishing. pp. 331–357.

Thussu, D.K. (2000). *International Communication: Continuity and Change*. London: Hodder.

?

Can the recorded music industry survive the global peer-to-peer, free down-loading of its products?

Television entertainment

This sector has become the key source for people's leisure worldwide. This industry is strongly affected by developments in the world economy at large and thus the world mar-ket is its determining context. The absolutely crucial factor in this industry is distribution, and the windows of distribution have increased, for example, theatres, home video, satellite transmission, pay-TV, and rentals.

A feature is also differential pricing, meaning that products have different prices in different buying markets. The seller will set a price that the buyer is willing to pay. It is also important to note that most countries are import-dependent. This leads to regulatory restrictions in the form of quota, for example. This implies the contradiction that in times of deregulation and privatization the regulatory measures are on the increase. The export prices of TV programmes are below the average production costs of sometimes US$1.5 million for one-hour episodes. (For more information on export prices for TV programmes, important sources are *Television Business International, Variety, Video Age,* and *TV World*.)

Film

Films, especially Hollywood feature films, are commodities that are sold worldwide. It is a high-risk industry! One of its problems is that buyers have to buy the products before they know whether they like them. The film industry is highly concentrated, with economies of scale, and thus with large barriers to new entrants. Only a few products account for the revenues of the total industry.

Distribution is essential and also very costly. Some films cost US$50 million in advertising and marketing. In order for the industry to survive and grow, product placement (the watches that actors wear, the cigarettes they smoke, the whiskies they drink, or the cars they drive) has become increasingly important and has even developed an industry of its own. To boost revenues, film production companies also use merchandising: film-related products are sometimes sold before the film is released. For the film *Jurassic Park*, over 1,000 products were sold as related merchandise, from boxer shorts to toothbrushes. The industry has been seriously affected by changes in production, distribution, and exhibition, and by piracy in global markets. Although there is some resistance against Hollywood worldwide and in spite of more local productions, the big Hollywood companies continue to do very well indeed. For filmed entertainment, the USA continues to be a leading exporter and its largest importer is Europe. There is also a growing demand for Hollywood films in China (Thussu, 2006: 158). (For further study on the film industry, there is a source for European TV revenues – the European Audiovisual Observatory – and an industry source for the US-based film industry – the website of the Motion Picture Association: www.mpaa.org.)

Children's television

There has been a proliferation of children's television channels (a useful source is *Screen Digest*). Among the most important networks are the Viacom-CBS-owned Nickelodeon (probably the first kids TV channel) that began in 1979, the Cartoon Network (owned by AOL-Time-Warner), the Disney Channel, and Fox Kids Worldwide (owned by the News Corporation). A large proportion of children's TV programmes use animation. The USA leads in exports of children's TV programmes, such as *Sesame Street*.

The industry entertains very effective links with the toy industry: "With their powerful marketing resources and huge programme libraries, the commercial children's channels can provide schedules of new services at low cost – which local companies find hard to compete with" (Thussu, 2000: 149).

The global advertisers

Advertising represents a key link between the global communication industry and the global economy. The global advertising agency has become an indispensable part of global communication.

Advertising emerged as a typical North American phenomenon. It grew worldwide with the expansion of transnational corporations (such as Procter & Gamble – the largest global advertiser – Coca-Cola, Ford, Shell, Unilever and Nestlé) towards global market shares as a result of their need to stimulate consumer demand worldwide. Important factors in the growth of global advertising were, in addition to the globalization of major companies, the growth of free market economies around the world, the availability of new communication technologies (from satellite broadcasting to the Internet), and the politics of communication deregulation (since the 1989s) that facilitated the emergence of commercial media outlets worldwide that were in need of advertising income.

Advertising grew very rapidly in the 1960s as many TNCs wanted the services of advertising agencies for their foreign markets. As a result, these agencies (mainly headquartered in the USA) established offices in many countries around the world. According to Noreene Janus, "What the agencies offer their transnational clients is now a total communication package, including product design, packaging, testing, and positioning in the market. This 'total communication package' represents the marketing experience gathered by the agency on a global basis over the past decade" (Janus, 1981: 306). This served the preference of the largest advertisers to work with one global agency.

In the process of global expansion and consolidation a good deal of merging between agencies took place. As Armand Mattelart wrote, "Concentration produces more concentration. Fear of the competitor initiates a spiral of further rapprochements. This is what is revealed by the process of formation of specialized companies for the purchase of advertising space" (Mattelart, 1991: 17). Thomas McPhail has suggested an answer to the question why there are so many mergers. "First, in some cases, the firms want to acquire creative talent not available in house. Second, others seek to acquire a strategic niche to complement current strengths. And third, some firms realize they have to be aggressive and expand before a competitor attempts a take-over of either them or a rival they are looking at" (McPhail, 2002: 164). Mergers are not without problems that often start "with the question of client confidentiality, when the client begins to worry about the cross-links with agencies that handle their competitors' budgets, and with whom they are therefore liable to come into conflict" (Sinclair, 2012: 18).

The globalization of advertising can also be seen from increases worldwide in the proportions of GDP spent in advertising and there seems to be still space for more. The economic problems of the late 1990s slowed down growth somewhat. "Even in the developed markets of western Europe, for example, most nations still spend no more than one half the US amount on advertising per capita" (McChesney, 2000: 192). In the early twenty-first century there were also rapidly emerging new markets for advertising in Brazil, Russia, India, and China, the so-called BRIC countries.

Global advertising is most visible through the rise of the global brands (Moor, 2007; de Mooij, 2013), such as Adidas, Apple, Coca-Cola, McDonalds, Nike, Ralph Lauren, and IKEA. These brands have achieved almost iconic status and are inseparably linked with the global spread of modern ideas and lifestyles.

? Try to identify the most popular global brands in your country and discuss why they have achieved such national popularity.

The global advertising industry is structured so that the top tier of the industry is dominated by four global groups. These are Omnicom, WPP, Interpublic, and Publicis Groupe.

Omnicom

One of the key networks within Omnicom is BBDO. This agency is known for the high level of its creative products and was often the winner in global advertising festivals. DDB Worldwide is another important advertising network within the Omnicom orbit. In the 1990s Omnicom acquired the French agency TBWA. Among the clients of Omnicom are BMW, Volkswagen, and Mercedes.

WPP

The famous agency Young & Rubicam Brands is, since 2000, a wholly-owned subsidiary of WPP. Ogilvy & Mather Worldwide (established in 1948 by advertising legend David Ogilvy) is also part of WPP. Since 1987 WPP also owns JWT (the official name for J. Walter Thompson), one of the most famous brands in advertising history and probably the world's first advertising agency. Among the clients of WPP are Ford, IBM, Johnson & Johnson, Procter & Gamble, and Microsoft.

Interpublic Group of Companies

Since 1961 this agency, which was formerly called McCann-Erikson, provides in over 100 countries worldwide services in consumer advertising, marketing, public relations, and media buying. In 2011 its revenues totalled US$7 billion. Among the clients of the Interpublic Group are General Motors, Microsoft, and Unilever.

Publicis Groupe

In 2003 the Publicis Groupe acquired the large global marketing Bcom3, created by the Leo Burnett agency – the legendary creator of Uncle Ben and the Marlboro Man. Since

2000 the well-known network of Saatchi & Saatchi is also housed in the Publicis Groupe. Among the clients of the Publicis Groupe are Toyota, Nestlé, and Coca-Cola.

Challenge

A special challenge for the advertising industry is the issue of regulation. "While there is some statutory regulation governing advertising in the US ... the UK ... and Australia, the advertisers and agencies in these and many other countries, in the face of pressure from consumer, community and environment groups, have sought strenuously to keep statutory regulation to a minimum and to set up their own self-regulation arrangements instead" (Sinclair, 2012: 90). Sinclair concluded that such arrangements have proven to be much more satisfactory to the industry than to consumers and their organizations (2012: 91).[2]

? What could be the global cultural effects of advertising? Discuss this question in the light of the following quote: "Transnational advertising poses a particular problem because the content of promotional messages are sometimes culturally laden and can have a significant influence on the values, economies, and politics of host nations" (Holwerda and Gershon, 1997: 61). Will global brands persuade people around the world to buy the same products and will they thus create a uniform global consumer culture?

Notes

1. Websites of global communication companies:

    AFP = www.afp.com

    Al Jazeera = www.aljazeera.et/english

    Apple = www.apple.com

    Associated Press = www.ap.org

    BBC World Service = www.bbc.co.uk/worldservice

    Bertelsmann = www.bertelsmann.com

    CNN = www.cnn.com

    Deutsche Welle = www.dwelle.de

    Disney = http://disney.go.com

    INTELSAT = www.intelsat.com

    Inter Press Service = www.ips.net

    MTV = www.mtv.com

    News Corporation = www.newscorp.com

    Microsoft = www.microsoft.com

    Reuters = www.reuters.com

    Sony Corporation = www.world.sony.com

    Time Warner = www.timewarner.com

    Viacom = www.viacom.com

    Vivendi = www.vivendi.com

2. Sinclair (2012) provides evidence through case studies on child obesity and green advertising.

Reading spotlight

Advertising

Klein, N. (1999). *No Logo*. Toronto: Knopf Canada.

> The author focusses on the issue of global branding and deals with topics such as Asian sweatshops, culture jamming and corporate censorship. She gives critical attention to companies such as Nike, McDonalds, Shell, and Microsoft. The four parts of the book are "No Space", "No Choice", "No Jobs", and "No Logo".

Music

Wikström, P. (2009). *The Music Industry*. Cambridge: Polity Press.

> This is an important study on the changes in the music industry in the beginning of the twenty-first century. The author gives us a global survey of the music industry and analyzes how music is produced in the interaction between global music corporations, independent music companies and the audience.

News

Van Ginneken, J. (1998). *Understanding Global News*. London: Sage.

> In this easily readable and well-documented book Van Ginneken offers a critical analysis of the construction of news about the world. He addresses such questions as "who gets to speak in the news", "when does something become news", and "where does the news come from". The focus of the book is on the social representation of the world by North American and West-European news media.

Online resources

Visit the book's companion website at **https://study.sagepub.com/hamelink** to watch the author discussing the theme of this chapter: **Global News**

Visit the book's companion website at **https://study.sagepub.com/hamelink** to access the following journal articles free of charge:

Abramson, B.D. (2002). Country music and cultural industry: mediating structures in transnational media flow. *Media, Culture & Society*, 24(2): 255–274.

Boyd-Barrett, O. (2000). National and international news agencies: issues of crisis and realignment. *Gazette*, 62(1): 5–18.

Cottle, S. and Rai, M. (2008). Global 24/7 news providers: emissaries of global dominance or global public sphere? *Global, Media and Communication*, 4(2): 157–181.

Fuchs, C. (2009). Information and communication technologies and society: a contribution to the critique of the political economy of the Internet. *European Journal of Communication*, 24(1): 69–87.

Nanwawy, M. and Powers, S. (2010). Al-Jazeera English: a conciliatory medium in a conflict-driven environment? *Global Media and Communication*, 6(1): 61–84.

Smythe, D. (1960). On the Political Economy of Communications. *Journalism & Mass Communication Quarterly*, 37(4): 563–572.

Wilke, J., Heimprecht, C. and Cohen, A. (2012). The geography of foreign news on television: a comparative study of 17 countries. *International Communication Gazette*, 74(4): 301–322.

Further reading

On global news

Boyd-Barrett, O. and Rantanen, T. (eds) *The Globalization of News*. London, Sage.

Hachten, W. (1999). *The World news prism: changing media of international communication*. Ames, Iowa State University.

Mattelart, Armand (1991). *Advertising International*. London: Routledge.

McPhail, Th. (2002) *The Roles of Global News Agencies. In McPhail, Th. Global Communication*. London, Allyn and Bacon, pp; 145–160.

On global entertainment

Guback, T.H. (1985). Hollywood's international market. In Ballo, T. (ed.), *The American Film Industry*. Madison, WI: University of Wisconson Press. pp. 463–486.

Hoskins, C., McFadyen, S. and Finn, A. (1997). *Global Television and Film: An Introduction to the Economics of the Business*. Oxford: Oxford University Press.

Sirois, A. and Wasko, J. (2011). The political economy of the recorded music industry. In Wasko, J., Murdock, G. and Sousa, H. (eds), *The Handbook of Political Economy of Communications*. Oxford: Blackwell Publishing. pp. 331–357.

Wasko, J. (1997). Hollywood meets Madison Avenue: the commercialisation of US films. In Sreberny, A., Winseck, D., McKenna, J. and Boyd-Barrett, O. (eds), *Media in a Global Context*. London: Arnold, pp. 113–130.

On global advertising

Ewen, S. (1976). *Captains of Consciousness: Advertising and the Social Roots of the Consumer Culture*. New York: McGraw-Hill.

Ewen, S. and Ewen, E. (1982). *Channels of Desire: Mass Images and the Shaping of American Consciousness*. New York: McGraw-Hill.

Moor, L. (2007). *The Rise of Brands*. London: Bloomsbury Academic Publishers.

RESEARCH ASSIGNMENT

What are the main sources of global news in a popular daily newspaper in your country?

What are the main sources of global news in a TV news programme that is watched by many people in your country?

What method(s) will you use to identity relevant news sources?

How would you analyze whether there are differences between newspaper and TV news sources?

How much time and money would be needed for a valid investigation of these questions?

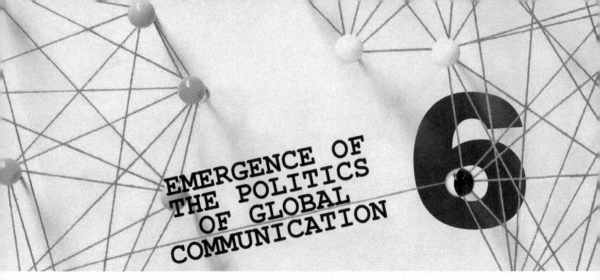

EMERGENCE OF THE POLITICS OF GLOBAL COMMUNICATION

6

From Heather Hudson I learned about the political, economic, and the social impact of global communication satellites. She inspired me with the insights her work offered on understanding the interactions between modern communication technology and institutional policies, and the potential risks and rewards involved.

Heather Hudson (1947–)

Hudson analyzed in critical detail the role of satellite technology in developing countries and explored how (national) policymaking can shape the impact of this technology upon business, health care, and education. Hudson was Director of the Telecommunications Management and Policy programme at the University of San Francisco from 1987 to 2009 and moved from there to Anchorage to become Professor and Director of the Institute of Social and Economic Research at the University of Alaska in 2010. She was specialist in such fields as international communication policy and planning and communication policy for rural development.

Important readings for the study of global communications are: *When Telephones Reach the Village: The Role of Telecommunication in Rural Development* (1984); *Communication Satellites: Their Development and Impact* (1990); "Converging technologies and changing realities: toward universal access to telecom in the developing world" (1997); and *From Rural Village to Global Village: Telecommunication in the Information Age* (2009).

For the study of global communication, Heather Hudson taught us to critically reflect on who makes policies and for what purposes.

This chapter introduces you to politics in the field of global communication. It traces its developments from the early nineteenth century to the late twentieth century.[1] The following chapter will then look at more recent shifts and trends in the early twenty-first century.

Governance

When the politics of communication (national, regional, or global) is discussed in the literature or at conferences, almost inevitably the word "governance" pops up. Its frequent use is not without confusion and contestation.

Governance, as a concept, gained wide recognition with the 1995 report of the UN Commission on Global Governance. In *Our Global Neighbourhood*, the Commission proposed that "Governance is the sum of many ways in which individuals and institutions, public and private, manage their common affairs. It includes formal institutions and regimes empowered to enforce compliance as well as informal arrangements that people and institutions either have agreed to or perceive to be in their interest" (UN Commission on Global Governance, 1995: 2). The UNDP *Human Development Report* of 1999 followed this direction and stressed that "governance does not mean government" but "the framework of rules, institutions and established practices that set limits and gives incentives for the behaviour of individuals, organizations and firms" (UNDP, 1999: 8). To this UNDP description should be added that governance is best understood as a process rather than as an institutional arrangement.

Precisely because of the broad conceptualization of governance, the concept can be used in a variety of contexts. Among its many different uses in the current literature are the following:

- Governance is used by the World Bank and Western donor countries in the sense of "good governance", which refers to the requirement for developing countries to demonstrate that their societies recognize democratic practices, respect human rights and the rule of law.
- In the business management literature, governance is used as "corporate governance", which refers to the requirement of transparency in corporations towards the shareholders.
- With civil society organizations governance is popular as "global governance", which refers to a global civil ethic as the basis for world management without government.
- Governance can also mean "corporate public management", which refers to new forms of public management by which public institutions are managed as if they are corporations.
- In neo-liberal economic schools, governance means "market governance", which refers to the self-regulatory potential of market forces.

The common denominator in the different uses of governance is the reference to ways of managing critical issues in the public, the semi-private, and the private spheres of modern societies. In past decades important shifts have taken place in the institutional arrangements for this management. New governance arrangements came about that involved a multitude of governmental and non-governmental agencies. In some arrangements governments retained the essential power of decision-making. Other stakeholders may be consulted, or be partners in debates, but the national states have the leadership and other actors are marginalized. In other arrangements the market forces of supply and demand are in control and only voluntary, self-imposed rules without enforcement mechanisms can intervene. Yet other arrangements are stakeholder-driven and imply forms of joint governance by all stakeholders, as in trilateral arrangements between states, commercial firms, and civil society organizations.

Governance on the national level can be described as a different way of managing national societies that emerged in response to the failure of conventional representative democracies and the need to accommodate the interests of new actors. Since, on the international level, there is no global government, the international community has begun to explore new forms of multi-stakeholder management of common issues.

Regarding the management of media issues in modern societies, governance arrangements are typically confronted with challenges related to the equity of access, the diversity of content, the protection against harmful content, the freedom of communication, the limits to cross-ownership, the corporate concentration in media markets, the global trade in media products, the protection of intellectual property rights, the public's right to know, and the future of public service broadcasting. For the management of these common affairs, governance arrangements in democratic societies will have to confront the essential normative criteria of legitimacy and accountability.

Legitimacy of governance refers to the adoption of a consensus among all stakeholders about rules, to the mutual trust between rulers and ruled, and to mechanisms of appeal whenever decisions are contested by stakeholders. Accountability of governance refers to the readiness of decision-makers to respond to inquiries, complaints, and contestations in relation to their actions and to mechanisms of remedy and redress.

Governance of global communication politics began with rules for postal communication, telegraphic communication, and the protection of the rights of authors. In the early twentieth century there were also concerns about rules for the social impact of the mass media.

Postal communication

From the sixteenth century a postal system had developed in Europe that served several countries. The system was governed through bilateral arrangements that accommodated the specific needs of the countries involved. The technical developments in railway transportation and steam engines for shipping began to necessitate changes in the complex set of bilateral rules for the calculation of rates in different currencies and according to different scales. In the nineteenth century the awareness arose that with the modernization of transport, the administrative formalities would also have to be standardized.

The first international meeting to address this was convened in 1862 by the US Postmaster-General, Montgomery Blair. The conference, held at Paris on May 11, 1863, brought delegates together from Austria, Belgium, Costa Rica, Denmark, France, Great Britain, the Hanseatic Towns, Italy, the Netherlands, Portugal, Prussia, the Sandwich Islands, Spain, Switzerland, and the United States of America. Several general principles were adopted by the conference as the first step towards a common postal agreement. These principles were to regulate the conventions that postal administrations would conclude between each other. However, the application of commonly accepted principles within bilateral agreements failed to meet the demands imposed by changing international relations. In 1868 Heinrich von Stephan, a senior official in the postal administration of the North German Confederation, prepared a proposal for an international postal union. Through his government this plan was submitted to a Plenipotentiary conference that was held at the invitation of the Swiss government at Berne on September 15, 1874. The 22 countries present at the conference founded, through the treaty of Berne, the General Postal Union.[2] The convention entered into force on July 1, 1875. In 1878 the name of the organization was changed into Universal Postal Union (UPU). The 1874 Berne conference introduced basic norms and rules that still hold today. Among these are the guaranteed freedom of transit within the territory of the Union and the standardization of charges to be collected by each country for letter-post items addressed to any part of the Union's territory.

Telegraphic communication

The development of telegraphy in the early nineteenth century brought about the need for standardization and cooperation across national borders. The first telegraph lines stopped at national borders and messages had to be transcribed and then hand-carried across the frontier. A similar problem was faced by early railway traffic when countries deployed different sizes of rails.

Next to standardization, inter-state cooperation was also necessary to guarantee the free passage of messages and to organize international tariffing.

By 1865 the need was felt to substitute a multiplicity of bilateral, trilateral, and quadrilateral arrangements for a multilateral agreement. In that year, France invited the European states to an international conference that became the founding meeting of the International Telegraphy Union (May 17, 1865). With the establishment of this predecessor of today's International Telecommunication Union (ITU), the first treaty to deal with global communication was adopted: the International Telegraphy Convention. The original text of the Convention stated that the signatories desire to secure for their telegraphy traffic the advantages of simple and reduced tariffs, to improve the conditions of international telegraphy, and to establish a permanent cooperation among themselves while retaining their freedom of operation.[3]

The Convention adopted the Morse code as the first international telegraph standard. Among the basic norms that were adopted were the protection of the secrecy of correspondence, the right of everybody to use international telegraphy, and the rejection of all liability for international telegraphy services. The Contracting Parties also reserved the to stop any transmission that they considered dangerous for state security, in violation of national laws, public order or morals.

As a result of significant technical inventions made during the First World War, radio was advancing rapidly in the years immediately after the war. Radio became an attractive commercial commodity and a vital tool for propaganda. All this contributed to the post-war need for domestic and international regulation. In particular, the emergence of short-wave broadcasting made it necessary to formulate standards for international radio communications. The first Radio Conference after the First World War was held at Washington in 1927. Eighty countries attended to draft a new Radio Convention and Radio Regulations.

A key element of contention at the conference was the different perceptions of the role of the state in telecommunication. Whereas "the companies in the United States did not want a document that would further broaden the appearance or reality of government control over them", most of the participating governments "viewed state control as necessary in order to maximize equitable use of the medium" (Luther, 1988: 28). In 1932 the Thirteenth International Telegraph conference and the Fourth International radio-telegraph conference were held at the same time in Madrid. The joint meetings led to the adoption of a single convention and to the establishment of the International Telecommunication Union.

The protection of author's rights

The emergence of the need for multilateral arrangements on author's copyright in the nineteenth century is linked with the expansion of international trading and the related need to protect works created in one country and sold in another. The expansion of international contacts increasingly confronted authors with the fact that intellectual property rights had very limited value if there was no international recognition and if the crucial question of the treatment of foreign authors was not resolved.

In the early bilateral treaties there was recognition of the principle of "national treatment" or "assimilation". Foreigners were granted the same protection as nationals. Gradually, however, this shifted to the adoption of the "reciprocity" principle. This means that foreigners could only be awarded the right they might enjoy in their home countries. Generosity gave way to the mundane preference to treat foreigners no better than they would be treated at home. The French–Russian treaty of 1861 left little doubt about the significance of the "reciprocity" norm. The text said "it is understood that the reciprocal rights accorded only extend to those authors whose countries extend the same rights" (Cavalli, 1986: 77). The bilateral treaties assisted the proliferation of the notion of legal protection of author's rights, but at the same time the proliferation of treaties created a very complex situation that was not always to the benefit of authors who could not, as a rule, grasp all the legal implications of so many arrangements.

More important, however, was the problem that several treaties were primarily based on trading relations between states and the force of the copyright arrangement would largely depend on the quality of commercial relations. In addition to this, the possibility of war between states seriously eroded any legal security for authors. International protection could easily be undermined as a result of national politics. The protection of foreign authors was limited because the "reciprocity" principle applied and because many states had a priority interest in the commercial protection of their domestic authors rather than in promoting the international accessibility of literature.

The inadequacy of the bilateral arrangements pushed the creation of the Berne Union. Its establishment was also facilitated by a series of literary and artistic congresses that had addressed the urgency of multilateral arrangements. A significant preparation for Berne was the first international conference on copyright held in Brussels in 1858, which resolved, among other things, that the principle of the international recognition of the property of literary and artistic works should be applied on the basis of national treatment. In June 1878 the international literary congress, organized by the "Société des gens de lettres en France", took place in Paris. The society, set up in 1838, had among its members famous authors such as Honoré de Balzac and Victor Hugo. Using the occasion of the 1878 universal exposition at Paris, the society convened a congress that primarily focused on an international right for the protection of literary property.

One of the tangible results of the congress was the establishment of the international literary and artistic association, ALAI. The association, which still exists today, had as its first objective the defence of the principle of literature as intellectual property. The participants of the congress stressed the national treatment principle in one of the resolutions and they proposed the initiative for a multilateral convention on literary property. The next step towards Berne was the International Congress on Artistic Property of September 1878 at Paris. Again the principle of national treatment was supported, but more importantly the congress proposed the constitution of a multilateral union for the adoption of uniform legislation on literary property (Cavalli, 1986: 138).

In the development of author's rights the basic principles have been to ensure remuneration for an author by protecting his work against reproduction (for fifty years after the author's lifetime), to demand respect for the individual integrity of the creator, to encourage the development of the arts, literature and science, and to promote a wider dissemination of literary, artistic, and scientific works.

Social concerns about mass media

With the proliferation of printed and especially broadcast media (in the late nineteenth and early twentieth centuries) serious concerns about the social impact of the mass media emerged. There was considerable excitement about the positive and constructive contribution of the media to peaceful international relations. Such positive expectations were expressed in the 1933 Convention for Facilitating the International Circulation of Films of an Educational Character. This convention was signed in Geneva on October 11, 1933. The contracting parties to the convention, which was registered with the secretariat of the League of Nations, considered the international circulation of educational films which contribute "towards the mutual understanding of peoples, in conformity with the aims of the League of Nations and consequently encourage moral disarmament" highly desirable. In order to facilitate the circulation of such films the signatories agreed to exempt their importation, transit, and exportation from all customs duties and accessory charges of any kind.

There was, however, also a serious concern about the negative social impact of the mass media. A moral, educational concern was expressed regarding the spread across borders of obscene publications. This concern resulted in the adoption of the 1910 and 1924 treaties on traffic in obscene publications. The 1924 International Convention for the Suppression of the Circulation of and Traffic in Obscene Publications declared it a punishable offence "to make or produce or have in possession (for trade or public exhibition) obscene writings, drawings, prints, paintings, printed matter, pictures, posters, emblems, photographs, cinematograph films or any other obscene objects". It was also punishable to import or export said obscene matters for trade or public exhibition and persons committing the offence "shall be amenable to the Courts of the Contracting Party in whose territories the offence … was committed".

Concern about the negative impact of the mass media also arose from the increasing use of the mass media (in the course of the nineteenth century) as instruments of foreign diplomacy. Although this was particularly the case with the newspapers, the development of wireless radio increased the potential for this new form of diplomacy. Increasingly diplomats shifted from traditional forms of silent diplomacy to a public diplomacy in which the constituencies of other states were directly addressed. In most cases this in fact amounted to the propagandistic abuse of the medium. During the First World War an extensive use was made of the means of propaganda. This psychological warfare continued after the war had ended and international short-wave radio began to proliferate.

By 1923 American radio amateurs had discovered the long-range features of high frequencies (HF) and conducted two-way transatlantic communications. Soon several states began to use HF for international broadcasting. In 1926 there were in Europe already some 26 stations that had international transmissions. The Dutch began with broadcasts to the East-Indies colonies in 1929, the French started their overseas service in 1931, the BBC followed suit with an Empire Service in 1932, the Belgians in 1934. In 1930 the USSR began using short-wave broadcasting to reach foreign audiences.

In the immediate post-war period, the League of Nations initiated discussions about the contribution of the international press to peace. The underlying concern with the role of the press in international relations found expression in a resolution that was adopted on September 25, 1925 by the Assembly of the League of Nations. This resolution called for a committee of experts representing the press of the different continents "with a view to determining methods of contributing towards the organisation of peace, especially: (a) by ensuring the more rapid and less costly transmission of press news with a view to reducing risks of international misunderstanding; and (b) by discussing all technical problems the settlement of which would be conducive to the tranquillisation of public opinion" (Kubka and Nordenstreng, 1986: 71). The resolution referred to the press as "the most effective means of guiding public opinion towards that moral disarmament which is a concomitant condition of material disarmament".

In August 1927 the League convened a first conference of press experts in Geneva to deal with such problems as the provision of information that would "calm down public opinion in different countries" (Kubka and Nordenstreng, 1986: 54). The conference made the appeal to the press "to contribute by every means at its disposal to the consolidation of peace, to combat hatred between nationalities and between classes which are the greatest dangers to peace, and to prepare the way for moral disarmament". In September 1931, the Assembly of the League of Nations adopted a resolution that requested the Council of the League to consider the possibility of studying with the help of the Press, "the difficult problem of the spread of information which may threaten to disturb the peace or the good understanding between nations". The increasing concern of the League for moral disarmament evidently reflected the actual historical developments of the period, such as the emergence of Nazism in Germany.

When the World Disarmament Conference opened in February 1932, the press was given great importance in moving public opinion towards moral disarmament.

A second conference with press experts was convened in Copenhagen (1932) and one of its resolutions addressed, among other issues, the problem of inaccurate news. Following the Copenhagen conference, a conference of governmental press bureaux and representatives of the press was held at Madrid in November, 1933. This conference adopted a resolution on the right to correct false information.

In 1931 the League of Nations decided to ask the Institute for Intellectual Cooperation (the predecessor of UNESCO) to conduct a study on all questions raised by the use of radio for good international relations. In 1933 the study was published ("Broadcasting and Peace") and it recommended the drafting of a binding multilateral treaty. Under the threat of war emanating from Germany after 1933, the treaty was indeed drafted and concluded on September 23, 1936, with the signatures from 28 states. The fascist states did not participate. The International Convention concerning the Use of Broadcasting in the Cause of Peace entered into force on April 2, 1938 after ratification or accession by nine countries: Brazil, the United Kingdom, Denmark, France, India, Luxembourg, New Zealand, the Union of South Africa, and Australia. Basic to the provisions of the Convention was the recognition of the need to prevent, through rules established by common agreement, broadcasting from being used in a manner prejudicial to good international understanding. These agreed-upon rules included the prohibition of transmissions which could incite the population of any territory "to acts incompatible with the internal order or security of contracting parties" or which were likely to harm good international understanding by incorrect statements. The contracting parties also agree to ensure "that any transmission likely to harm good international understanding by incorrect statements shall be rectified at the earliest possible moment". In 1994 the Convention was still in force and had been ratified by 26 member states of the United Nations.

> Are the social concerns around the early twentieth century fundamentally dif-
> ferent from today's social concerns about public communication?

Developments after the Second World War

It is always somewhat hazardous to identify the key components of historical processes and there is probably always an element of subjective preference and (by implication) of distortion in the exercise. Surveying the past decades of world politics in the substantive issues of global communication it would appear that among the most important factors affecting its development and orientation were the multilateral institutions that to a great extent became the negotiating platforms for state and non-state actors, the North–South and East–West confrontations, the growing importance of the non-state actors, and the economic and technological changes in the world.

The emergence of multilateralism

With the creation of the United Nations and its specialized agencies, a crucial group of institutions for multilateral policy evolution and policy coordination entered the international system. The General Assembly of the UN (particularly through the International Law Commission and several sub-commissions) and the International Court of Justice became the primary movers in the progressive development of the norms and rules that make up the current system of international law.

The UN General Assembly has contributed to global communication politics through a vast number of resolutions that address such divergent issues as the jamming of broadcasts, the protection of journalists on dangerous missions, direct satellite broadcasting, or human rights aspects of science and technology. Multilateral policy is also made by the specialized agencies of the United Nations and several of these became important regulators for the field of communication. This is particularly true for such organizations as the International Telecommunications Union (ITU), the Universal Postal Union (UPU), UNESCO, and the World Intellectual Property Organization (WIPO).

To a far lesser extent, the International Labour Organization (ILO) became involved through employment questions relating to communication professionals, and the World Health Organization (WHO) and Food and Agriculture Organization (FAO) through work in the field of standards for advertising and marketing of health and food products. Standards affecting world communications are also set in the International Civil Aviation Organization (ICAO), which has adopted rules for aircraft telecommunications systems, and the International Maritime Organization (IMO), which has addressed issues of maritime communications.

In addition to the already existing multilateral fora that became UN specialized agencies, new regulatory bodies were also established, such as the meanwhile defunct

Intergovernmental Bureau for Informatics (IBI) and UNCTAD, the United Nations Conference on Trade and Development, which has adopted standards in such fields as intellectual property and transfer of technology.

An important multilateral organization which does not belong to the United Nations family is the General Agreement on Tariffs and Trade (the GATT was replaced in 1995 by the World Trade Organization (WTO). Among the other important multilateral bodies with participation of national governments are the organizations that have been established for the operational application of space telecommunications technology. These are primarily the intergovernmental satellite systems – established by treaty – INTELSAT and Inmarsat.

Three other intergovernmental multilateral institutions should be mentioned, although they are not as broadly representative and in fact are more regionally oriented. However, they have made very significant contributions to world communication politics. These are the Organization for European Economic Cooperation (OECD), the Conference on Security and Cooperation in Europe, and the Council of Europe. In such fields as the freedom of information, and protection of transborder flows, the standard-setting work of these organizations has had an important impact on global communication governance.

The United Nations and its specialized agencies have from their inception involved non-governmental organizations (NGOs) in their policymaking processes. In the development of international human rights law, for example, the international non-governmental organizations (INGOs) have played a very important role. INGOs, such as Amnesty International, have contributed to the implementation of human rights standards. In UN agencies such as the ITU, WIPO, and UNESCO, INGOs have made very significant contributions to the formulation of world communication politics.

The growth of non-governmental organizations

In the post-1945 phase of the evolution of world communication politics, an important contribution was offered by a rapidly growing group of INGOs. INGOs are partly international, in terms of membership and activities, and partly nationally based. Obviously, they do not have the legal power to issue binding decisions, but they can influence the policymaking processes of the intergovernmental organizations as expert groups or as lobbying agents. They can also define standards for their own conduct that may have a political significance beyond the members of the group they represent. Illustrations are the efforts of the international professional bodies in journalism to arrive at a self-regulatory code of conduct, or the self-regulatory codes that are adopted by the International Public Relations Association and the International Advertising Association.

The United Nations and its specialized agencies have from their inception involved nongovernmental organizations in their policymaking processes. In the development of international human rights law, for example, INGOs have played an important role. INGOs such as Amnesty International have contributed to a crucial instrument for the implementation of human rights standards: "the mobilization of shame". Another example is provided by those INGOs that keep the World Health Organization informed of acts by multinational companies that violate the WHO code on the marketing of breast-milk substitutes. In the field of development cooperation, new policy insights have been forced upon public institutions through INGO pressure regarding concerns about women, population, health, and the environment. Various resolutions by the UN General Assembly have accorded special significance to the contributions of organizations representing scientists, employers, and workers' unions in negotiations on a code of conduct for transnational corporations

The East–West confrontation

The East–West confrontation had a significant influence on the multilateral negotiations. Its overall effect was that most of the issues on the political agenda were located in the context of the "super power" conflict, which made their resolution complex and often unattainable. For example, Cold War suspicion and distrust made it difficult to reconcile different positions on the management of the radio frequency spectrum and largely obstructed planning for the High Frequency bands. It also brought special regulatory issues to the agenda, such as those related to the phenomenon of "jamming". When in 1947 the Voice of America established Russian and Eastern European language services, the Soviet Union decided to begin operating full-time jamming against these services. With the heating up of the Cold War, jamming increased and as it continued throughout the 1950s and 1960s multilateral efforts to negotiate a settlement remained unsuccessful. The fundamental debate on freedom of information was strongly affected by the East–West adverse positions, as were the debates on Third World demands for a restructuring of the international provision of information. During the past decades there was in many instances an allegiance between the position of the Soviet bloc and the Third World community. On the one hand, this meant that hegemonic positions of the Western bloc (particularly the United States) could be challenged with at least the (largely theoretical) capacity to outvote the minority of affluent market economies. On the other hand, the alliance did not necessarily benefit the developing countries as their most legitimate demands were also conveniently put into the unproductive bi-polarity of mutually exclusive world views.

The North–South confrontation

Next to the East–West tension, the demise of the colonial powers could not fail to have an impact on the politics of world communication. In the post-war period a large number of new, post-colonial states emerged in Asia and Africa. In their struggle to become sovereign entities, they confronted, in addition to political and economic dependencies, the cultural legacy of former colonial relations.

The first generation of post-colonial nationalist leaders was intent on creating national integration in state structures that were internally threatened by the existence of multiple nationalities (often artificially thrown together) and externally beleaguered by a forceful cultural diplomacy enacted through Western foreign policy and business interests. In the early 1950s the first collective performance by the post-colonial states began. In those years the political cooperation between African and Asian countries, in particular, was at stake, as the 1955 Bandung conference demonstrated. In the 1960s this coalition was extended to include the Latin American countries, which brought especially economic problems to the agenda. Actually, since the mid-1960s, the non-aligned movement has given increasing attention to strategies for the development of economic links among the countries of the South. Alongside the non-aligned movement, the so-called Group of 77 came into existence at the first UNCTAD conference in 1964. These two overlapping groups were both affected by the ambivalent effort of the South to strengthen horizontal linkages and to cope with the remaining links with the former colonial powers.

It became clear in the early 1970s that these latter links had an important cultural component. In particular, the non-aligned summit in Algiers (1973) began to extend South–South cooperation to the area of cultural development.

Throughout the 1970s the debate on the information issue (which took place primarily in UNESCO) developed in the context of an economic dialogue between the North and the South which was largely inspired by the threat of a North–South confrontation over oil prices. In the context of this threat, the United Nations General Assembly adopted (in 1974) the Declaration and Programme of Action on the Establishment of a New International Economic Order. In the same year the Charter of Economic Rights and Duties of States was adopted. In 1976 the UNCTAD IV at Nairobi adopted the Integrated Programme for Commodities and a new financial institution was created to support the effort to stabilize the world's commodity markets, the Common Fund. In the reality of world politics all this meant very little.

As a matter of fact, by the end of the 1970s the North withdrew from this dialogue as the oil-threat had subsided. The UNCTAD V in 1979 at Manila marked the point at which the North–South round of negotiations on a fundamental restructuring of the world economy effectively ended. A few efforts to renew the dialogue in the early 1980s (such as the Cancun Summit, 1981, or the UNCTAD VI in 1983) met with no success.

In 1958 the UN General Assembly requested the Economic and Social Council (ECOSOC) to formulate "a programme of concrete action and measures on the international plane which could be undertaken for the development of information enterprises in under-developed countries" . The United Nations specialized agencies were invited to contribute to this initiative.

UNESCO was assigned to survey the problems involved in the development of communication. Among the other specialized agencies to become active in North–South issues was the International Telecommunication Union. As a matter of fact, already in 1959, the ITU Convention made reference to the need of cooperation and coordination related to development assistance. Also, the Universal Postal Union got involved with development assistance. This was seen to fall within its mandate to contribute to the organization and development of postal services and the fostering of international postal cooperation. Through the United Nations Development Programme (UNDP), the UPU contributed to various training programmes and institutions for postal administrations and to the technical cooperation among developing countries.

Other UN agencies that became engaged in development assistance in the communications field were the FAO (particularly assistance to develop support communication projects), the WHO (projects on media and health/nutrition), the UNFPA(United Nations Population Fund with projects for communication in family planning), UNICEF (communication for social development projects), and in particular UNDP (United Nations Development Programme).

The developing countries did not merely provide the incentive for cooperation programmes, they also challenged the existing international industrial property system and the conventional copyright conventions. Similar challenges were launched against dominant telecommunications arrangements. For example, they took issue with such conventionally adopted policy principles as "first come, first served" in resource allocations.

In the field of space resources, the developing countries were instrumental in introducing the concept of "common heritage" in the 1979 Moon Treaty. Herewith, a claim was laid to equitable access to space resources following the formulation of such basic principles in the 1967 Outer Space Treaty as "the exploration and use of outer space, including the Moon and other celestial bodies, shall be carried out for the benefit and in the interests of all countries, irrespective of their degree of economic or scientific development, and shall be the province of all mankind".

The global economy

Trading across borders grew exponentially after 1945 and added to the volume of movements of goods, services, capital, people, and information worldwide. World exports increased from US$63 billion in 1948 to over US$400 billion by 1977. The need to regulate world trade led to the establishment of such important trade and monetary negotiating platforms as the GATT, the International Monetary Fund and the OECD. The transnational corporations became vital actors in the world economy. Since the early 1950s there has been a rapid rise of transnational industrial and financial companies. These spread their affiliates across the globe and began marketing, advertising, and trading in many of the developing countries. As part of the growing world business system, the branch of communication conglomerates developed into one of the leading sectors.

Increasingly, the world flows of news and entertainment began to be controlled by ever fewer companies, often closely interlocked among themselves and with other industrial and financial interests. The increase in scope of industrial activities led to a rapidly growing need of extensive information networks. Telecommunications became critical to the coordination of the dispersed activities of transnational corporations. To support marketing, advertising, and public relations, large companies began to develop their own media production capacities. As a result of these developments the transnational business system emerged as a formidable lobby in multilateral negotiations.

The world economy also created a new environment for global communication politics. The increase of private consumption of goods and services implied a growth of information-intensive activities such as airline reservations, hotel bookings, entertainment, consumer electronics, and the use of credit cards. The increasing significance of these services and their trading across borders raised new regulatory issues.

Technological innovations

Rapid developments in the field of communication technology created the need to fill a regulatory vacuum in several areas. Technology also became economically more significant and this brought about a greater need to protect national economic interests and a greater pressure to enact industrial property protection legislation. The international patent system became increasingly important to the transnational corporations.

The post-Second World War years also saw the emergence of an international telephone system that developed from a situation of largely uncoordinated and fragmented national systems. Next to the internationalization of telephony (and later of data communications) the most important technological development was the growth of television.

Technology played a double role. It gave rise to new regulatory controversies, such as on the allotment of the Geo Synchronous Orbit (GSO), but also resolved such problems, for example through enlarging Radio Frequency Spectrum (RFS) capacity. Particularly influential for the development of global communication politics were the innovations in space technology, reproduction technology, and computer technology.

What can we learn from a key project in global mass media politics?

During the 1970s a coalition of politicians, media activists, and communication researchers committed itself to the creation of a New International Information Order (NIIO), also referred to as New International Information and Communication Order or New World Information and Communication Order (NWICO). This concept is described in more detail in Chapter 8.

The coalition aspired towards a new order that would be democratic, that would support economic development, enhance the international exchange of ideas, share knowledge among all the people of the world, and improve the quality of life. This aspiration was first publicly expressed through a meeting of Non-Aligned Heads of State in 1973 at Algiers. This meeting started a project that – after several years of much commotion and anger and little concrete achievement— would again disappear from the world's political agenda.

Among the various factors that contributed to the NIIO failure, the most critical one was the lack of people's participation.

The effort to democratize communication in the 1970s was never a very democratic process. The debate was mainly an exchange among governmental and commercial actors. Ordinary people were not on the playing field. The whole project was engineered by political and intellectual elites. Little or no attention was given to people's interests or even to the need to involve ordinary people in the debate. The NIIO debate was firmly rooted in the realist paradigm of international relations.

This paradigm conceived the world as a state-centric system and failed to take serious account of the numerous non-state actors that had become essential forces in world politics. As a result, the NIIO debate never explicitly promoted the notion that the effective protection of democratic rights could not be guaranteed under the conventional nation-state system. A critical problem was that the realist paradigm glossed over the internal dimension of state sovereignty while focusing on external factors. As a result, the nation-state was seen as protecting the liberties of its citizenry against external claims made by other states. However, the outwardly sovereign state tends also to appropriate sovereign control over its citizens in the process. This follows the vision of the philosopher Thomas Hobbes (1638–1709), who proposed that only the absolute sovereignty of the state (which he referred to as the Leviathan) can control the eternal strife among civil actors. This position ignores that state sovereignty represents more than the emancipation from the powers of emperors, popes, and nobility.

The development of legitimate sovereign states went together with the development of egalitarianism, in which subjects became citizens. The French Revolution and the American Revolution gave birth both to independent nation-states and to citizens with basic civil rights. As a matter of fact, the French Revolution recognized the primacy of the people's sovereignty. This recognition was not taken up in the NIIO project. It was not a people's movement. In so far as it aspired towards a democratic order, it was a "democratization from above".

Just like the NIIO project, the project for the construction of a Global Information Infrastructure (GII), which was strongly promoted by the Clinton/Gore administration, was equally steered by the interests and stakes of governments and corporations. Also, this project in the 1990s became the bilateral playing field of "princes" and "merchants", with ordinary people being occasionally addressed as citizens or consumers, but not as essential players.

A concern for the GII elite was actually that people may not be as excited about the digital future as the elite themselves are. It might well be that ordinary men and women are not eagerly waiting to believe that virtual reality can resolve the problems of their daily lives. Therefore, many of the official reports on the information society stressed the need to promote awareness among consumers. A key concern of the constructors of the information superhighway was that consumers may be hesitant about adding digital services to the present media supply, certainly if they have to pay for them. The GII project therefore needed to persuade people that the information society will bring them great improvements in lifestyle, comfort, and general well-being.

This makes people important targets for propaganda and marketing. However, no serious involvement of people's movements is on the agenda. No trilateral negotiations were taking place between governments, industrialists, and social movements to share decision-making on our preferred common future. Like the project of the 1970s, the 1990s GII project was about "democratization from above" and was unlikely to be effective in making world communication more democratic.

Notes

1. For more historical detail, see Hamelink, C.J. (1994). *The Politics of World Communication*. London: Sage.
2. The countries present at the conference were Austria, Belgium, Denmark, Egypt, France, Germany, Great Britain, Greece, Hungary, Italy, Luxembourg, the Netherlands, Norway, Portugal, Romania, Russia, Serbia, Spain, Sweden, Switzerland, Turkey, and the United States.
3. The following states attended: Austria, Baden, Bavaria, Belgium, Denmark, France, Hamburg, Hanover, Italy, the Netherlands, Norway, Portugal, Prussia, Russia, Saxony, Spain, Sweden, Turkey, and Würtemburg. Great Britain was excluded because its telegraph network was privately owned. The unions also decided in 1858 that French and German were to be the official languages for international telegrams.

Reading spotlight

Politics of Global Communication

Hamelink, C.J. (1994). *The Politics of World Communication*. London: Sage.

An examination of the political processes and decisions that determine the global communication environment. Analysis of negotiation processes and their outcomes from the perspective of international human rights.

Siochru, S.O., Girard, B. with Mahan, A. (2002). *A Beginner's Guide to Global Media Governance*. Boulder, CO: Rowman & Littlefield.

Presented as beginner's guide this book is indeed very readable. However, it is more than a textbook for 'dummies'. It is an essential guide to understanding which actors shape the future of global communication and how they do it. Excellent material for students, policymakers, and practitioners. The text introduces the key global governance institutions, important trends and forms of global media regulation.

Information Society

Webster, F. (1995). *Theories of the Information Society*. London: Routledge.

The author questions the usefulness of the widely popular concept of the information society. He does this through a critical analysis of theoretical propositions offered by Daniel Bell, Anthony Giddens, Herbert Schiller, Jürgen Habermas and Manuel Castells. He concludes that despite of the information explosion it is more sensible to talk about the informatisation of relations in society than about an information society.

Online resources

Visit the book's companion website at **https://study.sagepub.com/hamelink** to watch the author discussing the theme of this chapter: **Global Politics**

Visit the book's companion website at **https://study.sagepub.com/hamelink** to access the following journal articles free of charge:

Padovani P. and Nordenstreng, K. (2005). From NWICO to WSIS: another world information and communication order? *Global Media and Communication*, 1(3): 264–272.

Raboy, M. (1998). Public broadcasting and the global framework of media democratization. *International Communication Gazette*, 20(2): 167–180.

Voorhoof, D. and Cannie, H. (2010). Freedom of expression and information in a democratic society: the added but fragile value of the European Convention on Human Rights. *International Communication Gazette*, 72(4–5): 407–423.

Zhao, Y. (2004). Between a world summit and a Chinese movie: visions of the "Information Society". *Gazette*, 66(3-4): 275–280.

Further reading

Frau-Meigs, D. (2011). *Media Matters in the Cultural Contradictions of the "Information Society": Towards a Human Rights-based Governance*. Strasbourg: Council of Europe.

Hamelink, C.J. (1994). *The Politics of World Communication*. London: Sage.

Vincent, R.C., Nordenstreng, K. and Traber, M. (eds) (1999). *Towards Equity in Global Communication*. Cresskill, NJ: Hampton Press.

Wells, C. (1997). *The UN, UNESCO and the Politics of Knowledge*. London: Macmillan.

RESEARCH ASSIGNMENT

You would like to find out what important players in your country (government, business, media practitioners and social movement) contributed to the emergence of global communication politics over the past 100 years. Who was present during crucial international negotiations and what positions were taken?

What effects, if any, did the agreements on the global level have for national communication policymaking?

Discuss how to approach this piece of historical research. What sources can you use and which archives may be accessible?

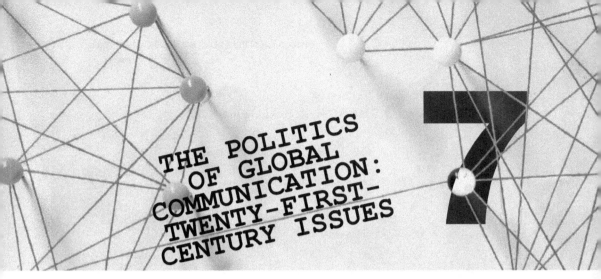

THE POLITICS OF GLOBAL COMMUNICATION: TWENTY-FIRST-CENTURY ISSUES

The inspirational source for this chapter (and actually for all chapters) is Joseph Haydn.

Joseph Haydn (1732–1809)

I guess that mentioning the eighteenth-century Viennese composer Joseph Haydn may come as a surprise. Did he write academic articles on global communication? Not that I would know. I know, however, that he wrote music of an exquisite refinement with innumerable variations and inventions. For me, his music (and especially his piano trios and string quartets) was constantly a great source of inspiration for thinking and writing about global communication.

In past decades, I have had the privilege to draft a series of documents that in a modest way contributed to developments in global communication politics. Among them were the "People's Communication Charter", the "Voices 21" position paper, and the "Declaration on the Right to Communicate". People often asked me what music I listen to while working on such texts. The answer is always the music of Joseph Haydn.

Shifts in global communication politics

Over the past decade the arena of global communication politics has seen major changes. Among the most important ones are the following:

The international governance system for communication operated during the past 100 years mainly to coordinate national policies that were independently shaped by sovereign governments. Today's global governance system to a large extent determines supra-nationally the space that national governments have for independent policymaking.

Global communication politics is increasingly defined by trade and market standards and ever less by political considerations, with a noticeable shift from a predominantly political discourse to a largely economic-trade discourse.

Evidence of this can be found in the growing emphasis on the economic importance of intellectual property and the related priority of protection for investors and corporate producers. In the telecommunications field, the standards of universal public service and cross-subsidization have given way to cost-based tariff structures. In the area of transborder electronic data flows, politics has changed from political arguments about national sovereignty and cultural autonomy to such notions as trade barriers and market access.

The most powerful private players have become more overtly significant. The invisible hand of the economic interests that have all along guided political decision-making became in recent years more and more visible. Transnational corporations became prominent players in the arena and played their role explicitly in the foreground. The locus of policymaking shifted from governments to associations of private business actors.

? Are the recent shifts in global communication politics also reflected in the national communication politics of your country?

The World Trade Organization

Global communication policies were traditionally made in such intergovernmental forums as UNESCO, the World Intellectual Property Organization (WIPO), and the International Telecommunication Union (ITU). These organizations were relatively open to the socio-cultural dimension of developments in the information and communication technologies. Moreover, they offered a platform where the interests of developing nations could also be voiced. In recent years the position of these international governmental organizations, or intergovernmental organizations (IGOs), was considerably weakened, as the major players began to prefer a forum that was more conducive to their specific interests. This forum is the successor to the General Agreement on Tariffs and Trade: the World Trade Organization (WTO). The WTO was established as one of the outcomes of the GATT Uruguay Round of multilateral trade negotiations, which was completed in December 1993.

The WTO is generally more favourable to the trading interests of the major industrial countries than are other intergovernmental bodies. Among its main policy principles are the worldwide liberalization of markets and the non-discrimination principle, which

117

provides for national treatment of foreign competitors in national markets and for treatment as most favoured nations. Actually, it should surprise no one that communication politics has shifted to this trade forum, given the increasing economic value of communication networks and information services.

The case of the WTO Telecommunication Treaty

In 1994 the Marrakech Agreement Establishing the World Trade Organization (WTO) completed the eighth round of multilateral trade negotiations held under the GATT (Uruguay Round). Part of the final treaty was a General Agreement on Trade in Services (GATS).

Of the 125 signatory countries of the Marrakech Agreement, some 60 made commitments to open their markets for telecommunication services, although most did not commit themselves on the issue of basic telecommunications. The commitments range from full competition for all telecommunication services to exceptions for basic telecommunication services or cellular services or for local services.

The Marrakech meeting established the Negotiating Group on Basic Telecommunications (NGBT), which was to deal with telecommunication services and concluded its work by April 1996. The NGBT failed to reach agreement by this date. Several issues remained inconclusive, such as the liberalization of satellite services and the settlement arrangements for international telecommunication rates. The negotiations did lead, however, to an agreement on some basic rules that were provided in a so-called Reference Paper, which deals with competitive safeguards, interconnection, universal service obligations, transparency of licensing criteria, independence of the regulator, and allocation and use of scarce resources.

A new group, called the Group on Basic Telecommunications, continued the work after July 1996. The main mandate of the group, which was open to all WTO member states and held monthly meetings, was to stimulate more countries to make commitments to deal with the issue of liberalizing satellite services, and to solve a number of issues related to the provision of telecommunications services.

The new series of negotiations focused on the matter of restrictions on foreign ownership, among other things. The US government pushed particularly hard for allowing maximum foreign ownership in domestic telecommunications. In making their commitments, restrictions on foreign ownership were fully waived by many countries; others, however, retained between 25 and 80 per cent of domestic control. Whereas some countries consider foreign ownership an opportunity to attract necessary foreign investment (ITU, 1997: 102), others perceive it as a threat to national sovereignty. Although national governments have full control over the scope, the phasing, and the timing of their commitments, once they have made those commitments, they cannot in the future change their concessions. A complex matter for the negotiations became the issue of mobile services provided through satellites. Although the allocation of satellite frequencies is the responsibility of the ITU, a trading aspect arises when national governments use national procedures for spectrum allocation as barriers to trade. Following the provisions of the GATS, such procedures should not be discriminatory.

On February 15, 1997, the Fourth Protocol of the General Agreement on Trade in Services was signed by 72 WTO member states (representing some 93 per cent of the world trade in telecommunication services). On February 5, 1998, the protocol entered into force. This World Telecommunications Agreement demands that participating states liberalize their markets. They are allowed some leeway to implement universal access in ways they deem desirable, but significant qualifications in the agreement seriously limit the national political space.

The agreement has far-reaching implications for the governance of the basic infrastructures of telecommunications. On the issue of universal service, it states: "Any member has the right to define the kind of universal service obligation it wishes to maintain. Such obligations will not be regarded as anticompetitive *per se*, provided they are administered in a transparent, non-discriminatory and competitively neutral manner and are not more burdensome than necessary for the kind of universal service defined by the member" (WTO, 1998). This seriously limits the space for independent national policymaking on access.

Since foreign industries cannot be placed at a disadvantage, the national standards for universal service have to be administered in a competitively neutral manner. They cannot be set at levels "more burdensome than necessary". If a national public policy would consider próviding access to telecommunication services on the basis of a cross-subsidization scheme rather than on the basis of cost-based tariffs, this might serve the interests of the small users better than those of telecommunication operators. Foreign market entrants could see this obligation as "more burdensome than necessary". As a consequence, the policy would be perceived as a violation of international trade law. It would be up to the largely obscure arbitration mechanisms of the WTO to judge the legitimacy of the national policy proposal.

The focus of the agreement is on the access that foreign suppliers should have to national markets for telecommunication services, rather than on the access that national citizens should have to the use of telecommunication services. The simplistic assumption is that these different forms of access equate. As a result, social policy is restricted to limits defined by the commercial players.

Trade interests rather than socio-cultural aspirations determine national telecommunication policy. By the year 2004 most trading partners had agreed to liberalize their domestic markets. The establishment of worldwide free markets for any type of services does not, however, necessarily imply the availability of such services or the equitable use of these services for all who could benefit from them.

Governments pursue privatization and/or liberalization policies for quite different reasons. These policies may – especially in poorer countries – be more related to trouble-some economies than with the desire to improve and upgrade telecommunication services. They may be related to the political wisdom of the day (for example, neo-liberalism) or with the hope to get technology transferred in the process. The new policies are neither an unequivocal recipe for disaster nor do they guarantee successful economic and technolog-ical performance. Results will be different in different countries and much more study is needed to establish which social conditions determine benefits and costs.

The arguments that are used to support privatization point to the expansion and upgrading of networks, the improvement of services, and the lowering of tariffs for access and usage of networks. Experiences are, however, varied. One of the results of privatization is often the expansion of the telecom network. In several countries (for example, Peru in 1997, and Panama in 1997) privatization considerably improved teledensity. The added telephone lines benefit, of course, those users who can afford the service. The privatization scheme does not necessarily enlarge the group of citizens who have the purchasing power that is required for the use of telecommunication networks.

In several countries tariffs have gone down but mainly for big corporate users, whereas the telephone bills for ordinary consumers have hardly benefited. Experiences with the pro-vision of services are also differentiated. This is partly due to the fact that the expectation of more competition and more choice as a result of privatization was not always fulfilled. As a matter of fact, in smaller and less advanced states national telecommunication oper-ators have lost against big global coalitions, the new monopolists. It is highly questionable whether markets controlled by a few global operators will actually benefit the consumer. It remains dubious how much competition in the end will remain. The reduction of prices and the increase in investments for technological innovations tend to shake competitors out of the market and as a result market liberalization almost everywhere tends to reinforce market concentration. This follows the historical experience that free markets inevitably lead to the formation of monopolies since competitors will shake contenders out of the market or will merge with each other.

Changing the account rate settlement system

An important component of global telecommunication politics is the so-called account rate system. Traditionally, the telecommunication system was based in bilateral relations between telecom carriers. The general regulatory framework for the settlement of charges between carriers (often the monopoly telecom operators) was provided by the International Telecommunication Regulations, a treaty administered by the ITU and last revised at the World Administrative Telegraph and Telephone Conference (WATT-C) in 1988. Over the past years, with the innovations in technology, the drive towards liberalization, and privatization, this regime came under severe pressure. Today, not only will more and more private commercial companies be the operators in both countries of origin and destination, but they will also offer new services (such as phone-cards or Internet telephony) that bypass the settlement system.

One of the essential motives of telecommunications regulation, as it was enacted in the first International Telegraph Convention (1865), was to find an adequate system for the division of revenues from international calls among countries of origin, transit, and destination. Basically, the public telecommunication operator (PTO) in the country of origin would charge the customer a certain price, then the PTO in the country of destination and the PTO in the country of origin would agree a price for the services by the destination PTO (providing international lines and switching and delivering calls to local customers). This is called the account rate. This amount forms the basis for the charges of operators in destination countries to operators in originating countries. These charges are called account settlement rates.

The general recommendation by the ITU has been to divide the charges on a 50/50 basis between carriers. This worked well in situations where monopolies dealt with other monopolies and where international telecommunications was seen as a jointly provided service. This is all changing with the availability of more private operators and more competition and more technical options to bypass the existing system.

For some time now a reform of the existing account rate settlement system has been discussed by the OECD (since 1991), by the ITU (since 1992), and by the WTO. In the past, the existing system has served the interests of the developing countries well. Since developing countries have usually applied relatively high charges for the completion of international calls at their end, the account rate settlement was an important source of foreign exchange. According to the ITU, each year up to US$10 billion may go to developing countries in net payments. This income can – at least in principle – be used to support access to the telecom infrastructure for people in rural areas who would otherwise remain disconnected.

When negotiations about reform did not progress quickly enough, the US administration decided to announce its preferred solution. The Federal Communications Commission in the USA argued that the US lost billions of dollars each year in payments to other countries. It therefore introduced (in November 1996) the Notice of Proposed Rulemaking, which went into force in January 1998). The revised system that was proposed determined how much US operators could pay to operators in foreign countries. This would, on average, be half of what was paid in the past. The European Commission was inclined to follow the US example. The shape of future politics on account rates undoubtedly had a critical impact on issues such as accessibility of telecommunication in poor countries since lowering the account rate payments will lead to an increase in costs to local customers in those countries.

Intellectual property rights

At present the essential governing institutions in the field of intellectual property rights are the World Intellectual Property Organization and the World Trade Organization. The WTO plays an increasingly important role because it oversees the execution of the legal provisions of the agreement on Trade-Related Intellectual Property Rights (TRIPS). This global agreement emerged under the GATT negotiations (as Annex 1C to the General Agreement on Tariffs and Trade in the Uruguay Round of multilateral trade negotiations, 1993). TRIPS contains the most important current rules on the protection of intellectual property rights (IPRs). It is implemented within the WTO regulatory framework. In this agreement, the economic dimension of IPR protection is reinforced. As Venturelli (1998: 63) correctly summarizes: "The balance has tipped entirely toward favoring the economic incentive interests of third-party exploiters and away from both the public access interests of citizens and the constitutional and human rights of creative labor". As IPRs have achieved a prominent place among the world's most important tradable commodities, the current trade-oriented IPR-regime favours the corporate producers (publishers, broadcast companies, music recording companies, advertising firms) against individual creators. The provisions of the TRIPS agreement protect the economic rights of investors better than the moral rights of creative individuals or the cultural interests of the public at large. For the dissemination of their products, the performing artists, writers, and composers increasingly transfer their rights to big conglomerates with which they sign contracts. Ultimately, these companies determine how creative products will be processed, packaged, and sold.

One of the serious problems with the current trend in IPR protection is that the emerging regulatory framework stifles the independence and diversity of creative production around the world. The regime is particularly unhelpful to the protection of the "small" independent originators of creative products. It establishes formidable obstacles to the use of creative products because it restricts the notion of fair use, under which – traditionally – these products could be freely used for a variety of educational and other purposes. The narrow economic angle of the current trend focuses more on the misappropriation of corporate property than on the innovation of artistic and literary creativity.

A particularly worrying phenomenon is that the current rules provide that once knowledge in the public domain is put into electronic databases, it will come under IPR protection. This will imply a considerable limit to freely accessible sources. Moreover, the present system of governance threatens to transform the new global forum that cyberspace potentially offers (through the new digital technologies) into a marketplace where a controlled volume of ideas will be traded.

The one-dimensional emphasis upon the commercial facets of copyright protection is reinforced by the progressive shifting of negotiating forums from the WIPO to the WTO. In this process the protection of intellectual property becomes part of the global free trade agenda. This implies that the public interest is secondary to the economic interest of the largest producers of intellectual property. The social value and common benefit of cultural products are not on the transnational corporate agenda.

These products (such as knowledge) tend to be seen as commodities that can be privately owned. A different point of view would contest this and propose that knowledge is part of the common heritage of humankind and cannot be the exclusive property of a few members of the community. The emphasis in the emerging system is rather exclusively on the rights of knowledge producers and almost completely bypasses the duties of rights holders. Such duties include the obligation of disclosure – the obligation to provide information and supporting documents concerning corresponding foreign applications and grants. The rights holder can be obliged to work a patent in the country where the patent was granted and can be required to refrain from engaging in abusive, restrictive, or anti-competitive practices.

Current intellectual property rights tend to benefit only the industrial nations, but they can also stimulate free innovation in poorer nations. Rather than strengthening the control of transnational corporations over technology and reinforcing the monopolistic rights of technology providers, the technological capabilities in the developing countries could be strengthened. The pressure to create a uniform global system of IPR protection constrains the flexibility that developing countries need in order to adapt the IPR system to their specific needs and interests.

One can expect that in the years to come the domain of intellectual property rights will continue to be a crucial battlefield of conflicting interests.

The mass media

The main issues in relation to the mass media concern concentration of ownership and the trade in media products. The mega-media mergers of the 1980s and early 1990s renewed in many countries concerns about media concentration. On the international level, only minimal concern is being expressed. The essential guideline for policymakers seems to be the deregulation of the marketplace. The common argument in favour of an unregulated marketplace in the provision of information is that it guarantees creative and competitive forums that offer a diversity of contents. Abundant empirical evidence, however, suggests that concentration in the mass media promotes market control by a few companies that tend to produce a limited package of commercially viable contents only.

The World Trade Organization's rules, for example, stress the need for competition. However, the major concern is that public policies should not be anti-competitive in the sense of hampering free access to domestic markets. Current competition rules mainly address the dismantling of public services and the liberalization of markets, not the oligopolization of markets or the conduct of the dominant market parties.

The WTO Basic Telecommunications Agreement of February 15, 1997, governs market access but has little to say about the conduct of parties on the market. It does not guarantee an effective, open competition between commercial actors. The non-discrimination principle that provides for most-favoured nation treatment of foreign competitors is inadequate to secure competition on domestic markets.

The WTO provisions on anti-competitive practices do not exclude the possibility that local media markets would be controlled by only three or four foreign suppliers. The lack of a serious competition policy supports unhindered market concentration and reinforces foreign ownership of essential market domains, particularly in developing countries.

One of the main policy issues is the question of whether the info-com market is substantially different from markets for other commodities (such as automobiles or detergents) so that it should be treated in a different way. Is the question whether public intervention for cultural products should be different from that for food products? Could it be that even if the shopping mall functions best when the state does not intervene, even if the mall is the main provider of information and culture?

The key arguments against attempts to regulate media concentration are the following. There is no empirical proof that concentration has indeed such negative effects. On the contrary, it can be argued that strong consolidated companies can offer much more diversity and can mobilize more independence in their dealings with governments than smaller companies. Moreover, strong media can "rescue" loss-making media that otherwise would disappear, and thus their contribution to diversity is retained. It is also argued that more competition does not guarantee more diversity, because competitors may all try to reach the largest share of the market with a similar product. Even if regulatory measures against industrial consolidation would be successful in stimulating more competition, an increase in product diversity is not guaranteed. Markets tend inevitably towards identical, though marginally distinct, products because, of necessity, they address the largest possible number of buyers. A problem is that allowing competition in the marketplace does not necessarily lead to more diversity. There is some evidence that the deregulated, competitive broadcast systems of Western European countries reflect less diversity in contents than the formerly regulated public monopolies. This type of situation occurs largely because the actors in a competitive market all try to control the largest segment by catering to rather similar tastes and preferences of that market segment.

The trading of media services has become global business with an expanding and profitable market. In the years ahead, the international media market is generally expected to reach the US$3 trillion mark. This expanding market is to a large extent due to the concurrent processes of deregulation of broadcasting and the commercialization of media institutions. These developments imply a growing demand for entertainment. The related important process is globalization – in terms of markets, but also in terms of products and ownership.

Worldwide, a clear trend towards an increasing demand for the American-brand entertainment is seen. An important feature of the trend towards globalization is that the trading by the mega-companies is shifting from the international exchange of local products to production for global markets.

Global communication politics today

Current global communication politics is dominated by a set of eight essential issues that will largely shape the future of global communication. The governance of these issues is complicated because the political agendas in the world community are strongly divided and conflicting, and define these issues in very different ways. The neo-liberal political agenda is commercially oriented and market-centred.

This agenda proposes the liberalization of national markets, the lifting of trade restrictions, and the strengthening of the rights of investors. Opposed to this, one finds a humanitarian political agenda that puts the interests of citizens at the centre of global policymaking and that wants human rights to be taken as seriously as property and investment rights in global communication politics.

Access

The neo-liberal agenda perceives people primarily as consumers and aspires to provide them with access to communication infrastructures so they can be integrated into the global consumer society. The humanitarian agenda perceives people primarily as citizens and wants them to be sufficiently literate so that communication infrastructures can be used to promote democratic participation.

Knowledge

On the neo-liberal agenda, knowledge is a commodity that can be processed and owned by private parties, and the property rights of knowledge producers should be strictly reinforced. On the humanitarian agenda, knowledge is a public good that cannot be privately appropriated.

Global advertising

The neo-liberal agenda has a strong interest in the expansion of global advertising. This implies, among other things, more commercial space in media (mass media and the Internet), new target groups (especially children), more sponsorships (films, orchestras, exhibitions), and more places to advertise (the ubiquitous billboards). The humanitarian agenda is concerned about the ecological implications of the worldwide promotion of a consumer society and the growing gap between those who can shop in the (electronic) global shopping mall and those who can only gawk. Moreover, the humanitarian agenda has a strong interest in defending public spaces against their commercial exploitation.

Privacy

The neo-liberal agenda has a strong interest in data mining: the systematic collection, storage, and processing of masses of data about individuals to create client profiles for marketing purposes. The humanitarian agenda has a strong interest in the protection of people's privacy and the creation of critical attitudes among consumers to guard their personal information more adequately.

Intellectual property rights

The neo-liberal agenda has a strong interest in the strict enforcement of a trade-based system for the protection of intellectual property rights that provides a large degree of freedom for the transnational commercial rights owners to exploit those rights. Equally, these IPR owners have an interest in expanding the period of protection as well as the materials that can be brought under this protection. The humanitarian agenda is concerned that the present system sanctions the grand-scale resource plunder of genetic information (biopiracy) from poor countries and serves the interests of corporate owners better than the interests of local communities or individual artistic creators. This agenda has a strong interest in protecting the interests of communal property of cultural resources and in protecting resources in the public domain against their exploitation by private companies.

Trade in culture

The neo-liberal agenda has a strong interest in the application of the rules of international trade law to the export and import of cultural products. Under these rules countries are not allowed to take measures that restrict cultural imports as part of their national cultural policy. The humanitarian agenda is interested in having culture exempted from trade provisions and in allowing national measures for the protection of cultural autonomy and local public space.

Concentration

The neo-liberal agenda has a strong interest in creating business links (acquisitions, mergers, joint ventures) with partners in order to consolidate controlling positions on the world market and wants to create a sufficiently large regulatory vacuum in which to act freely. The humanitarian agenda is concerned that today's global merger activities have negative consequences for both consumers and professionals in terms of diminishing diversity and creating the loss of professional autonomy.

The commons

The neo-liberal agenda wants the private exploitation of such commons as the airwaves and promotes the auctioning of these resources to private parties. The humanitarian agenda wants to retain the public property of the human common heritage so that public accountability and community requirements remain secured.

Civil advocacy

At present the battle between these two conflicting agendas is fought with inequality of arms. The commercial agenda is supported by a strong constituency of the leading members of the WTO and powerful business lobbies (such as the Business Software Alliance and the Global Business Dialogue). The humanitarian agenda, although increasingly active in the economic arena, is still in search of an active constituency in the global communication arena. Although civil advocacy would be up against formidable opponents, a global movement could pose a serious political challenge. It would represent the interests of democratic citizenship and thus present a stronger claim to credibility than business firms. Because it would be inspired by such fundamental notions as universal human rights, it would have a moral authority, which is superior to those who are driven by commercial interests. It could use the court of public opinion more effectively than corporations and use this to get major concessions from its commercial opponents. A global civil movement would be made up of citizens who at the same time are consumers and thus clients of the media industries, which would make them a forceful lobby.

On December 20, 2000, the *International Herald Tribune* used for one of its articles the following lead: "Small Advocacy Groups Take Big Role as Conscience of the Global Economy." In the same way, it should be possible to state: "Small Advocacy Groups Take Big Role as Conscience of Global Communication Politics." The intervention by public interest coalitions in the arena of global communication politics will not come about spontaneously. It demands organization and mobilization. A modest beginning has been made to achieve this through the Platform for Cooperation on Communication and Democratization. The platform that was established in 1995 is at present made up of the World Association of Community Radio Broadcasters (AMARC), the Association for Progressive Communications (APC), Article 19, CENCOS, Cultural Environment Movement, GreenNet, Grupo de los Ocho, IDOC, International Federation of Journalists, IPAL, International Women's Tribune Center, MacBride Round Table, MedTV, OneWorld Online, Panos, People's Communication Charter, UNDA, Vidéazimut, the World Association for Christian Communication (WACC), WETV–Global Access Television, and Worldview International Foundation. Members of the platform have agreed to work for the formal recognition of the right to communicate. They emphasize the need to defend and deepen an open public space for debate and actions that build critical understanding of the ethics of communication, democratic policy, and equitable and effective access.

127

The right to communicate was also the central concern of the so-called People's Communication Charter (PCC) (www.pccharter.net). The People's Communication Charter is an initiative that originated in 1991 with the Third World Network (Penang, Malaysia), the Centre for Communication and Human Rights (Amsterdam, the Netherlands), the Cultural Environment Movement (United States), the World Association of Community Radio Broadcasters (AMARC), and the World Association for Christian Communication. The charter provides the common framework for all those who share the belief that people should be active and critical participants in their social reality and capable of governing themselves. The People's Communication Charter could be a first step in the development of a permanent movement concerned with the quality of our cultural environment.

Eventually this movement could develop into a permanent institution for the enforcement of the PCC, perhaps in the form of an ombudsman's office for communication and cultural rights. This idea largely follows a recommendation made by the UNESCO World Commission on Culture and Development, chaired by Javier Pérez de Cuéllar, in its 1995 report *Our Creative Diversity*. The Commission recommended the drawing up of an International Code of Conduct on Culture and – under the auspices of the UN International Law Commission – the setting up of an International Office of the Ombudsperson for Cultural Rights (World Commission, 1995: 282). As the Commission writes:

> Such an independent, free-standing entity could hear pleas from aggrieved or oppressed individuals or groups, act on their behalf and mediate with governments for the peaceful settlement of disputes. It could fully investigate and document cases, encourage a dialogue between parties and suggest a process of arbitration and negotiated settlement leading to the effective redress of wrongs, including, wherever appropriate, recommendations for legal or legislative remedies as well as compensatory damages. (World Commission, 1995: 283)

Ideally, the proposed ombudsman's office would have full independence both from governmental and from commercial parties, and as an independent agency it would develop a strong moral authority on the basis of its expertise, its track record, and the quality of the people and the organizations that would form its constituency. Given the growing significance of the global communication arena and the urgency of a humanitarian agenda for its politics, the building of this new global institution constitutes one of the most exciting challenges in the twenty-first century.

Voices 21

In December 1998, Cees J. Hamelink and Cilla Lundström (then General Manager APC, the Association for Progressive Communications) wrote the first draft for "A Call and Proposal for a Movement for People's Voices in Media and Communications in the 21st

Century". The proposal, entitled "Voices", aimed to call for a movement where civil society and NGOs form an international alliance to address concerns and to work jointly on matters around media and communications. The authors believed that a new social movement in this field was needed and should be ready to act internationally. Civil society organizations that use media and communication networks in their work for social change could unite under the umbrella of:

- the awareness of the growing importance of the mass media and communication networks for the goals they try to achieve;
- the concerns about current trends in the field of information and communication towards concentration, commercialization, privatization, and liberalization;
- the lack of public influence on these trends in both developed and developing countries, in democracies, and under dictatorships.

The central focus of the movement would be to address problems and show solutions to one of the greatest challenges of our time: that the voices and concerns of ordinary people around the world are no longer excluded!

As joint activities of the people and organizations participating in the movement were suggested: Access and accessibility, The Right to communicate, Diversity of expressions, Security and privacy, and protection of the cultural environment.

? How do you rate the possibility of the mobilization of consumer movements around the world for the establishment of public accountability in the field of global communication?

The United Nations World Summit on the Information Society

In 1996 the Executive Board of UNESCO explored the possibility of convening an International Conference on Information and Communication for Development to be held in 1998 jointly with other UN agencies, such as the ITU. Unfortunately, this conference never took place as the international community resolved to plan for a world summit on the information society that would be administered by the ITU. In the process, a concrete topic for international negotiations was replaced by the nebulous and contested concept of the "information society" and the UN organization with a broad mandate in the field of culture and communication and with much experience with non-state actors (the UNESCO) was replaced by the UN organization that champions the "information society" mainly in terms of a technologically-determinist view of the global future (the ITU). It should have come as no surprise to any critical observer that the Clinton/Gore US administration that propagated universal access to the 'Global Information Infrastructure' played a crucial role in these developments.

When the UN began to announce the World Summit on the Information Society (WSIS) in 2001, there was criticism of the lack of careful reflection before the UN rushed into this third major global diplomatic event in the politics of global communication. The first time had been the 1948 UN conference on the Freedom of Information and the second time had been the UN involvement with the 1970s debates on a new international information order. Both earlier projects had largely failed for different reasons. This should have raised a warning flag for the third attempt in the early twenty-first century. Even so, there was also the positive and constructive expectation – both among diplomats and civil advocates – that the WSIS might provide a global forum to address the most burning issues of communication politics and, moreover, there was the aspiration that this global gathering could become a genuine multi-stakeholder exercise.

After a series of Preparatory Committee meetings (so-called Prepcoms), the first phase of the WSIS took place in December 2003 in Geneva. It turned out to be a summit that was only partly different from earlier UN summits. There was a massive input from well-organized and highly motivated civil movements, particularly under the umbrella of the Communication Rights in the Information Society (CRIS) campaign. However, the WSIS remained largely an inter-state, diplomatic gathering with no participation of non-state actors in the final decision-making process. The summit ended with two separate Declarations. The Declaration of Principles by states (www.wsis.org), and the Civil Society Declaration *Shaping Information Societies for Human Needs* (www.wsis-cs.org). Moreover, the two most burning global issues were not resolved and were referred to the second phase of the summit that was held in November 2005 in Tunisia. The unresolved issues were the financing of efforts to bridge the global digital divide and the global governance of the Internet. If one takes a positive attitude towards the outcome of the WSIS process, one might conclude that for the first time global civil movements were effectively mobilized to address the key issues of the politics of global communication. Since many of the civil advocates see the WSIS as an ongoing process, these issues will remain on the public agenda and will hopefully attract the political attention from citizens worldwide as well as from their elected representatives in national parliaments and supra-national institutions, such as the European Parliament.

The summit offered a unique opportunity for the international community to address the need for global governance institutions in the domain of information and communication. However, the summit was unfortunately not well equipped to deal with content issues. Its orientation was largely towards infrastructural and funding issues. The summit was strongly influenced by the techno-centric discourse that is characteristic of current "information society" discussions and negotiations.[1]

A common assumption in much of the WSIS discourse was that information and communication technologies (ICTs) have the capacity to advance human development and that human potential can be achieved through ICT and access to knowledge. Such statements are puzzling because of their generality. They seem to assume that ICTs under whatever conditions and in whatever environment have this constructive power. This represents a technological determinism in its crudest sense. The WSIS discourse suggested that technological development leads to productivity and economic growth and subsequently to the improvement of the quality of life. Apart from the fact that there is no convincing empirical evidence about such causal connections, one could equally well argue that technological development and economic growth destroy the quality of life. This totally depends upon how one defines "quality of life". It obviously makes a fundamental difference whether one chooses a material versus a spiritual definition of "quality".

The most striking feature of the official WSIS final texts is the lack of any serious and critical structural analysis of the politico-economic context. It would seem that the WSIS discourse takes place in a societal void, without any awareness of the politico-economic environment within which statements are made about information and communication technologies and their possible applications. Already during the preparatory proceedings, most of the visions on the Information Society as they were presented by the various stakeholders were heart-warming and uplifting. Most of the texts described a vision of the Information Society as inclusive and open for the broadest possible participation and access. The Information Society should create an enabling environment and support capacity building. Governance of the Information Society should be democratic. Primary goals are sustainable development, cultural diversity, and gender sensitivity. The general feeling is that the Information Society can yield an unprecedented win-win situation and can contribute to a better life for all citizens.

Although all these intentions are very laudable, it should be noted that they are offered as visions without any empirical evidence as to why the Information Society would offer this potential. In the preparations for the summit, one looks in vain for a serious and critical analysis of the socio-political context in which all the promises of the Information Society would have to be realized. This is troublesome because most of the laudable visions on what the Information Society is or should be, are part of a well-known international agenda for a better world. All the buzz-words from past decades were back: democracy, diversity, capacity, participation, gender, bridging the gap. The nagging question is, however, why such aspirations have so far not been taken seriously by the international community. Why has the international community been unwilling – in past decades – to engage in real efforts to implement what it preaches?

The WSIS discourse steered away from such political questions and remained unclear (probably intentionally) about questions of power and control. These notions were not part of the official WSIS discourse. And yet, it can be argued that the question of the distribution and execution of political, economic, and military power, and the

131

control they exercise, is essential to a meaningful discussion about global communication governance.

?   Could the WSIS-process have evolved into a genuinely democratic multi-stakeholder arena for the politics of global communication?

Perspectives on global communication politics

Over the past 150 years, the players in global communication have designed and adopted (by legislation or by self-regulation) rules, institutions, and practices that have provided limits and incentives for their conduct. In all these years, the substantive domains of the arena have largely remained the same. They encompass the fields of telecommunication (now including data communication), intellectual property rights, and mass communication. By and large, the core issues of today's communication politics are still to be found in these domains. It is obvious that technological developments have added new dimensions to these issues.

In the domain of telecommunication the main issues continue to concern accessibility, allocation, and confidentiality. The accessibility issue refers today not only to basic telephony, but also to advanced computer networks. The allocation issue concerns today, in addition to frequencies and settlement rates, the new field of domain names for the use of the Internet. The confidentiality issue has gained increased urgency through the global proliferation of data networks and data collection activities, and new forms of electronic surveillance.

The issues in the domain of intellectual property rights have acquired more urgency through the application of new technologies that make large-scale copying of copyrighted materials very easy. Commercial content providers have a strong interest in the strict enforcement of a trade-based system for the protection of intellectual property rights that provides a large degree of freedom for the private owners of such rights to their exploitation. Equally, these rights-owners have an interest in expanding the period of protection as well as the materials that can be brought under this protection. Against this there is growing concern that the present system serves the interests of corporate owners better than the interests of individual artistic creators. There are also strong arguments raised in favour of the abolition of the system of IPR-protection.

- The system makes access too expensive and thus prohibitive for the world's majority!
- It stifles creativity because of its concentration on a limited number of star cultural producers. Once the IPR system has gone there will be space for a greater number and variety of creative artists.

- It poses a serious threat to the public domain. Increasingly, freely available cultural products (which are in the public domain, meaning there are no longer copyrights claims against users, as in the case of works by Shakespeare or Mozart) are stored in digital format and deposited in electronic databanks. Such databank collections are entitled to copyright protection, as a result of which public access is restricted.

In the domain of the mass media the basic controversy about contents continues to be focused upon the tension between harmful content and free speech. The regulation of content on the Internet is today an urgent new issue on the agenda of communication regulators. In 1865 the first international treaty to deal with global communication (the International Telegraph Convention) secured the freedom (in the sense of "secrecy") of correspondence across national borders. At the same time, however, governments reserved the right to interfere with any message they considered dangerous for state security or in violation of national laws, public order, or morality. This tension between freedom and interference remained over the years a much debated topic among politicians, regulators, content carriers, and users. The ambiguity of the freedom of global flows versus the need to interfere with this freedom posed a challenge for attempts at global governance. On the side of the freedom of content one finds classical civil and political rights arguments in favour of "free speech". On the side of interference there are arguments about "national sovereignty" and about the responsibility of speech *vis-à-vis* the rights and reputations of others. The "free speech" argument promotes an unhindered flow of messages into and out of countries. The "sovereignty" argument provides for protective measures against flows of messages that may impede the autonomous control over social and cultural development. The "responsible speech" argument claims the right to protection against the harmful effects of such free flows. Over the years, the international community and individual national governments have repeatedly tried to establish governance mechanisms (rules and institutions) to deal with the "freedom versus interference" concern. The conclusion is that no satisfactory arrangement has been produced. No satisfactory rules for balancing freedom versus interference have been developed and no relevant global institutions have emerged to deal with this.

In these different domains a contested issue remains the scope and reach of regulation. There are sharply divided opinions about regulation, re-regulation and deregulation. This is compounded by the fact that players may want robust regulation in one domain (the protection of intellectual property rights, for example) and prefer no regulation in another domain (trading of telecommunications services, for example). There may also emerge new political coalitions such as in the field of encryption where commercial firms and private individuals share an interest in the protection of confidentiality against the interests of security agencies, law enforcement institutions, and tax authorities.

The governance of global communication typically represents a complex system of actors, institutions, rules, and practices. This implies that decision-making on choices in relation to governance issues largely takes place under conditions of uncertainty and ignorance. There is no certainty or knowledge about the future effects of choices that may affect the lives of large numbers of people. The future is open, precisely because we have no information about it. If we had such information, there would be no real choice. As Brian Loasby (1976: 5) has remarked: "If choice is real, the future cannot be certain; if the future is certain, there can be no choice."

The greatest challenge this poses for those in governance positions is the possibility of error. As David Collingridge (1982: 17) wrote: "If the possibility of error is unavoidable, we must learn to live with it. We must be prepared to discover our mistakes and to remedy them. In making a decision under ignorance two things are essential: the ability to discover information which would show the decisions to be wrong, and the ability to react to this information if even comes to light". This is not so easy as there is – particularly in governments – a strong insensitivity to error. This persisting in error was called "the imbecility of government" by Barbara Tuchman. She wrote, "Practitioners of government continue down the wrong road as if in thrall to some Merlin with magic power to direct their steps" (Tuchman, 1985: 480). For this obstinate imbecility arguments are used such as "It was the only choice that could be made" or "By the time we knew, it was too late". However, "there is always freedom of choice to change or desist from a counterproductive course if the policy-maker has the moral courage to exercise it" (Tuchman, 1985: 481). This is what the governance of global communication needs more than anything else; the moral courage to discover and admit the wrong choice and to change direction.

? Are special governance measures and institutions needed for the governance of the Internet?

Notes

1. For a critical analysis of the World Summit on the Information Society, see Hamelink, C.J. (2004). "Did WSIS achieve anything at all?" *International Communication Gazette* (special issue), 66(3–4): 281–290.

Reading spotlight
Global Media Policy

Chakravartty, P. and Sarikakis, K. (2006). *Media Policy and Globalization*. Edinburgh: Edinburgh University Press.

Pertinent to students of global communication. Well-structured and argued analyses, written in an easy and accessible manner, rich empirical material and useful case studies. Three key parts: context, domains and paradigms. Describing historical shifts in world communication politics the authors show how a variety of governmental, business and civil actors have negotiated the rules of governance in telecommunication and broadcasting. In the part on policy paradigms the authors take issue with the notion of the "information society" and argue how this concept provides a legitimising discourse for policymaking that is strongly inspired by the twentieth century struggle for hegemony. They also deal with the question of global governance and focus on the new civil society actors in the policy-making arena.

Mansell, R. and Raboy, M. (2011). *The Handbook of Global Media and Communication Policy*. Oxford: Blackwell.

A comprehensive guide to the understanding of the key policy issues in global communication.

Online resources

 Visit the book's companion website at **https://study.sagepub.com/hamelink** to watch the author discussing the theme of this chapter: **Global Politics**

Visit the book's companion website at **https://study.sagepub.com/hamelink** to access the following journal articles free of charge:

Dakroury, A. and Hoffmann, J. (2010). Communication as a human right: a blind spot in communication research? *International Communication Gazette*, 72(4–5): 315–322.

Hamelink, C.J. (2004). Did WSIS achieve anything at all? *International Communication Gazette*, 66(3–4): 281–290.

Padovani, C. (2004). The World Summit on the Information Society: setting the communication agenda for the 21st century? An ongoing exercise. *Gazette*, 66(3–4): 187–191.

Raboy, M. (2004). The World Summit on the Information Society and its legacy for global governance. *Gazette*, 66(3–4): 225–232.

Further reading

Raboy, M. (ed.) (2001). *Global Media Policy for the New Millennium*. Luton: University of Luton Press.

Raboy, M. and Landry, N. (2005). *Civil Society, Communication and Global Governance: Issues from the World Summit on the Information Society*. New York: Peter Lang.

RESEARCH ASSIGNMENT

Make a design for a multilateral institution for global communication governance that brings together representatives of national governments, executives from business corporations, and members of civil society organizations.

Make an analysis of the existing multilateral institutions and analyze their strengths, weaknesses, opportunities and threats (SWOT analysis) in terms of spaces where the relevant stakeholders in global communication can negotiate.

How would you identify the pertinent data for this exercise? And how would you collect them?

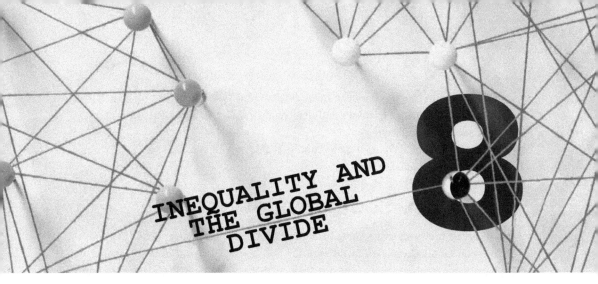

INEQUALITY AND THE GLOBAL DIVIDE

8

He has been a founding father of critical communication research on development issues and is the essential inspirational source for this chapter.

Luis Ramiro Beltran (1930–)

Beltran worked as a journalist, film script writer, taught at Ohio State University and Stanford University in the USA, and was a consultant for organizations such as UNESCO. He is the recipient of many awards, including the McLuhan-Teleglobe Canada Award.

For the study of global communication, his important publications are: "Communication in Latin America: Persuasion for Status Quo or for National Development", PhD thesis, Michigan State University (1970); "Communication for development in Latin America: a forty years appraisal" (1976); "Communication: forgotten tool of national development" (1997); *Que comunicacion para el desarrolo?* (1993a); and *La communication para el desarrollo en Latinoamerica* (1993b).

For the study of global communication, Luis Ramiro Beltran taught us to critically reflect on the different understandings that exist between the North and the South of the notion of "development".

This chapter confronts you with one of the persistent characteristics of global communication: inequality. I will take the following route:

- From the 1948 UN conference on Freedom of Information through the 1970s debates on a New International Information Order and to the 2003/2005 UN World Summit on the Information Society (WSIS) the equality standard was at the core of international debates on the development of communication.

- Little, if any, progress has been made since the late 1940s and it can be argued that "equality" remains a contested and challenging standard in the policies and practices of social communication.
- The international community has not been able or willing to find satisfactory solutions to the inequality issue.

The North–South divide

In the earliest meetings of the United Nations Economic and Social Council (ECOSOC) the inadequacy of information facilities in the less developed countries was highlighted. Diplomats representing these countries stressed that with the existing disparities there could be no reciprocity and equality in global communication.

Several resolutions by the Council and by the General Assembly expressed the need to improve information enterprises in the less developed countries and in 1957 the General Assembly requested the ECOSOC Commission on Human Rights to "give special consideration to the problem of developing media of information in under-developed countries".

One year later the United Nations General Assembly requested ECOSOC to formulate "a programme of concrete action and measures on the international plane which could be undertaken for the development of information enterprises in under-developed countries". The specialized agencies were invited to contribute to this initiative.

UNESCO was asked to study the mass media in the "less developed countries" to survey the problems involved in the development of communication. This was no new terrain to the organization. In its early history there had been an effort to reconstruct and develop mass communication media in war-devastated countries. At its third General Conference in 1948 a resolution was adopted that added to this "the provision of raw materials, equipment and professional training facilities … for under-developed areas". This was the beginning of assistance to Third World countries which received special impetus when in 1958 the General Conference explicitly requested the Director General "to help develop media of information in the underdeveloped countries". In response to the request of the General Assembly, UNESCO organized a series of expert meetings (in Bangkok, 1960, Santiago, 1961, and Paris, 1962) to assess communication needs and to design ways to meet these needs. The organization also prepared a report that was presented to the UN General Assembly in 1961. This report on *Mass Media in Developing Countries* formulated minimal levels of communication capacity and concluded that for some 70 per cent of the world population this minimum was not available (UNESCO, 1961).

The report recommended that communication development should be considered part of the overall United Nations development effort and thus be incorporated in the UN Technical Assistance Programme. In response to the report, ECOSOC suggested in 1961 that the developed countries should assist the developing countries in the "development of independent national information media, with due regard for the culture of each country".

In 1961 ECOSOC recommended to the General Assembly that the UNESCO programme should get its place within the efforts of the First United Nations Development Decade.

In 1962 the UN General Assembly (UNGA) confirmed this by stating that "development of communication media was part of overall development". Herewith a multilateral programme of technical assistance to the development of mass communication capacity was launched that was unanimously supported by the UN member states. The technical assistance programme that lasted throughout the 1960s was primarily oriented towards the transfer of resources and skills.

It is understandable that because of the stark disparity in communication capacity between the industrialized countries of the North and the Third World countries, there was considerable concern about Third World acquisition of communication in technology. This has to be seen within the broader context of the quest of Third World countries to complete the decolonization process and to achieve a level of self-reliant development.

The access to technical knowledge became a concern for the Third World countries only in the 1970s. Earlier on, most of the newly independent countries were mainly interested in attracting foreign investors, particularly transnational corporations, with the expectation that they would transfer the much needed scientific and technical know-how. It was assumed in the 1950s that science and technology, which had lifted the advanced industrial countries to unprecedented levels of material wealth, would do the same for the Third World. In the remarkably rapid economic growth that North America and Western Europe experienced after the industrial revolution, science and technology were crucial factors.

Since they had progressed through laborious and expensive trial-and-error processes, it seemed a well-advised policy for those who came late to exploit the most recent state of the art. "Rarely did the countries at each stage of the decision-making process raise basic questions such as: Does the country have the technology? Can it develop it? Can it adapt imported technology? How long will it take? What resources will be needed? What are the trade-offs between importing technology now and waiting to develop it at home? Why not import now, but plan in such a fashion that there will be no more repetitive imports in the future?" (UNCTAD, 1985: 162). By and large, policymakers in the developing countries were concerned with the availability of maximum volumes of technological products rather than with the more complex problems of their political, economic, and cultural integration. Little or no attention was given to the infrastructural requirements for a productive assimilation of imported science and technology in the recipient countries.

Throughout the First United Nations Development Decade it did seem that the transfer of the latest and the best from the developed countries to the Third World was the optimal instrument for rapid development. In the course of the 1960s there was a considerable increase in the volume of technology transferred between the developed market economies and the developing countries. In the process, many recipient countries became aware that the transfer usually consisted of end-products rather than of technology *per se*, that much of the transfer took place as intra-firm movements, that the conditions under which transfer took place were often disadvantageous for them, and that much of the technology was inappropriate, obsolete, over-priced, or all of these together.

In 1970 the tenth session of the UNCTAD Trade and Development Board decided to establish an Intergovernmental Group on Transfer of Technology (IGGTT). At its first session the IGGTT drew up a programme of work for UNCTAD in the field of transfer of technology. Herewith a strong involvement of UNCTAD in technology issues began that would soon lead to such activities as the negotiations on an international code of conduct on the transfer of technology and the revision of the industrial property system.

As the science and technology issues moved on to an essential position in multilateral negotiations, it also became clear that there were important differences in positions taken by the developed and the developing countries. These were largely based upon the conflicting interests of the protection of knowledge as private property versus the availability of knowledge as public resource. The Third World countries began to claim a right of access to scientific and technological (S&T) information in the early negotiations on the UNCTAD Code of Conduct on the Transfer of Technology where they stressed the definition of S&T information as a common good. They claimed that knowledge resources should be transferred to them. These claims were expressly formulated in UNGA Resolutions on the Establishment of a New International Economic Order (NIEO).

One of these resolutions observed that "The benefits of technological progress are not shared equitably by all members of the international community". Therefore, it was seen as imperative to give "to developing countries access to the achievements of modern science and technology and the creation of indigenous technology for the benefit of the developing countries in forms and in accordance with procedures which are suited to their economies". The developed countries opposed these claims and did not support the NIEO programmes and declaration.

Despite Western opposition, the UNGA resolutions on the NIEO led to the preparations of the United Nations Conference on Science and Technology for Development. This conference was eventually held at Vienna in 1979 and on August 31 the UNCSTED adopted the Programme of Action on Science and Technology for Development. The Vienna Programme responded to Third World demands for access to and transfer of knowledge, and addressed the creation of conditions under which the developing countries could improve their autonomous capacity for research and development. The programme contained a series of action proposals for the resolution of the North–South disparity in scientific and technical information. Its essential components were strengthening the scientific and technological capacities of the developing countries, restructuring the current pattern of international scientific and technological relations, strengthening the role of the UN with regard to science and technology for development, and creating the financial provisions to this end.

NIIO and NWICO

In the 1970s the Non-Aligned countries began to recognize that technical assistance did not alter their dependency status, that information inequality persisted, and that in fact their cultural sovereignty was increasingly threatened. They therefore opened the debate on the need of normative standard-setting regarding the mass media. The key agenda issue for this debate was the demand for a new international information order. This demand expressed the Third World concern about disparity in communication capacity along three lines.

There was concern about the impact of the skewed communication relations between North and South on the independent cultural development of the Third World nations. Actually, the first Non-Aligned summit in Bandung, Indonesia, in 1955 already referred to the impact of colonialism on culture. "The existence of colonialism in many parts of Asia and Africa, in whatever form it may be, not only prevents cultural co-operation but also suppresses the national cultures of the peoples. ... Some colonial powers have denied their dependent peoples basic rights in the sphere of education and culture". The 1973 Non-Aligned summit at Algiers expressed its concern about cultural colonialism as the effective successor to the earlier territorial modes of colonialism.

Then there was concern about the largely one-sided exports from the North to the countries of the Third World and the often distorted or totally absent reporting in the media of the North about developments in the South. The Algiers summit called for the "reorganization of existing communication channels, which are a legacy of the colonial past and which have hampered free, direct and fast communication between developing countries". This disequilibrium in the exchange of information between the North and the South controlled by a few Western transnational information companies began to be criticized by the Non-Aligned movement as an instrument of cultural colonialism.

The Tunis symposium of 1976 stated: "Since information in the world shows a disequilibrium favouring some and ignoring others, it is the duty of the non-aligned countries and other developing countries to change this situation and obtain the decolonization of information and initiate a new international order of information". The New Delhi Declaration on Decolonization of Information stated that the establishment of a New International Order for Information is as necessary as the New International Economic Order.

A third line of concern addressed the transfer of media technology. On balance, it was concluded in the early 1970s that precious little technology had been transferred and that by and large only technical end-products had been exported from the industrial nations. This was often done under disadvantageous conditions so that in the end the technical and financial dependence of the receiving countries had only increased. As from its Algiers summit in 1973, the Non-Aligned movement continuously articulated its position of strong support for the emancipation and development of media in the developing nations. UNESCO became the most important forum for this debate.

Already in 1970 the minutes of the UNESCO General Conference read: "Delegates from a number of developing countries stressed the need to ensure that the free flow of information and international exchanges should be a two-way operation. They asserted that the programme must continue to emphasize the rights of less privileged nations, to preserve their own culture."

In a first phase (1970–1976) the debate was characterized by the effort to "decolonize". In this period political and academic projects evolved that fundamentally criticized the existing international information order and that developed proposals for decisive changes.

Several years of declarations, resolutions, recommendations, and studies converged into the demand for a New International Information Order (NIIO).

The concept surfaced at the Tunis information symposium in March, 1976. With this concept (formally recognized by Non-Aligned Heads of State in August 1976 in Sri Lanka) a clear linkage was established with the proposal for a fundamental restructuring of the international economy that was put forward in 1974 (the New International Economic Order, NIEO). Both new orders were deeply inspired by the human rights principle of equality. Although the precise meaning of the NIIO was not defined, it was evident that it aspired to a level playing field for the international information exchange.

During the Nineteenth General Conference of UNESCO in 1976 at Nairobi, a draft resolution proposed by Tunisia was discussed and adopted. The resolution invited the Director General "to pay special attention to the activities of the bodies responsible for co-ordinating and implementing the information programme of the non-aligned countries ... to strengthen the intellectual, technical and financial resources provided for under the Regular Programme through an appreciable and appropriate increase in the proposed growth rate for communication and information activities...".

The Twentieth General Conference of UNESCO in 1978 at Paris adopted a request to the MacBride Commission to propose measures that could lead "to the establishment of a more just and effective world information order". In fact, this Conference was a turning point in the debate in so far as at this meeting the hostile opposition towards the idea of a new order was softened. There began to be almost unanimous acceptance that Third World countries had justifiable complaints and that concessions must be made by the industrialized states. The original formula coined by the Non-Aligned movement, NIIO, was replaced by the proposal for a "new, more just and effective world information and communication order", NWICO. According to the interpretation of United States Ambassador John Reinhardt at the 1978 General Conference, this new order required "a more effective program of action, both public and private, to suitable identified centers of professional education and training in broadcasting and journalism in the developing world ... [and] ... a major effort to apply the benefits of advanced communications technology ... to economic and social needs in the rural areas of developing nations". The new order (NWICO) that was now acceptable to all UNESCO member states was mainly interpreted as a programme for the transfer of knowledge, finances, and technical equipment. The problem of the international information structure was being reduced to mere technical proportions. In response to this, an intergovernmental programme for support to the development of communication was launched as a Western initiative in 1980.

The Twenty-first General Conference in 1980 at Belgrade adopted by consensus a resolution concerning the establishment of the International Programme for the Development of Communication (IPDC).

During the UNESCO General Conferences of 1976, 1978, and 1980, the Western minority managed to achieve most of its policy objectives against the expressed preference of the majority of member states. In the end, the debate did not yield the results demanded by the developing countries. Their criticism of the past failures of technical assistance pro-grammes was answered by the creation of yet another such programme: the International Programme for the Development of Communication. This programme was seen by many Third World delegates as the instrument to implement the standards of the NWICO. The UNESCO General Conference of 1980 had stated that among these standards were the elimination of the imbalances and inequalities which characterize the present situation, the capacity of the developing countries to achieve improvement of their own situation, notably by providing infrastructure and by making their information and communication means suitable to their needs and aspirations, and the sincere will of developed countries to help them. The IPDC was not going to meet these expectations. Apart from the inherent difficulty that the IPDC represented a definition of global communication problems that had in the past not worked to the benefit of Third World nations, the programme would also from the outset suffer a chronic lack of resources. Although the Non-Aligned summit in Belgrade (September, 1989) reiterated its support for the NWICO, the UNESCO General Conference strove hard to reach consensus on formulations that represented conventional freedom of the press, pluralism of the media, freedom of expression, and free flow of infor-mation positions. According to the UNESCO Director General (in 1989), plans for a new information order no longer existed in UNESCO.

The MacBride Round Table

Throughout the 1980s and 1990s only some international non-governmental organizations (meeting as the MacBride Round Tables on Communications) kept expressing concern "that economic and technological disparities still characterise the current international system. The rapid advances in communication technologies in the affluent parts of the world have widened that gap between the 'haves' and 'have-nots'" (Harare Round Table in 1989). The Round Table of Prague, 1990, was concerned about the state of communication in the South:

> The rapid development of communication technology, which has drastically increased the capacity for information in industrialised countries, has bypassed many countries in the South. Essential technical infrastructures for communications are still not available there or are inaccessible to most of the people. Instead, foreign communication enterprises have, in alliance with many governments and elitist interests, created an artificial commercial culture which is accessible only to an affluent few ... a new basis and new methods for North–South co-operation, must be found which ensure greater equality and more genuine partnership.

The sixth MacBride Round Table (Honolulu, Hawaii, January 20–23, 1994) gave special attention to the inadequate communication capacity of the so-called Fourth World within the Third World, the indigenous peoples. The Round Table participants recognized "that the indigenous peoples of the world are marginalized from communicative links in the world

143

and within countries". The meeting also addressed the issue of the plans for "information superhighways" to be constructed by the USA, the European Union countries, and Japan. As the participants stated in the final document, "No 'information superhighway' is planned for the developing world. ... It is likely that the new information highways will widen the gap between the information rich and information poor, both within individual countries and between rich and poor regions of the world, to such an extent as to render it unbridgeable in the foreseeable future".

The international transfer of technology

Throughout the 1980s and 1990s the principle of equality in the literature and policy debates about information/communication met with a great deal of consensus. In 1991, for example, the non-discrimination standard was applied to the use of telecommunication satellites through a resolution by the General Assembly of the UN: "Communication by means of satellite should be available on a global and non-discriminatory basis" (Res. 1721 D [XVI] in 1961).

Yet, at the same time there was general agreement in the scientific literature and in public policy statements that the information/communication technology (ICT) gap between the developed and developing countries was widening. As the UNDP Development Report of 1999 stated: "The network society is creating parallel communication systems: one for those with income, education and, literally, connections, giving plentiful information at low cost and high speed; the other for those without connections, blocked by high barriers of time, cost and uncertainty and dependent on outdated information" (UNDP, 1999: 63).

At the turn of the century the worldwide distribution of ICT resources continued to be enormously unequal. In terms of availability, accessibility, and affordability of equipment and services as well as the mastery of technical and managerial skills there remained great disparities between affluent and developing countries, but also between different social groups within all countries.

The WSIS and the global digital divide

The information/communication inequality became one of the key issues of the United Nations World Summit on the Information Society (in Geneva, 2003, and in Tunis, 2005). There was a tendency in the WSIS debates to treat the digital divide mainly as a matter of the globally skewed distribution of information and communication resources. The divide was not primarily seen as a dimension of the overall global "development divide". Since this bigger problem was not seriously addressed, a romantic fallacy prevailed which proposed that the resolution of information/communication problems, and the bridging of knowledge gaps or inequalities of access to technologies, can contribute to the solution of the world's most urgent and explosive socio-economic inequities. This isolated the digital divide from the broader problem of the development divide. In reality, the digital divide is not more than one of the many manifestations of the unequal allocation of both material and immaterial resources in the world, both between and within societies. Its solution has little to do with information, communication or ICT. This is a matter of political will, which is lacking in a majority of nation-states. Instead of the strong political commitment that is needed, the WSIS discourse focused on the possibility of a global "Digital Solidarity Fund". This is an almost scandalous proposition in view of the fact that since the 1970s all the efforts to develop and sustain such funds for communication development, telecom infrastructures, or technological self-reliance have failed because of the lack of political will. The WTO Ministerial meeting in Cancún (September, 2003) demonstrated once again that not all stakeholders are equally intent on solving rich–poor divides. Fortunately, the poor countries understood that the rich countries (particularly the USA and the EU) intended to impose yet another set of demands on them that would be very detrimental to their societies and their people. In this sense, the Cancún meeting was a great success. That same sense of alertness did not inspire the poor country representatives at the December 2003 WSIS.

?

According to Castells (2001: 270), the digital divide is the "divide created between those individuals, firms, institutions, regions, societies that have the material and cultural conditions to operate in the digital world, and those who cannot, or cannot adapt to the speed of change". Could education play a role in bridging gaps in global digital densities?

The WSIS discourse on the digital divide did not critically question whether rich–poor divides can at all be resolved within the framework of the prevailing development paradigm. Following this, development is conceived of as a state of affairs which exists in society A and, unfortunately, not in society B. Therefore, through some project of intervention in society B, resources have to be transferred from A to B. Development is thus a relationship between interventionists and the subjects of intervention. The interventionists transfer such resources as information, ICT, and knowledge as inputs that will lead to development as an output. In this approach, development is "the delivery of resources" (Kaplan, 1999: 5–7). This position was reflected in the conceptual framework of the WSIS discourse that conceives development as delivery. This delivery process is geared towards the integration of its recipients into a global marketplace. There is no space for a different conceptualization of development as a process of empowerment that intends "to enable people to participate in the governance of their own lives" (Kaplan, 1999: 19).

A difficult problem is that if indeed greater global equality in access to information could be achieved, this would not guarantee an improvement in the quality of people's lives. "Even when these disparities are recognised and new organisational models such as telecentres are proposed, the policy emphasis is frequently biased towards improving access to networks rather than towards content creation and the social processes whereby digital content can be converted into socially or economically useful knowledge" (Mansell, 1999: 8). Including people in the provision of basic public services does not create egalitarian societies. The existing social inequality means that people benefit from these services in highly inegalitarian ways. Actually, the growing literacy in many societies did not bring about more egalitarian social relationships. It certainly did have some empowering effect, but did not significantly alter power relations. Catching up with those who have the distinct social advantage is not a realistic option. They too use the new developments, such as ICTs, and, at a minimum, the gap remains and might even increase. It is a common experience with most technologies that the powerful players know best how to appropriate and control new technological developments and use them to their advantage. In the process they tend to further increase their advantage.

Large disparities in access to the Internet continue to exist, particularly for developing countries. Africa, for example, still very much lags the rest of the world in both mobile and Internet penetration. One widely recognized reason for this is the high costs of international circuits for Internet connectivity between least developed countries and Internet backbone networks. A number of initiatives are under way to address this problem. These include consideration of new models for financial exchanges among operators as well as efforts to facilitate the creation of traffic aggregation within localities, countries, or regions in developing countries in order to avoid the sending of this traffic over satellite or cable links used for intercontinental traffic – for example, between Africa and Europe or North America. The latter would aim to maximize the retention of local and national traffic within these regions and thus reduce the dependence on international communications links. To give a sense of the scale of the problem, over 75 per cent of Internet traffic in Europe remains intra-regional compared with only 1 per cent in regions like Africa.

Information/communication inequality is, however, not merely a matter of access to technological infrastructures and thus cannot be resolved by providing equal access to the technology. When new technologies are introduced in societies, the chances to benefit from them are always unequally distributed. Some people will benefit, others will mainly experience the negative impact. This is a recurrent pattern. When a technology that promises financial benefits is introduced in social situations where unequal power relations prevail, a small group will enjoy advantages and the majority will often experience regressive development. Access to the global network society is mainly available to those with good education and those living in the OECD countries with sufficient disposable income. In most countries, men dominate access to the Internet and young people are more likely to have access than the elderly. Ethnicity is an important factor and in many countries the differences in use by ethnic groups has widened. "English is used in almost 80% of Websites and in the common user interfaces – the graphics and instructions. Yet less than 1 in 10 people worldwide speaks the language" (UNDP, 1999: 62).

146

A particularly skewed distribution of ICT resources and uses concerns the position of women across the world. An immediate problem is the fact that ICT skills are largely based on literacy. Actually, "…it seems likely that the vast majority of the illiterate population will be excluded from the emerging knowledge societies" (Mansell and Wehn, 1998: 35). This affects women especially, since around the world illiteracy rates for women are higher than for men. In terms of sharing ICT knowledge, women are also disadvantaged since their numbers in enrolment for science and technology education lag far behind the figures for male enrolment. ICTs offer potentially new forms of communication that enable women to break through their often isolated social situation. They also create new opportunities of employment for women in jobs that require new skills. However, the technologies themselves will not achieve this. Unless robust policies are in place and are enforced, the possible benefits of ICTs will have no impact on women's lives. The realization of opportunities that are in principle created by the deployment of ICTs will depend upon such social variables as cultural capital, class, and age. "Although faced with these changing skill requirements and the need for continuous upgrading of skills, few women have access to the relevant education and training" (Mansell and Wehn, 1998: 249).

The French sociologist Pierre Bourdieu (1985) has proposed that the position of social actors is not only determined by economic capital, but also by their cultural, social, and symbolic capital. Cultural capital is made up of such features and skills as knowledge about wines, fine arts, music and literature, good manners, and mastery of foreign languages. Social capital is based upon the social networks that people develop. Symbolic capital represents social prestige and reputation.

To these forms of capital, the category of "information capital" should be added. This concept embraces the financial capacity to pay for network usage and information services, the technical ability to handle network infrastructures, the intellectual capacity to filter and evaluate information, but also the motivation to actively search for information and the ability to translate information into social practice.

Just like other forms of capital, information capital is unequally distributed across societies. Its more egalitarian distribution would require an extensive programme of education, training, and conscientization. To just have more "surfers" on the Web does not equate the equal possession of information capital.

It needs to be questioned, however, how realistic the expectation is that this disparity can indeed be narrowed, let alone be eliminated. It may well be an illusion to think that ICT-poor countries could catch up or keep pace with the advancements in the Northern countries. In the North, the rate of technological development is very high and is supported by considerable resources. It would be wasting scarce resources if poor countries did attempt to follow a "catching up" policy which would, in the end, only benefit the designers and operators of ICTs. This does not mean that poor countries should not try to upgrade their ICT systems. They should not do this in the unrealistic expectation that those who are ahead will wait for them. As a result, the situation may improve for the poorer countries, but the divide will not go away. As long as ICTs are embedded in the institutional arrangements of a corporate-capitalist market economy, the equal entitlement to information and communication resources will remain a normative standard only.

The present discussion on the ICT gap provides no convincing argument that the owners of technology will change their attitudes and policies towards the international transfer of technology. Throughout the past decades the prevailing international policies on transfer of technology have erected formidable obstacles to the reduction of North–South technology gaps. Today, there is no indication of a radical change in the current practices of technology transfer. This makes it very unlikely that the relations between ICT-rich and ICT-poor countries will change in the near future.

The equitable sharing of communication infrastructures (the electronic highway systems created by telecom carriers such as satellites, cables, fixed lines, and mobile transmissions), computing capacity (computers, peripherals, networks), information resources (databases, libraries), and ICT-literacy (intellectual and social capabilities to deploy ICT in beneficial ways) demands an enormous effort on behalf of the international community. Massive investments are required for the renovation, upgrading, and expansion of networks in developing countries, for programmes to transfer knowledge, for training of ICT skills – in particular, for women.

Distribution of effects

A fairly common assumption about ICTs is that they have mainly benign effects and that these will be equally distributed. Informational developments and their supporting technologies obviously have a certain societal impact. In the business and political community, references to "social effects of technology" are usually made with great ease. From the academic literature it is clear that the issue of impact is far from unequivocal, and indeed is very complex. In a conventional reading of social sciences, "effects" may be conceived of as measurable variables because it is accepted that there are regularities in social processes, there are cause–effect chains, and identifiable causes of effects. In a more advanced understanding of social realities – such as those inspired by chaos theory conceptions – this has all fundamentally changed. We know far less about effects than we may want to admit. Moreover, there is no realistic possibility to anticipate with any degree of reliability and validity the future impact of technological developments. The complexity of social reality implies that technology assessment in the sense of forecasting is pretentious and misleading. We could and should think in the future sense, but then in terms of possible futures (always in the plural), both negative and positive ones.

Realistic thinking about future technological impact will have to accept both benefits and risks. ICTs may have some benign effects, but they are equally likely to have effects that are not so benign. It seems that the Information Society euphoria blinds policymakers in both politics and industry to the undesirable effects, such as the loss of privacy, growing digital dependence, or cyberwarfare.

The assumption that effects would be equally distributed betrays a considerable lack of historical insight. Whatever societal effects technological developments – such as industrial machinery in the eighteenth century or automation in the twentieth century – had, there was always an unequal distribution. Those on top of the social hierarchy usually had more benefits than those lower down in the system, who often had to live with most of the risks.

Already in 1975 a meeting of experts (in September at Geneva) recommended to the United Nations the establishment of an international machinery for the assessment of new technologies from the point of view of human rights. The assessment would have to include the evaluation of possible side-effects and long-range effects of technological innovations and would weigh possible advantages against possible disadvantages. The General Assembly never acted upon this recommendation, which would seem as urgently needed today as it was in the 1970s.

The issue of inclusion

There seemed among participants in the World Summit on the Information Society a strong consensus on the proposal that the Information Society should be inclusive and accessible to all. Apart from the fact that nowhere is the notion of inclusion defined or elaborated, this presumes without further questioning that everyone also wants to be included. What does "inclusion" mean? Is this the same proposition as that everyone should be included in the free market economy? The notion is presented as inherently benign. Without explanation about the entity within which everyone should be included, it is unclear as to whether one should welcome or mistrust "inclusion". How far is being included a free choice? Is it possible to consider that there may be people who would prefer not to live in whatever the Information Society might be. If, for example, an Information Society implies a societal dependence upon fallible, unreliable, and ill-understood technologies which imply great social risks, could it make sense for sensible people to let the opportunity pass by? If an Information Society means that all included people get more information, but if that information consists mainly of commercial messages and disinformation, propaganda or hate speech, could some people say they would rather be excluded?

What are the real motives behind the drive towards inclusion? Is the anxiety about digital illiteracy fed by the same motive as earlier alphabetization campaigns in European history. These were often not motivated by a strong desire to empower ordinary people but served to facilitate the functioning of a system that with too many people unable to read or write would not efficiently operate.

Moreover, a puzzling question remains how the proponents of the inclusion thesis expect that – if information is a key resource and if access to such a resource has historically always been skewed – it could be any different today. Are there any socio-economic and political conditions that make universal accessibility to essential resources a realistic claim in the early twenty-first century?

? How does digital inequality relate to broader forms of societal inequality (such as income disparities or dual occupational structures) as documented in the UNDP Human Development Reports?

Communication for development

This chapter began by honoring Luis Beltran for his work in a field in which equality issues were always on the agenda. It is a field that has been described in many different ways, as Development Communication, Communication for Development, and, more recently, as Communication for Sustainable Development and Social Change. There is a small library of good books on the origins and growth of studies in this field and the most important ones you will find in the further reading section (Melkote and Steeves, 2001; Gumucio-Dagron and Tufte, 2006; Servaes, 2008; McAnany, 2012; and Wilkins, Tufte and Obregon, 2013). In the 2010s it continues to be a very productive area of research on such topics as environmental communication, health communication, peace communication, and rural communication. Among the essential notions that inspire all this work are human rights (especially the right to communicate), participation, and empowerment. Although the study of global communication primarily addresses communicative practices that cross national borders, the issue of (local and regional) development has become a matter of global interest that requires the synergy of global communication, development communication, and intercultural communication. A particularly interesting approach to the study of communication for social change can be found in a book by Mohan Dutta (2011). He proposes to situate this research in the realm of post-colonial studies.[1] By taking this route, Dutta opens new perspectives on oppression, exploitation, and resistance, and in his own words he "creates a discursive space for engaging with the role of communication to bringing about social transformation" (2011: 28).

Note

1. I return to the issue of post-colonialism in Chapter 13.

Reading spotlight

Communication Inequality

Galtung, J. and Vincent, R.C. (1992). *Global Glasnost: Toward a New World Information and Communication Order?* Cresskill, NJ: Hampton Press.

This book addresses communication inequality in the context of global problems. It analyzes the 1970s debates on proposals for new economic and information orders. The notion "glasnost" points to the need to develop better global understanding through the improvement of global news flows.

Hamelink, C.J. (1983). *Cultural Autonomy in Global Communications*. New York: Longman. This book explores the cultural dimensions of the global communication divide. Develops proposals for national communication policies on the basis of the theoretical proposition of "dissociation".

Communication and Development

McAnany, E. (ed.) (1980). *Communications in the Rural Third World: The Role of Information in Development*. New York: Praeger.
After the introductory reflections by McAnany on the role of information and communication in development, access, exposure and impact of mass media for development are analyzed by Larry Shore. This is followed by three case studies: Ivory Coast, Guatemala and Brzail.

Servaes, J. (1999). *Communication for Development*. Cresskill, NJ: Hampton Press.
The text moves from a theoretical analysis of modernization, dependency and multiplicity to policy and planning for social change. Concrete case studies on participatory policymaking and research.

Online resources

Visit the book's companion website at **https://study.sagepub.com/hamelink** to watch the author discussing the theme of this chapter: **The Global Divide**

Visit the book's companion website at **https://study.sagepub.com/hamelink** to access the following journal articles free of charge:

Chakravartty, P. (2004). Telecom, national development and the Indian state: a post-colonial critique. *Media, Culture & Society*, 26(2): 227–249.

Deursen, A. van and Van Dijk, J. (2011). Internet skills and the digital divide. *New Media & Society*, 13(6): 893–911.

Padovani, C. (2005). Debating communication imbalances from the MacBride Report to the World Summit on the Information Society: an analysis of a changing discourse. *Global Media and Communication*, 1(3): 316–338.

Servaes, J., Polk, E., Reilly, D. and Yakupitijage, T. (2012). Towards sustainability indicators for "communication for development and social change projects". *International Communication Gazette*, 74(2) : 99–123.

White, R. A. (2004). Is "Empowerment" the answer? Current theory and research on development communication. *Gazette*, 66(1): 7–24.

Wilkins, K.G. and Enghel, F. (2013). The privatization of development through global communication industries: Living Proof? *Media, Culture & Society*, 35(2): 165–181.

Further reading

Bordenave, J.D. (1977). *Communication and Rural Development*. Paris: UNESCO.

Casimir, F. (ed.) (1991). *Communication in Development*. Norwood, NJ: Ablex Publishing.

Gumucio-Dagron, A. and Tufte, T. (eds) (2006). *Communication for Social Change Anthology: Historical and Contemporary Readings*. South Orange, NJ: Communication for Social Change Consortium.

Hancock, A. (ed.) (1984). *Technology Transfer and Communication*. Paris: UNESCO.

Hedebro, G. (1982). *Communication and Social Change in Developing Countries: A Critical View*. Ames, IA: Iowa State University Press.

Lerner, D. (1958). *The Passing of Traditional Society: Modernizing the Middle East*. New York: Free Press.

McAnany, E.G. (ed.) (1980). *Communications in the Rural Third World: The Role of Information in Development*. New York: Praeger.

McAnany, E.G. (2012). *Saving the World: A Brief History of Communication for Development and Social Change*. Champaign, IL: University of Illinois Press.

McPhail, Th. (2009). *Development Communication: Reframing the Role of the Media*. Oxford: Wiley-Blackwell.

Melkote, S.R. and Steeves, H.L. (2001). *Communication for Development in the Third World: Theory and Practice for Empowerment* (2nd edn). London: Sage.

Rogers, E.M. (ed.) (1976). *Communication and Development*. Beverly Hills, CA: Sage.

Schramm, W. (1964). *Mass Media and National Development*. Stanford, CA: Stanford University Press.

Servaes, J. (1999). *Communication for Development*. Cresskill, NJ: Hampton Press.

Servaes, J. (ed.) (2008). *Communication for Development and Social Change*. London: Sage.

Wilkins, K., Tufte, T. and Obregon, R. (eds) (2014). *The Handbook of Development Communication and Social Change*. Oxford: Wiley-Blackwell.

RESEARCH ASSIGNMENT

Conduct a research project on the role of your country (its government, its diplomats) in the 1970s negotiations concerning the establishment of a new order for information and communication in the world.

How would you approach a historical analysis like this? Where could you find relevant sources? Are there experts you could interview? What questions would you ask?

More than anyone else, it was Noam Chomsky who helped me to understand the workings of propaganda.

Noam Chomsky (1928–)

Born December 7, 1928, he has been described as the father of modern linguistics and was for some 50 years Professor in the Department of Linguistics and Philosophy at the Massachusetts Institute of Technology. Next to the significance of his work on the universal grammar theory, he became well-known for his critical analysis of US foreign policy and modern capitalism. With Edward Herman he developed the propaganda mode for the purpose of critical media analysis.

For the study of global communication, important sources are: *Manufacturing Consent* (1988); *Necessary Illusions: Thought Control in Democratic Societies* (1989); and *Media Control: The Spectacular Achievements of Propaganda* (2002).

For the study of global communication, Noam Chomsky taught us to critically reflect on the delusions and illusions that global propaganda creates.

This chapter looks at the international political system as a communication network in which endless flows of messages are transported across the globe. The main forms of these flows, which are essential to global politics, are:

- propaganda
- diplomacy
- espionage

It is important to understand how these communicative genres create "soft power". They are storytelling vehicles. The propagandists spread stories to manage perceptions, diplomats exchange stories, and spies collect and process stories about friends and enemies.

A short history of political propaganda

The use of propaganda as a foreign policy instrument has a long history. The use of propaganda messages in international relations was well known in antiquity. Alexander the Great had what amounted to a public relations unit. "Reports written to serve his ends were sent to the Macedonian court, multiplied there and disseminated with propagandistic intent" (Kunczik, 1990: 73). Propaganda has been systematically carried out since the fifteenth century.

In the seventeenth-century Pope Gregory XV in 1622 founded the Sacra Congregatio de Propaganda Fide. The Congregation received among its briefs the call to propagate the catholic faith to the New World. In 1627 Pope Urban VII established a special training centre, the Collegium Urbanum de Propaganda Fide, where catholic propagandists received their training before spreading their religious ideas across the world.

The eighteenth century in particular provides many illustrations of hostile propaganda. It witnessed the work of one of history's greatest propagandists, Napoleon. "He engaged in a veritable propaganda battle with the rest Europe, a battle of big words. … Napoleon communicated selectively with foreign countries. The open appeal to the civilian population was something fundamentally new. Thus in 1796 he directed a manifesto to the Tyroleans to give up 'the hopeless cause' of their emperor" (Kunzcik, 1990: 75).

However, only in the twentieth century did propaganda become an issue that demanded a collective response. Although propaganda was exercised through newspapers, magazines, and movies, radio broadcasting became the essential medium. "The invention of radio in the late nineteenth century totally altered for all time the practice of propaganda" (Jowett and O'Donnell, 1986: 82). In spite of the availability of more advanced communication technologies, radio broadcast propaganda is still today a vibrant activity engaging vast sums of money around the world. There is an estimated audience of between 100 and 200 million listeners worldwide. Radio programmes are transmitted abroad for a variety of reasons. Among them are the contacts with nationals in foreign countries, the international dissemination of news, the distribution of information about a country's politics, economy and culture, and hostile propaganda.

During the First World War an extensive use was made of the means of propaganda.

WOODROW WILSON AND GEORGE CREEL

In April 1917 US President Woodrow Wilson established the Committee on Public Information (CPI) and appointed George Creel, a newspaper man, to be the chair. Creel urged the president to use propaganda in the true sense of the word, meaning the "propagation of faith". The mission of the CPI was to manage American public opinion towards support for participation in the First World War.

(Continued)

(Continued)

In his memoirs, Creel wrote: "In no degree was the Committee an agency of censorship, a machinery of concealment or repression. Its emphasis throughout was on the open and the positive. At no point did it seek or exercise authorities under those war laws that limited the freedom of speech and press. In all things, from first to last, without halt or change, it was a plain publicity proposition, a vast enterprise in salesmanship, the world's greatest adventures in advertising. … We did not call it propaganda, for that word, in German hands, had come to be associated with deceit and corruption. Our effort was educational and informative throughout, for we had such confidence in our case as to feel that no other argument was needed than the simple, straightforward presentation of the facts" (Creel, 1920).

Psychological warfare continued after the war had ended and international short-wave radio began its proliferation. Germany began with international radio broadcasting in 1915 and was followed in 1917 by the Soviet Union. During the 1920s there was a rapidly growing interest for international radio broadcasting and more nations became involved. By 1939 some 25 countries were actively engaged in broadcasting to foreign countries in a multitude of languages. Many broadcast programmes in this period contained propaganda and most of it was hostile. Programmes defamed other governments or their leaders, and made attempts to subvert foreign leadership or incited war.

From its establishment, the League of Nations (predecessor to the United Nations) was concerned about the role of the mass media in international relations and addressed such problems as the contribution of the press to peace. In 1931 the League of Nations had decided to ask the Institute for Intellectual Cooperation (the predecessor of UNESCO) to conduct a study on all questions raised by the use of radio for good international relations. In 1933 the study was published ("Broadcasting and Peace") and it recommended the drafting of a binding multilateral treaty. This treaty was indeed drafted and concluded on September 23, 1936, with signatories from 28 states. The fascist states did not participate. The International Convention concerning the Use of Broadcasting in the Cause of Peace entered into force on April 2, 1938, after ratification or accession by nine countries: Brazil, the United Kingdom, Denmark, France, India, Luxembourg, New Zealand, the Union of South Africa, and Australia. Basic to the provisions of the convention was the recognition of the need to prevent, through rules established by common agreement, broadcasting from being used in a manner prejudicial to good international understanding. These agreed-upon rules included the prohibition of transmissions which could incite the population of any territory "to acts incompatible with the internal order or security of contracting parties", or which were likely to harm good international understanding by incorrect statements. The contracting parties also agreed to ensure "that any transmission likely to harm good international understanding by incorrect statements shall be rectified at the earliest possible moment".

The Second World War led to an enormous expansion of radio propaganda and this continued in the years after the war. "As the dynamics of world politics were being played out, international radio broadcasting became a prominent weapon in the arsenal of propaganda" (Jowett and O'Donnell, 1986: 86). In response to harmful broadcasting there were attempts to impede the reception of radio signals from abroad. "Jamming" has been practised by many countries. Governments have tried to manipulate the effective receiving range of radio sets. Usually most of these attempts have not been very successful.

The United Nations General Assembly adopted a series of resolutions addressing the problem of war propaganda and the diffusion of false or distorted reports "likely to injure friendly relations between States" (UNGA Res. 127.II. of 1947). The concern about propaganda was codified in Article 20 of the International Covenant on Civil and Political Rights. Also, the UNESCO General Conference adopted a series of resolutions on the role of UNESCO in generating a climate of public opinion conducive to the halting of the arms race and transition to disarmament. For example, Resolution 1878 (20th session) recommended "...to pay particular attention to the role which information, including the mass media, can play in generating a climate of confidence and understanding between nations and countries as well as increasing public awareness of ideas, objectives and action in the field of disarmament...".

If one adopts the distinction proposed by Whitton (1979: 217–229), we can divide propaganda into three categories: subversive propaganda, defamatory propaganda, and war propaganda. The category of subversive propaganda, which incites to revolt, has been recognized in various legal instruments as an illegal act. It has been seen as a form of illegal intervention and as a form of aggression. A large number of multilateral treaties urge states to refrain from this type of propaganda. The category of defamatory propaganda, in which foreign leaders are vilified, has also been ruled illegal and a danger to international peace. A special problem in this context has been "the question of the publication of defamatory – especially false – news by the independent press and radio of a country". Although there is general agreement in the world community that false news should be prohibited, "there is wide discord over the best method to accomplish this" (Whitton, 1979: 223). There is no unequivocal collectively adopted agreement on this type of propaganda.

The consideration of propaganda for war as illegal is a typical development of the twentieth century. Earlier, "to declare war was considered one of the sovereign rights of every state" (Whitton, 1979: 225). War propaganda came to be seen as a serious danger to international peace by the League of Nations and later by the United Nations. The preliminary draft of the General Convention to Improve the Means of Preventing War by the League of Nations stated that aggressive propaganda could "take such offensive forms and assume such a threatening character as to constitute a real danger to peace". In various instruments the world community expressed its concern about war propaganda, but it never managed to establish a robust multilateral accord on the issue.

A peculiar problem in this area has been the fact that much hostile communication originates with private actors, and opinions have been divided over the extent of state responsibility in such cases. Moreover, only a limited number of states have adopted the prohibition of war propaganda in their domestic legislation. It remains a matter of dispute whether a state could be held responsible in case independent media under its jurisdiction were guilty of warmongering. It also remains unclear whether there is a precise definition of propaganda for war.

By and large the political practice has been characterized by discord and ambivalence. The ambivalence is clearly articulated in UN General Assembly Resolution 424 (v) of December 14, 1950. In para 3, the Resolution invites the governments of member states to refrain from interference with the reception of certain signals originating beyond their territories. At the same time it invites all governments to refrain from radio broadcasts which would mean unfair attacks or slander against other peoples anywhere. In several UN instruments jamming has been condemned, but this was never codified in binding law. Equally, there is no multilateral accord that would limit the contents of international radio broadcasts. In fact, it has been the prevailing practice of most players to broadcast as they wanted, largely unhindered since attempts at barring broadcast signals have usually been ineffective.

The Cold War

Since in the nuclear age international combat could hardly be a military confrontation, the world arena moved from armed conflict via diplomatic negotiations towards propaganda and counter-propaganda. As a result, the United States and the Soviet Union were engaged in a propaganda war.

On May 28, 1980, James Wright, Republican spokesman in the US House Representatives, stated that "the USA cannot risk losing the battle for minds in all countries of the world". This "battle for minds" was indeed supported by the US government with impressive resources, but equally important were the contributions made by private initiatives and the mass media. The Committee on the Present Danger (established in 1976), for example, conducted propaganda against treaties on the reduction of nuclear arms and gave special emphasis to the alleged Soviet desire to conquer the world. Among the distinguished members of this Committee were Jeane Kirkpatrick, Paul Nitze, George Schultz, and William Casey. In 1978, the Committee, together with the American Conservative Union and the Coalition for Peace through Strength, spent US$200,000 to broadcast a film called "Russian power and American myth" via 200 television stations as part of a campaign against ratification of the SALT 2 agreement. In 1982 the Centre for Strategic and International Studies at the University of Georgetown, Washington, DC, hosted a Reader's Digest-sponsored meeting, during which an increase in psychological warfare was recommended. Among the participants were Jeane Kirkpatrick, Henry Kissinger, and Zbigniew Brezinski.

A special contribution to the propaganda war was also provided by US President Ronald Reagan. Illustrative was his reference to the Soviet Union as "the focus of evil in the modem world" in his speech to a meeting of evangelical Christians, in March 1983, in Orlando,

Florida. The Soviet Union was just as heavily engaged in propaganda. Soviet international propaganda found its origins in the Communist International Comintern), set up in 1919 as an aggressive disinformation agency. Among the purposes of post-war Soviet international propaganda were spreading the idea of the revolution in other countries, breaking up existing alliances against the Soviet Union by exploiting differences between the allies, and weakening individual Western countries by stirring up internal tensions. The KGB (the Soviet intelligence service) also used journalists in many countries to influence public opinion and official decision-making. In 1959 a special department for disinformation was established. A great variety of manufactured stories were put in foreign newspapers across the world. Among the very many illustrations is the forged speech that Jeane Kirkpatrick was alleged to have given to the United Nations in her function as the US ambassador.

Soviet propaganda stepped up particularly since 1975. According to the Soviet government, this became necessary when Western countries began using extensive propaganda against the Soviet Union after the signing of the Helsinki Final Act. The Soviet authorities called their activities an "offensive in counter-propaganda". This offensive used among its weapons political cartoons in the newspapers *Pravda* and *Izvestia*. A key argument was that the Western press operated an instrument of aggressive NATO strategists, that Western journalists were allies of the CIA, that they maintained the myth of a Soviet threat and that the political programme of US President Ronald Reagan was full of deceit, violence, and bribery.

The battle for minds

Warfare has considerably changed in recent times. Modern wars are no longer classic battles between regular armed forces but are confrontations between regular armies and guerrilla groups, non-state militias, and terrorist networks. These wars are termed counter-insurgency (COIN). The opponents are highly mobile and easily blend in with civilian populations. This requires deep knowledge of local relations, tribal constructions, attitudes, and belief systems. Therefore, more intelligence is needed and cultural awareness. It is crucial to win the opponents' "hearts and minds".[1] These wars are more about politics than about fighting. Politics in the information age is about the framing of an event as the most credible story.

At its core, propaganda is the management of perceptions. In order to do this effectively governments will often rely on the so-called "spin doctors". These professionals have to sell wars as attractive products. They do this with lies, half-truths, and the fabrication of myths. During the Gulf War some infamous myths were reproduced by journalists around the world with little or no critical probing. Among these were the Patriot success story and the oil spill story. It was reported that the Patriot missile had been very effective in intercepting Iraqi Scud missiles launched against Israel. General Norman Schwarzkopf told correspondents it was a one hundred percent success. Only after the war did the truth emerge. "A US Army Services Committee report quoted in the *Guardian* of August 17, 1993,

159

concluded, 'A post war review of photographs cannot produce even a single confirmed kill of a Scud missile'" (Knightley, 2000: 496). In a testimony before the House Armed Services Committee, former Defense Department official Pierre Sprey stated, "The country has been poorly served by shamelessly doctored statistics and the hand-selected video clips of isolated successes that were pumped out to the media during the war in order to influence post-war budget decisions" (Knightley, 2000: 497).

Most war correspondents were "pretty impressively ignorant about technology" and acted as unpaid publicists to help weapons manufacturers get government contracts.

The image of the dying cormorant choked by an oil slick that the Iraqis had released from Kuwait made Saddam Hussein an "environmental terrorist" in addition to being a brutal dictator. The story was a lie, "a brilliant piece of propaganda" (Knightley, 2000: 497). The oil slick that killed the cormorant was caused by the Americans, who had bombed an Iraqi tanker. "It was to take nearly another month before an Associated Press story said a Saudi official had confirmed that the first crude oil to wash up on Saudi shores had resulted from an American attack and that Allied attacks were responsible for about a third of the oil pollution in Saudi waters" (Knightley, 2000: 498).

Modern propagandists use a variety of techniques. They invent "brand-names" for wars such as "Operation Just Cause" for the US invasion of Panama in 1989 or "Restoration Hope" for the US intervention in Somalia in 1992. The first Gulf War (1991) was sold as "Operation Desert Storm", the war in Afghanistan (2001) as "Enduring Freedom", and the war against Iraq as "Operation Iraqi Freedom".

Among the images that the "spin doctors" use are the portrayal of the enemy as the great evil, archtypical images such as the killing of innocent babies, and the demonstration of the attractiveness of one's own moral values, lifestyles, cultural achievements, or superior strength. It is important for the politics of propaganda that it should be credible. Exaggerated propagandistic claims can easily undermine credibility. Illustrative of this was the case of the suggested presence of weapons of mass destruction in Iraq or the stories about the links between Saddam Hussain and Al-Qaeda. Essential is also that advertising political values only works if these values are respected in the originating country. US propaganda for democracy in Iraq was eroded when at home the enforcement of the Patriot Act was seen as a violation of basic democratic principles.

Media and political propaganda

It is understandable that governments, when they plan to engage in a war that is not popular with their electorates, will employ mind managers. These professionals obviously need wide-ranging public platforms – international news media – for their propagandistic messages in words and images. The essential problem here is that, by and large, media are too gullible and not sufficiently critical and suspicious so that too many deceptive messages reach out to publics worldwide. It is inherent in common media logic that there is a strong pressure to answer the classical "5W" questions in a news report.

The five Ws (what, where, when, who, and why) were designed to improve objectivity in journalism. In real practice, they often stand in the way of this objectivity. The what, where, and when questions can often be answered without too much difficulty. The trouble arises with the who and why questions. They often require more time, more research, and more prudence. Mainstream journalism has serious problems with these requirements. There is a lot of editorial pressure on journalists to provide answers quickly and with certainty. Much journalism is haunted by an obsession with certainty that often, in all honesty, cannot be provided. However, the spin doctors that assist the political leaders in conflicts claim to have all the answers. In the 9/11 attacks, for example, they knew immediately that the "who" were Al-Qaeda terrorists and the "why" was hatred of American freedoms and lifestyles. This is a tempting offer for news producers and – regrettably – journalists, who easily fall into the traps of the propagandists (Knightley, 2000: 496).

As long as journalists do not find the courage to honestly say "I have no idea", they remain vulnerable to the perception management by spin doctors.

Propaganda can be summed up as the effort to propagate ideas, beliefs, or worldviews through professional means and with the aim to exercise (soft) power.

? Philip Taylor ends his book on war propaganda with this statement "the challenge is to ensure that no single propaganda source gains a monopoly over the information and images that shape our thoughts" (1990: 232). In times of war, how can a multiplicity of sources of information be maintained?

Diplomacy and global communication

International diplomacy is largely storytelling, stories about national interests, grievances, and threats. Diplomacy is likely to have started with the Egyptians, with the Eighteenth Dynasty in the sixteenth century BC. The pharaohs sent their representatives abroad. They were often recruited from the nobility. The Greek cities received and sent out diplomats, usually elders. "Reflecting and practicing its democracy, and suspicious of its own envoys, the Greek Assembly sent several ambassadors on one mission, each representing different parties and points of view" (Van Dinh, 1987: 13). The Greek cities also knew the figure of the *proxenos*, who as "a native of the city in which he resided [functioned] more or less like the present-day honorary consul" (Van Dinh, 1987: 13). The Roman empire was more inclined to use force than to engage in diplomacy.

After the demise of the empire, the Byzantine emperors developed protocols for international diplomacy and brought their ceremonies to the Venetians, who perfected them: "The Venetians set the communication patterns for other Italian states in the fifteenth century by initiating the practice of exchanging resident ambassadors. At first they were not called ambassadors, but "resident orators." The title of ambassador, derived from a Celtic word meaning "servant," became current only in the middle of the sixteenth century" (Van Dinh, 1987: 14). Resident embassies were established (by the mid-sixteenth century), and a diplomatic community developed with its own procedures, language, and methods of communication.

In the seventeenth century, diplomacy became a profession. Cardinal Richelieu set up the first Ministry of Foreign Affairs in order to claim a prominent role for France in international diplomacy. Until 1919 French was the lingua franca of diplomats.

Between the First and the Second World War the first international negotiating forum for multilateral diplomacy was established in the League of Nations. Through this platform the role of the public (as represented in senates or parliaments) grew and public opinion became a factor to reckon with. After the Second World War – often resulting from media–diplomacy interactions – public diplomacy began to develop. Public diplomacy is in fact global communication with the publics of foreign countries.

Whereas conventional diplomacy concentrates on exchanges between governments, the main purpose of public diplomacy is to influence the perceptions and attitudes people in foreign countries and hereby the foreign policies of their governments. As in the case of propaganda, at its core public diplomacy is the management of people's collective perceptions. This requires the manipulation of words, ideas, and symbols. The final goal of the exercise is to achieve power by making people do and believe things they would otherwise not do or believe. Contrary to the coercive (hard) power of warfare and economic sanctions, public diplomacy (as propaganda) uses discursive (soft) power.

Diplomacy and media

With the advent of the mass media (at first the printed press) journalists began to inform the public so that it could begin to assess the achievements of diplomacy.[2] From the early twentieth century the media and diplomats began to engage in a complex relationship of enmity and symbiosis.

The key challenge of the diplomacy–media relationship is that what one seeks to conceal (diplomacy) the other seeks to reveal (the press). This tension is present since secret diplomacy remained important in international politics, as the case of the secret Oslo negotiations between Israel and the Palestinians in 1993 demonstrates. There was no media coverage and the public was excluded.

Secret diplomacy is, for journalists, a failure. The news media often fail to recognize signs pointing to secret talks because they cannot imagine arch-enemies talking to each other. As a result of these misconceptions, the media discarded reliable pieces of information that were available on the secret negotiations and failed to adequately follow the leads that could have enabled them to uncover the secret talks.

Secret diplomacy involves lying to the media and thus to the public. Can you find situations where these means are justified by the final diplomatic goal?

A milder form of relating to the media is "closed door" diplomacy, such as in the Camp David (the meeting between president Anwar Sadat of Egypt and prime minister Menachem Begin of Israel in 1978 at the invitation of US President Carter) or the Dayton negotiations (in 1995 between the presidents of Serbia, Bosnia, and Croatia at the invitation of US President Clinton), which were known to take place but were not open to the media.[3] The media coverage of closed-door diplomacy is limited and thus very frustrating for journalists. In the absence of hard news, most of the coverage is confined to "background stories, human interest stories, speculation, vague assessments, ..." (Gilboa, 2000: 285).

The most open form is public diplomacy as media diplomacy. This takes place through briefings, press conferences, and interviews. A serious danger of this public openness is the oversimplification of complex issues. Can television news sufficiently cover international negotiations for audiences to develop well-founded positions?

There is also a form of media diplomacy in which the media are deliberately employed for diplomatic purposes. They function as channels to transmit messages. For example, US Secretary of State Baker issued an ultimatum to Saddam Hussein (during the 1990–1991 Gulf conflict) not through the official US diplomatic representative in Iraq but through CNN. In his 1973–1974 shuttle diplomacy in the Middle East, Henry Kissinger used top US TV correspondents to transmit messages. International journalists such as Walter Cronkite (in connection with Egyptian president Sadat's visit to Jerusalem in 1977), Ted Koppel (with Nightline TV programmes in 1985 from South Africa and in 1988 from Israel), or John Scali, the ABC correspondent (who was used by Soviets and Americans to transmit messages during the Cuban missile crisis in 1962), have played roles as mediators between negotiating parties. It should be realized, however, that in the end the political leaders call the shots and they are in control as prime sources and manipulators of global news! "The media ... have transformed diplomacy more through providing leaders and officials with new tools than in functioning as independent actors" (Gilboa, 2000: 305).

All states – even if they are hostile to each other – feel the need to directly communicate with each other. One of the inventive means for direct talks are the so-called "working funerals". Funerals of heads of state are often the platforms for considerable diplomatic activity. As Berridge (1994: 60) writes, "the working funeral is now the most important ceremonial occasion in the world diplomatic system". Funeral diplomacy grew significantly since the 1960s, mainly as a result of improvements in such technologies as air transport, refrigeration, and television. It was a happy coincidence for peace that between 1982 and 1985 Brezhnev, Andropov, and Chernenko died at a time when the Soviet Union wanted to get out of Afghanistan, and sought better relations with both the USA and China. The major drawback of the working funeral is that it cannot be organized on schedule, so there is often too short notice for well-informed preparatory procedures. On the other hand, funerals create a unique ambiance that is very conducive to the diplomacy of reconciliation. "International funerals are usually times of political truce" (Berridge, 1994: 70).

Diplomatic communication has demonstrably played an important role in maintaining peace between states. The US–Soviet hot line provides a good illustration of this. The hotline was established in June 1962 after the Cuban Missile Crisis when the absence of direct communication between the governments of the USA and the USSR caused almost fatal misunderstandings.[4]

HOT LINE

The hotline was used (1967) for the first time during the six-day war between Egypt and Israel. Messages were exchanged between Chairman Kosygin and President Johnson to address the necessity to cooperate towards the ending of the military conflict in the Middle East. The hotline became particularly important when the *USS Liberty* was hit by torpedoes from an unknown attacker. This could have been the Soviet Union or its ally Egypt. In both cases, this could have been the beginning of nuclear warfare. By means of the hotline, the parties were informed that the attack was an erroneous hit by the Israeli Air Force and Navy. The hotline was also used during the war between India and Pakistan in 1971, and when the Soviet Union invaded Afghanistan in 1979. In 2005 India and Pakistan set up their own hotline. Since 2008 there has also been a hotline between the USA and China.

? President Woodrow Wilson proposed that "diplomacy shall proceed always frankly and in the public view" (quoted in Williams, 1971: 79). Is this a realistic vision?

Espionage: global communication in secrecy

There have always been spies. Espionage is, after prostitution, the second oldest profession in human history. The Hebrew Old Testament narrates the story of the Philistine spy Delila, and the sixteenth-century ruler of the Mongols, Akbar, had a secret service comprising 4,000 agents.

Organized espionage as a branch of global communication began only in 1909 in Britain, with a small office. This was largely inspired by the fictional stories produced by writer and amateur spy William LeQueux, who was obsessed with the idea of the presence of German spies in Britain (Knightley, 2003: 12ff). After the establishment of the British Secret Service, similar organizations emerged in the USA (CIA and NSA), in the Soviet Union (KGB and GPU), and in Israel (Mossad).

States instruct their intelligence agencies to – secretly – collect intelligence about other states and sometimes about their own citizens. Illustrations of the latter are the infamous CIA programmes, such as CHAOS, which began in 1967 and which, according to the *New*

York Times, in 1975 had active files on 10,000 US citizens. Among those surveilled were Martin Luther King and Robert Kennedy. In the period 1952–1975 the National Security Agency collected files on some 75,000 US citizens. Part of the mission of intelligence agencies is also to disseminate "disinformation" to mislead potential or real enemies by planting distorted or completely false stories in news media.

The main techniques for the collection of intelligence are SIGINT and HUMINT.

SIGINT stands for the reception of signals usually through satellites and computers. The Echelon espionage project of the US National Security Agency, in collaboration with the British GCHQ and with the support of New Zealand, Australia, and Canada, uses enormous satellite disks (called vacuum cleaners) to collect all transatlantic electronic traffic and analyzes it with the assistance of intelligent robots that check keywords at a rate of 4 million characters a second.

HUMINT stands for the deployment of spies. Through popular media culture the spy speaks to the imagination of large publics. In films and novels, the spy is portrayed as the angel who rescues the world (James Bond) or as the operator in a dirty war and as part of corrupt bureaucracy (John Le Carré). The stories about Mata Hari (the dancer from Friesland who supposedly worked as a spy for the Germans in the First World War) inspired many women to become spies.

Today's intelligence services face several problems. As a result of globalization, the global reach of intelligence services has extended. Espionage is no longer a mere European business. All states do it and non-states have also moved – at a fairly large scale – into industrial espionage The result is that today everyone is spied upon. "An FBI study looking at 173 countries around the world discovered that 57 of them were running economic and technological spy operations against the USA. The Japanese came top of the list, closely followed by the South Koreans and the Taiwanese" (Knightley, 2003: 441).

Technological developments have made very sophisticated forms of vast data collections possible. However, this leads to the risk of combining information overload with limited analytical capacity to deal with all this information.

The size and mandate of intelligence services have expanded and so too their political role. Very often important political decisions are taken on the basis of information provided by the secret services. This raises the issue of the political management of the services. As president Harry Truman remarked in 1963, "For some time I have been disturbed by the way the CIA has diverted from its original assignment. It has become an operational and at times a policy-making arm of government" (in the *Washington Post*, December 22, 1963).

Then there is the challenge of the confusion that affected the international intelligence community by the end of the twentieth century. The security of the old enemies (US versus Soviet Union) had disappeared and thus a clear and transparent object for intelligence-gathering was gone. What new tasks are there today for spies? Should they engage in the war against drugs (but other agencies are already involved in this), or fight global terrorism, illegal (nuclear) arms trading, or expand into industrial espionage? The former spy can also write and sell spy stories as several of the ex-KGB spooks have done.

Whatever the future of the intelligence business is, its key characteristic is likely to remain its sustainability. Whatever their failures may have been, Knightley concludes (2003: 463) that the spies will be around for some time to come. "'Governments come and go', a British SIS officer once told me. 'But we go on for ever'".

Media and espionage

In the end, the West won the Cold War. It can be argued that in this process economic strength, technological ability, political institutions, geography, and population were far more important factors than intelligence. "The simple fact was that the Soviet Union was unable to prevent its citizens from learning about the West, and it was obvious from the way the young of Moscow dressed, and from the music they played, that they considered life abroad better than they had at home. You could claim with some justification that the media, not the spies, won the Cold War" (Knightley, 2003: 431).

? There exists a tension between parliamentary accountability (essential to democratic governance) and secret intelligence gathering (essential to national security). Should parliaments accept and sanction results obtained in secrecy?

Notes

1. This notion was coined by Field Marshall Gerard Templer during the British actions in Malaysia (1948–1975).
2. Like in the first war reporting (Crimean war, 1854–1856) by William Howard Russell.
3. President Carter explained the decision to exclude the media with "It was imperative that there be a minimum of posturing by Egyptians or Israelis, and an absence of public statements, which would become frozen positions that could not subsequently be changed" (quoted in Gilboa, 2000: 283).
4. "Memorandum of Understanding Regarding the Establishment of a Direct Communication Line" signed on June 20, 1963, in Geneva by representatives of the Soviet Union and the United States.

Reading spotlight

War Propaganda

Taylor, P.M. (1990). *Munitions of the Mind: War Propaganda from the Ancient World to the Nuclear Age.* Wellingborough: Patrick Stevens.

Philip Taylor gives a splendid historical overview of propaganda for war throughout the ages from ancient Greece and the Middle Ages to the First and Second World War and the Cold War. In his conclusion he argues that propaganda is a process of persuasion and a "necessary means of forging democratic consensus in a civilized world threatened by possible nuclear annihilation. If they disagree with the public, they must persuade the public of the merits of their case. But the public must be given access to their views and be trusted to respond in a responsible manner" (p. 232).

Online resources

Visit the book's companion website at **https://study.sagepub.com/hamelink** to watch the author discussing the theme of this chapter: **Propaganda and Spin**

Visit the book's companion website at **https://study.sagepub.com/hamelink** to access the following journal articles free of charge:

Gilboa, E.(2008). Searching for a theory of public diplomacy. *The ANNALS of the American Academy of Political and Social Science*, 616 (1): 55–77.

Louw, P.E. (2003). The "War Against Terrorism": a public relations challenge for the Pentagon. *Gazette*, 65(3): 211–230.

Nye, J.S. Jr. (2008). Public diplomacy and soft power. *The ANNALS of the American Academy of Political and Social Science*, 616(1): 94–109.

Winseck, D. (2008). Information Operations "Blowback": communication, propaganda and surveillance in the Global War on Terrorism. *International Communication Gazette*, 70(6): 419–441.

Further reading

On propaganda

Jackson, R. (2005). *Writing the War on Terrorism: Language, Politics and Counter-Terrorism*. Manchester: Manchester University Press.

Jowett, G.S. and O'Donnell, V. (1986). *Propaganda and Persuasion*. London: Sage.

Lasswell, H.D., Lerner, D. and Speier, H. (eds) (1979). *Propaganda and Communication in World History. Volume I: The Symbolic Instrument in Early Times*. Honolulu: East–West Center, University Press of Hawaii.

Lasswell, H.D., Lerner, D. and Speier, H. (eds) (1980) *Propaganda and Communication in World History. Volume II: Emergence of Public Opinion in the West*. Honolulu: East–West Center, University Press of Hawaii.

Lasswell, H.D., Lerner, D. and Speier, H. (eds) (1980) *Propaganda and Communication in World History. Volume III: A Pluralizing World in Formation*. Honolulu: East–West Center, University Press of Hawaii.

Miller, D. (ed.) (2004). *Tell Me Lies: Propaganda and Media Distortion in the Attack on Iraq*. London: Pluto Press.

Rampton, S. and Stauber, J. (2003). *Weapons of Mass Deception. The Uses of Propaganda in Bush's War on Iraq*. London: Robinson.

Taylor, P.M. (1990). *Munitions of the Mind: War Propaganda from the Ancient World to the Nuclear Age*. Wellingborough: Patrick Stevens.

Short, K.R.M. (ed.) (1983). *Film & Radio Propaganda in World War II*. London: Croom Helm.

Short, K.R.M. (ed.) (1986). *Western Broadcasting over the Iron Curtain*. London: Croom Helm.

On diplomacy

Lasswell, H.D. (2010). The theory of political propaganda. In Thussu, D.K. *International Communication: A Reader*. New York: Routledge. pp. 329–332.

Nelson, R. and Foad, I. (2009). Ethics and social issues in public diplomacy. In Snow, N. and Taylor, P.M. (eds), *Routledge Handbook of Public Diplomacy*. New York: Routledge. pp. 334–351.

Nye, J.S. Jr. (2010). Public diplomacy and soft power. In Thussu, D.K. (ed.), *International Communication: A Reader*. New York: Routledge. pp. 333–344.

Snow, N. (2009) Rethinking public diplomacy. In Snow, N. and Taylor, P.M. (eds), *Routledge Handbook of Public Diplomacy*. New York: Routledge. pp. 3–11.

Snow, N. and Taylor, P.M. (eds) (2009). *Routledge Handbook of Public Diplomacy*. London: Routledge.

Taylor, P.M. (2009) Public diplomacy and strategic communication. In Snow, N. and Taylor, P.M. (eds), *Routledge Handbook of Public Diplomacy*. New York: Routledge. pp. 12–16.

On espionage

Bungert, H., Heitmann, J.G. and Wala, M. (eds) (2003). *Secret Intelligence in the Twentieth Century*. London: Cass.

Fitzgibbon, C. (1978). *Secret Intelligence in the Twentieth Century*. London: Granada.

Knightley, Ph. (2003). *The Second Oldest Profession: Spies and Spying in the Twentieth Century*. London: Pimlico.

Wark, W.K. (2003). Canada and the intelligence revolution. In Bungert, H., Heitmann, J.G. and Wala, M. (eds) (2003). *Secret Intelligence in the Twentieth Century*. London: Cass. pp. 176–191.

RESEARCH ASSIGNMENT

Identify and analyze recent examples of the deceptive use of language by propagandists in international news media.

How would you go about this assignment? What method(s) would you use?

Would there be a theoretical framework that may be helpful?

Which media would you select for analysis?

GLOBAL COMMUNICATION AND CONFLICT

10

Writing about communication and conflict, it is impossible to not be inspired by the grand master of peace journalism, Johan Galtung.

Johan Galtung (1930–)

Galtung was born in 1930 in Norway and is the founder of the field of peace and conflict studies. In 1959 he established the Peace Research Institute in Oslo, and 1969 he was appointed to the Chair of Peace and Conflict Studies at the University of Oslo. For the study of global communication, his work on the selection of foreign news and on peace journalism is important.

Essential publications for the study of global communication are: *The True Worlds* (1980); *Johan Galtung: There are Alternatives* (1984); *Essays in Peace Research* (1988); *Global Glasnost: Towards a New World Communication Order?* (with R. Vincent) (1992); *Human Rights in Another Key* (1994); and *Economics in Another Key* (1997).

For the study of global communication, Johan Galtung taught us to critically reflect on the role of journalism in global peace-making.

In this chapter I want to focus on the role of communication in conflicts. The role of communication media in the representation of global violence is analyzed and a new form of diplomatic communication is proposed to strengthen the decline of violence.

- Free flow of information and peace
- Media logic and violence
- Peace journalism
- More and better information?
- Towards urban–global diplomatic communication

Early in its history, the UNESCO expresses the expectation that through the free flow of information people would understand each other better and that this would lead to peaceful relations. It can be established empirically that global information flows and communication networks have grown impressively in past decades.

It can also be documented that although since 1945 there is a decline in large-scale violence across the world. There have been several wars since 1945 and too many people have fallen victim to their violence, but there is historically a demonstrable trend that makes today's world less violent than ever before. In 1988, the study on homicide by evolution psychologists Daly and Wilson pointed to this, and in 2011 Steven Pinker brought a convincing set of historical data to support the decline of violence. We live in more peaceful times than ever before. Large-scale violence is on the decline in the twentieth and twenty-first centuries (Pinker, 2011). This seems an unlikely conclusion when one observes that the stories (in news, entertainment, and games) that media distribute globally do not project the image of an unprecedented peaceful world. There is daily warfare on TV screens and volumes of blood flow from the television set into households across the globe. The media around the world suggest that we live in a dangerous world. Popular titles such as are *World War IV* (by Norman B. Podoretz) and *We Are Doomed* (by John Derbyshire) are sold in millions of copies. There is also the observation that "The media in our modern information society have done much to perpetuate the myth of easy killing and have thereby become part of society's unspoken conspiracy of deception that glorifies killing and war" (Grossman, 1995: 35). James Bond and his entertainment colleagues suggest that killing is easy. Contrary to what much mediafare suggests, men have strong inhibitions against killing members of their own species. "The media's depiction of violence tries to tell us that men can easily throw off the moral inhibitions of a lifetime – and whatever other instinctive restraint exists – and kill casually and guiltlessly in combat. Men who have killed and talk about it, tell a different tale" (Grossman, 1995: 88).

Media have also in important ways provided public platforms for the propaganda of the elimination belief that encouraged ordinary Germans or Rwandans to slaughter other ordinary people. Although crimes can be committed without apparent motivation, the exercise of gross violence at a grand scale – as in crimes against humanity – need motivating beliefs. In order to get people to commit such crimes, they need to believe that their violent acts are right. Crimes against humanity often take place in situations where propagandistic disinformation about the "others" is systematically disseminated. The purpose of this propaganda is the incitement to and the justification of the social and/or physical elimination of an out-group. Members of such groups are often first targeted as "socially undesirable". They are publicly ridiculed, insulted, and provoked (often in the media). When the harassments are put into acts, the victims are beaten up and killed. In the propagation of "elimination beliefs", the "others" are dehumanized, whereas the superiority of one's own group is emphasized. The propagandists convincingly suggest to their audiences that the "others" pose fundamental threats to the security and well-being of society and that the only effective means of escaping this threat is the elimination of this great danger.

171

The use of violence in this process is presented as inevitable and thus not only acceptable, but absolutely necessary.

The elimination beliefs that motivate people to kill each other are not part of the human genetic constitution. They are social constructs, which need social institutions for their dissemination. Such institutions include religious communities, schools, families, and the mass media.

The story of the Holocaust – and other atrocities in history – demonstrates that ordinary people are capable of actively and enthusiastically committing the mass-slaughter of their fellow human beings once they are ideologically motivated to do so.

Because crimes against humanity are unthinkable without elimination beliefs, the institutional carriers of such beliefs (such as mass media) can be seen as perpetrators of crimes against humanity.

Media logic and violence[1]

Major conflicts are brought to the world's attention through international and national news media. Media are for most people around the globe the essential information source about the collective destruction of human dignity. It is obvious that without news media coverage there would be little or no knowledge about the hundreds of thousands who are victims of massive destruction and aggression in places such as Congo or Darfur. Without media reports, the victims would be non-existent. This "mediatization" of conflicts has important consequences for the ways in which media audiences (including leading policymakers) react to such events (Cottle, 2006). This is not without serious problems.

A first problem of global news reporting is that all media reporting is driven by "selective articulation" (van Ginneken, 1998: 16). This means that – inevitably – by a convergence of factors (political pressures, economic drives, personal preferences, professional styles, mechanisms of human perception) choices are made (e.g. not all conflicts are covered) and emphases are given. Some conflicts are considered more important than others (sometimes the reasons are access, resources, risks, embeddedness), and in selected conflicts some parties or dimensions get more attention than others. Selective articulation is inherent in the "media logic". This is the specific way of operating that one finds in most media. Media logic is characterized by the tendency to focus on incidents, to accentuate the sensational, dramatize social reality, and to decontextualize developments.

Media logic is largely responsible for the prevailing format of conflict reporting: war journalism. Reporting on armed conflict tends to focus on violence and its visible effects, is oriented towards zero sum thinking, focuses on winners and victories, employs us versus them distinctions, and portrays "them as the problem" (Shinar, 2008: 9). "Professional values – such as the tendency to visualize conflict and the expectation of war-oriented conflict results – are variables that stimulate the adherence to war journalism" (Shinar, 2008: 23). As Hackett and Schroeder write: "Conventional news routines and news values tend towards conflict escalation"(2009: 26). War news tends to take sides and provides little socio-political context and historical perspective.

A second problem is that newsmakers report about events by framing them. Conflicts are put within a specific definitional frame. They may be defined as insurgence, struggle of liberation, terrorism, or civil war. Frames are often constructed by the primary definers of the news, such as politicians, who use skilled "perception managers" to sell their interpretation of reality. By and large, media tend to frame conflicts in terms of either/or choices.

Journalism is the art of telling stories and the "narrative" format of news reporting implies the use of definitional frames. Through journalists, the parties in a conflict tell their stories and change their narratives as the conflict develops. This often "entails a transformation from a narrative of victimization to one of evolution and empowerment" (Pruitt and Kim, 2004: 203).

"Each side has its own narrative and, when conflict is severe, the two parties often interpret the same events in radically different ways. Thus, Israelis explain their military campaigns against Palestinians by talking about the Holocaust and the many times they have been attacked by the Arabs, who seem to be challenging their right to exist as a nation. Palestinians explain their assaults against Israel by talking about Israel's steady encroachment on their territory and freedoms" (Pruitt and Kim, 2004: 202).

In the narration of conflicts, metaphors play an essential role. "Some metaphors intensify a conflict and make it harder to solve" (Pruitt and Kim, 2004). Pruitt and Kim give the example of the metaphors used by the parties in the conflict in Northern Ireland. The Irish Republican Army used "colonialism" for the role of the British army and the British government used "criminality" for the IRA activities. These were very negative metaphors that needed to be discarded for the peace process to move ahead. After the 9/11 attacks governments and media routinely used the "war" metaphor. This focused attention on the military approach to the conflict and ignored attention for the problems that caused terrorist activities.

A third problem relates to a difficult question that media reporting about conflict confronts us with. Should the horrendous and bloody pictures of warfare be publicized? Susan Sontag writes about this in *Regarding the Pain of Others* (2002), and she argues that these pictures tell us what people do to each other and that we should never forget this. It would indeed seem important that worldwide TV audiences regularly watch the painful images of wounded and maimed children in the hospitals of Southern Iraq. We might otherwise forget that they are the victims of a Western military choice to use depleted uranium that poisoned the South of Iraq for many years.

This does raise the question as to whether showing the suffering of people will make audiences realize the insanity and the disgrace of the war? Or, would this rather motivate people to more violence and revenge? It is not certain what the effects would be. Maybe this is the wrong question altogether. We should probably ask what would be the effect if we did not permanently and realistically show the horrors of warfare. If we did not demonstrate to each other what we are capable of, this "obscuration" would make it easier for those who initiate and want war to get away with it and contend that their wars are necessary and legitimate. The masquerade provides politicians and the military with ample space to distort the truth about their wars. Shocking images and stories may not change the human propensity to lethal conflict. Yet, it can be seen as a minimal morality that we have to daily confront human-made damage. The least we can do is not to forget the victims. When Elie Wiesel received the Nobel Peace Prize in 1986 he said, "What all these victims need above all is to know that they are not alone, that we are not forgetting them, that when their voices are stifled, we shall lend them ours, that while their freedom depends on ours, the quality of our freedom depends on theirs".

Peace journalism

Various authors have suggested that a format in which communication could contribute to peace-making is "peace journalism". This notion was launched by Norwegian peace researcher Johan Galtung as a counterpoint to the dominant format of conflict reporting. An important promotor of peace journalism is academic and journalist Jack Lynch, at the Centre for Peace and Conflict Studies of the University of Sydney. Conventional war journalism focuses on war as a zero sum game with winners versus losers, is oriented towards "us" versus "them" propaganda, and uses victory and defeat metaphors. Peace journalism is more empathic, proactive, and focused upon the effects of violence. It exposes propagandistic lies and highlights peace initiatives. In short, peace journalism provides a more balanced news coverage, seeks alternative interpretations, focuses on context, is proactive, humanizes all sides in a conflict, exposes lies from all sides, exposes the suffering, pain and trauma of warfare, and de-anonymizes the evil-doers. The key hypothesis of peace journalism studies is that "conventional news routines and news values tend towards conflict escalation" (Hackett et al. 2008: 26). Suleyman Irvan (2006) defines peace journalism as a normative theory that obliges media to be socially responsible and promote peace. Peace journalism proposes what media should do in order to positively contribute to violent conflict. The literature on peace journalism is aware of essential obstacles to the realization of this normative position.

Conceptions of journalistic professionalism, ideas about news values, and objectivity can be impediments since they suggest that peace journalism threatens professional integrity and independent reporting of the news. Institutional impediments to peace journalism are the prevailing mode of organization and management of media that often operate as commercial enterprises driven by an obsession with market shares, ratings, and scoops. There are also obstacles in the form of nationalist sentiments. When the nation goes to war there is a strong inclination among media to follow the flag and become partisan to the conflict. The main question would not seem to be whether a peace journalism format is helpful to the de-escalation of conflict. It is pretty obvious that within reasonable limits a more balanced and less propagandistic, partisan and war-triumphalist news reporting provides for more serious questioning of the dangers of conflict escalation. It may also stimulate the uncritical bystanders in conflict situations to ask more questions. An important task for peace journalism could be to go beyond the focus on the reporting of present conflict and address issues of post-escalation situations.

A flaw in peace journalism is the lack of awareness of the necessity of societal receptivity to the offerings of the peace-promoting journalist. Unless societies (i.e. media audiences) at large care about the specific qualities of a more qualified, more contextualized, less sensationalist, less partisan, and more investigative conflict reporting, the journalistic effort is an exercise in futility. As suggested before, an essential question is whether the realities of news production as business, of news as commodity, of prevailing news-institutional interests and professional standard operations, can accommodate the routines and value orientations of media formats that accommodate peace journalism in both pre-escalation and post-escalation situations. This would definitely require a substantial change in the ways journalism is organized on the supply side. Even more importantly, though, is that this requires – on the demand side – a substantial change in the expectations of news audiences. Critical researchers may propose different news styles, but global audiences in massive numbers demonstrate no disturbing dissatisfaction with the "news as it is". The concern for mass media performance is not the sole responsibility of media producers. It also involves client communities. "The listening, viewing, reading public underestimates its power", wrote Wilbur Schramm in 1969 when he pointed to the shared responsibility of public regulatory bodies, the media themselves, and the general public for the quality of mass communication (Schramm and Rivers, 1969: 249). In 1993 journalist Mort Rosenblum also included the role of the general public in the inadequacies of international news reporting: "If the suppliers have not done better, it is because consumers have not demanded it" (Rosenblum, 1993: 287).

When armed conflicts begin, often the words of senator Hiram Johnson are heard: "In times of war truth is the first victim". But a good second victim would seem to be the public interest in knowing the truth. Often media audiences prefer not to know all the details of armed confrontations. Reliable media need good-quality audiences. Since the provision of information is of critical importance in democratic societies, citizens can be asked to be vigilant media consumers that actively and critically reflect on media content. Unless media consumers worldwide demand to be properly informed about conflicts in peace journalism formats, it is unrealistic to expect the news business to change winning horses. Media are part of the societal context within which they function. The more this context opens possibilities for people to address anxieties, to resist agitation, and to withstand disconnectedness from others, the better the media potential for de-escalation will develop. This obviously implies a position about the media–society relationship. Research evidence does indeed suggest that by and large media are followers and not leaders. In most important social debates, media may look like the initiators but they are usually the disseminators, the amplifiers, not the pioneers. Examples abound of political groups, activists, and religious movements that are the first definers of social issues such as gender, race, pacifism, or climate change.

More and better information?

The 1945 constitution of UNESCO provided that since wars begin in the minds of men, it is in the minds of men that the defences of peace must be constructed. The implied suggestion is that the minds of people need to be influenced (through the media) in order to develop a culture of peace. The expectation that the provision of information is a crucial exogenous variable in the decline of violence is, however, flawed, as I will argue below. Moreover, the idea that war begins in the minds of people is misleading. Wars among members of the human species start with the material, physical fact of their bodies. The human life form – like other life forms – is constantly involved in a struggle for life. Inevitable components of that struggle are aggression and violence. In such struggles, information campaigns directed at people's "hearts and minds" will do little to make conflicts less dangerous.

A problem with properly informing publics about what happens in the world is also the underlying assumption that people are predominantly rational beings who have their viewpoints defined by new information and who on the basis of new information change earlier positions and develop new insights. Reality is different! People often know already – on emotional and irrational grounds – what they should think. They filter away the information that does not match their expectations. Much information that threatens to undermine established opinions is simply discarded. People tend to believe their assumptions are correct and not in need of any questioning. The idea that people would want information in order to arrive at better decisions is based upon the assumption that processes of decision-making proceed in orderly and rational ways. More often than not, however, social and personal decision-making is a chaotic process driven by irrational and *ad-hoc* motives. If human beings were rational and logical information processing systems, they would more often change opinions and positions than they routinely do.

In analyzing the role of communication in violent conflicts one should address the often over-rated expectations about the provision of information. It is widely held that more and better information is essential for the prevention of escalation and that more and open communication contributes to the prevention of escalation. The underlying assumption here is that once people know more about each other, they will understand each other and be less inclined towards violent behaviour.

Such assumptions deserve a sceptical assessment. They are largely valid only if one believes that conflicts and their escalation into violence are primarily caused by insufficient and inadequate information. From this reasoning it follows that conflicts can be controlled once adversaries have correct information about each other. This suggests that if adversaries knew more about each other, it would be easier to reach agreement. It is, however, difficult to find empirical evidence for this and one can equally well propound the view that social harmony is largely due to the degree of ignorance that people have about each other. As a matter of fact, many societies maintain levels of stability because they employ rituals, customs, and conventions that enable their members to engage in social interaction without having detailed information about who they really are.

These assumptions neglect the fact that conflicts often address very real points of contention. Conflicts may be very dangerous precisely because adversaries have full information about each other's aims and motives. More information about the adversary may actually lead to more conflict. A critical component in nuclear stability between the USA and the USSR (during the Cold War) was that both powers lacked information about the exact location of their nuclear submarines. Since these were difficult to detect, they were difficult to target, might escape a first strike and render a debilitating second strike to the attacker. The ignorance about their location was a powerful deterrent against a first nuclear strike by either party.

Complete informational openness may enhance conflict and it could be argued that a functional level of secrecy is a positive contribution to societal security. A level of secrecy is also helpful in containing potential conflict escalation, since it leaves ample space for face-saving disclaimers in critical negotiations.

Another footnote is that in conflict situations the problem is often one of an abundance rather than a dearth of information. In decision-making, the flow of messages that needs to be evaluated may become dysfunctional once it reaches a critical mass. The overload may seriously impede rational decision-making since the means of coping with it (such as selective filtering, stereotyping, and simplistic structuring) yield misperception and incorrect interpretations.

For the study of media and violence, the complexity perspective is useful since it can help to move students away from the focus on causality that was discussed in Chapter 2.

The leading question is not: "Do media cause collective destructive aggression"? But: "Are they among the factors that facilitate – the killing and humiliating of fellow human beings?"

If there is indeed a decline of violence in contemporary history, as Steven Pinker presents in his 800-page study (2011), there is still no guarantee that this will continue. Pinker makes this point very clearly. A crucial question therefore becomes how this decline could become an ongoing process. It is somewhat disappointing to note that in Pinker's study (2011) there is no reference to communication. The role of diplomatic communication in the decline of violence is not even mentioned.

It is for scholars of global communication a challenge to reflect on how this field could make a contribution to a more peaceful world. One possibility to explore is the development of a new form of diplomatic communication that is less state-centric than conventional diplomacy and that involves global cities as partners.

Towards urban–global diplomatic communication

There is worldwide a tendency towards what is called citizen diplomacy. This is a form of public diplomacy in which relations between people (among others through exchange programmes or the use of music and fine arts) function as instruments of diplomacy.

Conventional diplomatic communication is primarily communication between states. However, states are no longer the only actors in global politics. States may also have interests that are more specific and provincial rather than universal and cosmopolitan. States control and use the physical instruments of (hard) power. In fact, global diplomacy should not be exercised merely by states but by "nations" (see Chapter 2). Nations are the communities of people that worldwide have an essential stake in peaceful relations. These people constitute in the early twenty-first century the first urban species. In 2009, half of the global population lived in urban areas and in the years to come this will become some 70 per cent. The city will be the space in which people have to find ways to live together and to deal with all the conflicts that go with urban spaces.

We are all locals in a global environment. Locality is the geographical and psychological place that forms our daily habitat. At the same time, though, these local places are affected by global flows of goods, finances, and stories. Daily life in localities is influenced by global perceptions. However, local communities can reach beyond their borders, network with other localities, and thus develop global countervailing power to the forces that threaten the survival of the planet.

The key strategic question for the social movements of our age is "how to reach the global from the local through networking with other localities? ... How can social movements use communication resources to network globally for the mobilization of counter power?" (Castells, 2009: 52).

Of paramount importance in the design of urban strategies for local urban media is networking with other localities in order to create glocal inter-city networks. This requires urban social movements dedicated to both survival and urban communication that understand that local and global survival are intrinsically connected, that form alliances with similar urban movements, and that begin to exchange (through their globalized local media) stories of hope and that lobby with local administrations to design and implement communication policies that contribute to publicly owned and managed urban communication systems. There is truth in Castell's proposal that the rise in self mass-communication creates new chances for social and political change (2009: 302).

Networked social movements can use these new chances for the building of countervailing power and the developing of alternative solutions. Crucial for this is the global effort to keep the Internet a free and open medium for social deliberation. It is evident that the new information and communication technologies offer unprecedented opportunities for the construction of global networks of local communities.

The world's cities are becoming globally interconnected systems. In many cities around the world fascinating and promising experiments are conducted in the use of cyberspace technologies. However, there is little concrete policy planning by local governments for this innovation and little reflection on how this can render cities nodes of global networks.

The inevitable question evidently is how realistic is the prospect of glocal networks for global survival. Given the formidable power of the driving forces of the dominant global order and the effective propaganda for the supporting belief system, this prospect would seem rather dim. Yet, against the current "globalization-from-above" a "globalization-from-below" (Falk, 1993: 39) is no longer a chimera.

Over the past decades local communities have demonstrated that global change is within their power. Today, millions of people around the world are involved with forms of local community-based activities that focus on global problems. A new type of world politics is emerging through these initiatives. They represent a shift from conventional international relations, mainly conducted by the national foreign affairs elites of statesmen, diplomats, and politicians, towards a world political arena in which ordinary people in local communities involve themselves directly in the world's problems, often bypassing their national officials. As these local communities begin to network and cooperate, a new formidable force in the shaping of world politics develops. Local communities no longer depend upon the national leadership to make the world a safer place to live. In this process, globalization of the local is countered by local communities going global! Local communities have begun to recognize responsibility for problems outside their boundaries and have put world problems on their policy agenda. Local initiatives provide people with the opportunity to address this responsibility and increase people's contribution to political life. People in local communities accept that the fundamental obligation to take the future in their own hands is inherent to the democratic ideal. As local communities around the world are presently engaged in such areas of activity as development, environment, and human rights, it could be argued that the achievement of a global production and distribution of stories of hope can be put on their agenda as a decisive contribution to human survival in the third millennium.

Saskia Sassen wrote that the global city has emerged as a site for the formation of new claims (2009: 92). Among those could be the claim to the continuation of the decline of violence in the world. Urban space could become a frontier zone for a new type of "glocal" communicative engagement with global peaceful relations.

Note

1. The following paragraphs were published earlier in Hamelink (2011), pp. 32–36.

Reading spotlight

Conflict

Hamelink, C.J. (2011). *Media and Conflict: Escalating Evil*. Boulder, CO: Paradigm Publishers.

> In this book the author struggles with the perennial and troubling question of human evil. Reflecting on the past and the future of evil he tries to understand the escalation of human conflict, explores the role of the media in processes of escalation, and proposes

thought-provoking responses: mindful communication, the communicative city and the international media alert system.

Genocide

Goldhagen, D.J. (1996). *Hitler's Willing Executioners: Ordinary Germans and the Holocaust.* New York: Vintage Books.

Goldhagen describes the crucial role of anti-Semitic eliminationist beliefs in the Holocaust. He shows how images of evil and dangerous Jews nurtured German society provided crucial motivation for genocidal killings.

Volkan, V.D. (1994). *The Need to Have Enemies and Allies: From Clinical Practice to International Relationships.* London: Jason Aronson Inc.

Volkan addresses with the insights from his psychiatric practice about the roots of human conflict the psychological need to have both enemies and allies. He provides an understanding of how internal representations of external enemies contribute to the escalation of conflicts particularly between groups and states.

Violence

Pinker, S. (2011). *The Better Angels of Our Nature: The Decline of Violence in History and its Causes.* London: Penguin.

Steven Pinker argues that contrary to popular belief which is inspired by the daily avalanche of media images of lethal conflict violence has declined over history. Today's societies are becoming progressively less violence through historical processes of pacification and civilization and through humanitarian and human rights revolutions.

Online resources

Visit the book's companion website at **https://study.sagepub.com/hamelink** to watch the author discussing the theme of this chapter: **Global Conflict**

Visit the book's companion website at **https://study.sagepub.com/hamelink** to access the following journal articles free of charge:

Bahador, B. (2011). Did the Global War on Terror end the CNN effect? *Media, War & Conflict,* 4(1): 37–54.

Hamelink, C.J. (2008). Media between warmongers and peacemakers. *Media, War & Conflict,* 1(1): 77–83.

Ottosen, R. (2010). The war in Afghanistan and peace journalism in practice. *Media, War & Conflict,* 3(3): 261–278.

Shinar, D. (2009). Can peace journalism make progress? The coverage of the 2006 Lebanon War in Canadian and Israeli media. *International Communication Gazette*, 71(6): 451–471.

Tumber, H. (2008). Journalists, war crimes and international justice. *Media, War & Conflict*, 1(3): 261–269.

Further reading

Gallagher, T. (1997). My neighbour, my enemy: the manipulation of ethnic identity and the origins and conduct of war in Yugoslavia. In Turton, D. (ed.), *War and Ethnicity*. Oxford: The Boydell Press., pp. 47–75.

Galtung, J. (1991). Visioning a peaceful world. In Paige, G. and Gilliat, S. (eds), *Buddhism and Nonviolent Global Problem-Solving*. Honolulu: University of Hawaii Press.

Graham, S. (ed.) (2004). *Cities, War, and Terrorism*. Oxford: Blackwell.

Irvan, S. (2006). Peace journalism as a normative theory: premises and obstacles. *Global Media Journal: Mediterranean Edition*, 1(2): 34–39.

Jackson, R. (2005). *Writing the War on Terrorism: Language, Politics and Counter-Terrorism*. Manchester: Manchester University Press.

Korzenny, F. and Ting-Toomey, S. (1990). *Communicating for Peace: Diplomacy and Negotiation*. London: Sage.

Richardson, L. (2006). *What Terrorists Want: Understanding the Enemy, Containing the Threat*. New York: Random House.

Seib, P. (2004). *Beyond the Front Lines: How the News Media Cover a World Shaped by War*. New York: Palgrave Macmillan.

Shaw, M. (2003). *War and Genocide*. Oxford: Polity Press.

Sontag, S. (2002). *Regarding the Pain of Others*. London: Hamilton.

Tumber, H. and Palmer, J. (2004). *Media at War: The Iraq Crisis*. London: Sage.

Tumber, H. and Webster, F. (2006). *Journalists under Fire*. London: Sage.

Volkan, V. (1988). *The Need to Have Enemies and Allies: From Clinical Practice to International Relationships*. New York: Jason Aronson.

Volkan, V. (2004). *Blind Trust: Large Groups and their Leaders in Times of Crisis and Terror*. Charlottesville, VA: Pitchstone Publishing.

Volkan, V. (2006). *Killing in the Name of Identity*. Charlottesville, VA: Pitchstone Publishing.

Waller, J. (2007). *Becoming Evil: How Ordinary People Commit Genocide and Mass Killing*. Oxford: Oxford University Press.

RESEARCH ASSIGNMENT

Explore the possibility of global urban diplomacy.

Define urban diplomacy and analyze its possible significance in global politics.

If it would work, what effect may it have on the de-escalation of dangerous conflicts in the world?

Design a research project on this exploration.

CULTURE AND GLOBAL COMMUNICATION

11

The study of intercultural communication is an inevitable confrontation with the complexities of the global conversation between us and the others. Edward Said gave us brilliant insights in the binary social relations between the Occident and the Orient, and helped us – as theorist and advocate – to deal with the links between culture and imperialism.

Edward W. Said (1953–2003)

Palestinian-American literary theorist and advocate for the Palestinian cause, Said was professor of English and comparative literature at Columbia University in New York. He was a well-known (and often controversial) public intellectual who combined a dual heritage of Western education and Palestinian/Christian origins. With Daniel Barenboim, he founded the West-Eastern Divan Orchestra that brings children from Israel, the Palestinian territories and Arab countries together.

The most important sources for the study of global communication are: *Orientalism* (1978); and *Culture and Imperialism* (1993). In *Orientalism*, Said argued that the Western study of the East is highly politicized and servant to the power of imperialist societies.

For the study of global communication, Edward Said taught us to critically reflect on biased perceptions of foreign worlds.

Our next focus is the cultural dimension of global communication. This means that attention has to be given to:

- Cultural imperialism and cultural rights
- The dominant paradigms on globalization and culture
- Intercultural communication
- Intercultural communication competence

What is culture?

Culture can be conceived of as the secondary artificial environment that humans create in order to adapt to their primary, natural (geographic or climatic) environment. Culture is a coping mechanism that is essential to human survival. To survive, the human species develops a variety of adaptive instruments, such as tools, symbols, language, values, and norms.

Cultural identity informs individuals and social groups about their past, defines their position in the present, and proposes expectations about their futures.

From an evolutionary perspective, cultural evolution takes shape alongside biological evolution with the emergence of Homo Sapiens. As Homo Sapiens develops self-consciousness and language, cultural adaptations to everyday problems become possible. This begins with the formation of beliefs about the surrounding world. Such beliefs concern the core issues of humanity, such as the origin, the meaning, and destiny of human life. As in the biological evolution, beliefs are copied to following generations (reproduction) and only the useful beliefs continue to function (natural selection). Some beliefs disappear ("the earth is flat"), others are sustained ("using wheels for transport").

An important driving force in the process is most likely the realization of mortality. The discovery of "self" also implies the discovery of the finiteness of this self. All major civilizations have struggled with mortality. Egyptians, Chinese, Americans have all designed different psychological mechanisms in order tell stories that made it possible to cope with death. The development of language made it possible to share stories (through myths and rites) about transcending death and give meaning to the self. Culture – on a universal level – is developed by the human species as a functional adaptive response to the existential problem of mortality. At the local level, there have been tools, symbols, and social forms developed to deal with the problems of day-to-day life.

Dynamism and diversity

Culture is not a static phenomenon. Culture is not the same as manifestations of traditional folklore in a museum. Culture is constantly evolving. A key characteristic is dynamism in combination with diversity. As a tool for human survival, cultures reflect the diversity of species and their processes of selection, in which useful ideas survive and bad ideas disappear. Globalization has spread the political, economic, and cultural practices of modernity around the globe. Practically everywhere countries have adopted modern forms of democratic government, constitutional law, and human rights. Equally, they have liberalized and opened up their markets, and have embraced such cultural icons as the yellow McDonald's arch, jeans, T-shirts, sneakers of global brands, and the ubiquitous cell phone. As the global spread of modern practices seemed to threaten local cultural identities, the international community began negotiations about the protection of cultural diversity. These were finally concluded by an agreement on the UNESCO Convention on the Protection and Promotion of the Diversity of Cultural Expressions that was adopted by the General Conference of UNESCO on October 20, 2005.

Culture is a learning process

Solutions to adaptive problems are transferred in non-genetic ways, for example through sharing information. Chimpanzees develop culture by learning the technique of cracking nuts. They teach this technique as a strategy of survival to the younger apes. Birds learn singing to seduce the females and intimidate their rivals. People learn cultural adaptations today largely through the great modern storytellers, such as the Disney studios. The Disney stories provide audiences globally with ideas and beliefs about the world in which they live. To understand this it is advisable to read the book that Armand Mattelart and Ariel Dorfman wrote about Donald Duck (Mattelart and Dorfman, 1975).

Cultural politics

Although the area of culture has been considered "low politics" for a long time, culture has begun to acquire agenda status in world politics. Over the past decades cultural diplomacy has been adopted as "the third pillar of foreign policy" (Willy Brandt, in Mitchell, 1986: 1). Today most countries have established cultural accords (often bilateral) as a common component of their foreign relations. Culture is often expected to contribute to peace, to improve political relations among countries, to reduce the stereotyped images that people in different countries may hold about each other, and to promote trade between countries.

In cultural diplomacy, states use culture deliberately as an instrument to promote their interests. The first systematic organization of cultural diplomacy was probably initiated by the French. Beginning with the cultural expansionism of such kings as Louis XIII (1610–1643) and Louis XIV (1643–1715), France managed to make its language the dominant diplomatic and scholarly language of eighteenth- and nineteenth-century Europe. In the early twentieth century, France established its educational institutions abroad. It was an example that would be followed by many other countries. Among them were Britain, Germany and Italy. Whereas until 1945 most cultural diplomacy is unilateral or bilateral, multilateral politics in the field of culture emerges only after the Second World War. The first multilateral forum for collective cultural diplomacy is UNESCO, established in 1945. Its Constitution (1945) departs from the notion that "wars begin in the minds of men" and therefore "it is in the minds of men that the defences of peace must be constructed". Among these mental defences of peace are the "wide diffusion of culture" and the cultural relations among the peoples of the world. On this basis UNESCO is committed to the spread, the protection, the development, and the diversity of culture.

The spread of culture

For the implementation of its mandate, the UNESCO General Conference adopted in 1948 and 1950 multilateral agreements on the circulation and import of cultural materials. In 1948 the so-called Beirut convention was adopted, the Agreement for Facilitating the International Circulation of Visual and Auditory Materials of an Educational, Scientific and Cultural Character. The key provision of the agreement is that each of the contracting states shall accord "exemption from all customs duties and quantitative restrictions and from the necessity of applying for an import licence in respect of the importation, either permanent or temporary, of material originating in the territory of any of the other contracting States".

The 1950 so-called Florence Agreement on the Importation of Educational, Scientific and Cultural Materials stated that the contracting states shall not levy customs duties or other charges on the importation of books, publications, documents and educational, scientific and cultural materials as listed in the Annexes to the convention. The contracting states also accepted to grant the necessary licences and/or foreign exchange for the importation of a variety of cultural materials. In 1976 a Protocol to the Florence Agreement was adopted that extends the materials listed in the Annexes, especially in the light of the needs and concerns of the developing countries.

In 1976 the UNESCO General Conference adopted a recommendation on the international exchange of cultural property. The recommendation urges states to adopt measures to develop the circulation of cultural property among cultural institutions in different countries. The basic rationale for this is the consideration that the extension and promotion of cultural exchanges contribute to the enrichment of the cultures involved. The circulation of cultural property is seen as a powerful means of promoting mutual understanding and appreciation among nations.

Cultural exchange and cooperation

The UNESCO General Conference adopted in 1966 (Res. 8.1.) a Declaration of the Principles of International Cultural Cooperation. The Declaration refers in its preamble to the UNESCO constitution and its emphasis on the wide diffusion of culture and to a variety of human rights instruments. It clearly states the human rights standards in connection with culture in Article I: "Each culture has a dignity and value which must be respected and preserved. Every people has the right and the duty to develop its culture." Among the aims of cultural cooperation, the Declaration mentions "to enrich cultures, and to enable everyone to contribute to the enrichment of cultural life". Cultural cooperation, which is seen as both a right and a duty for all peoples and all nations, is expected to contribute to the establishment of stable, long-term relations between peoples.

In a similar spirit, the CSCE (Commission on Security and Cooperation in Europe) Final Act of Helsinki (1975) contains fairly elaborate provisions on cultural cooperation and exchange. In the part of the Act dealing with humanitarian issues, the participating states consider that cultural exchanges and cooperation contribute to a better comprehension among people and among peoples, and thus promote a lasting understanding among states. States conclude to increase substantially their cultural exchanges in the conviction that this will contribute to the enrichment of their respective cultures. They declare to set themselves the following objectives: "To develop the mutual exchange of information with a view to a better knowledge of respective cultural achievements. To improve the facilities for the exchange and for the dissemination of cultural property. To promote access by all to respective cultural achievements. To develop contacts and co-operation among persons active in the field of culture. To seek new fields and forms of cultural co-operation."

Cultural heritage

The United Nations General Assembly adopted in 1973 a resolution (UNGA Res. 3148 (XXVIII) on the preservation and further development of cultural values. The resolution considers that the value and dignity of each culture, as well as the ability to preserve and develop its distinctive character, is a basic right of all countries and peoples. In the light of the possible endangering of the distinctive character of cultures, the preservation, enrichment, and further development of national cultures must be supported. It is important that the resolution recognizes that "the preservation, renewal and continuous creation of cultural values should not be a static but a dynamic concept...". It is recommended to the Director General of UNESCO to promote research that analyzes "the role of the mass media in the preservation and further development of cultural values". The resolution also urges governments to promote "the involvement of the population in the elaboration and implementation of measures ensuring the preservation and future development of cultural and moral values".

A specialized instrument on the protection of the world cultural heritage was adopted by the seventeenth session of the UNESCO General Conference in 1972. This was the Convention for the Protection of the World Cultural and Natural Heritage. The text noted that the world's cultural heritage is threatened, that this impoverishes the world and that effective provisions are needed to collectively protect the cultural heritage of outstanding universal value. In the Convention, the international protection of the world cultural heritage is understood to mean "the establishment of a system of international co-operation and assistance designed to support States parties to the Convention in their efforts to conserve and identify that heritage".

On the protection of cultural property, the world community has also adopted through UNESCO, the Hague Convention for the Protection of Cultural Property in the Event of Armed Conflict (1954), the Convention on the Means of Prohibiting and Preventing the Illicit Import, Export and Transfer of Ownership of Cultural Property (1970), and the Convention on the Protection of the World Cultural and Natural Heritage (1972). In 1973 the United Nations General Assembly adopted on its agenda the issue of the restitution of works of art to countries that were the victims of expropriation. UNGA Res. 3187 (XXVIII) of December 18, 1973 sees the prompt restitution of works of art as strengthening international cooperation and as a just reparation for the damage done. To implement this, UNESCO established the Intergovernmental Committee for Promoting the Return of Cultural Property to its Countries of Origin or its Restitution in Case of Illicit Appropriation. Throughout the 1980s the United Nations General Assembly stressed the issue, commended the work of UNESCO undertaken in this field, and called upon member states to ratify the relevant Convention.

In 1986 the General Assembly proclaimed that 1988–1997 would be the World Decade for Cultural Development. The objectives for the Decade were formulated as the acknowledgement of the cultural dimension of development, the enrichment of cultural identities, the broadened participation in cultural life, and the promotion of international cultural cooperation (UNGA Res. 41/187, December 8, 1986).

Other approaches of the world community to the protection of cultural property include the safeguarding of traditional culture and folklore. In 1989 the General Conference of the UNESCO adopted a recommendation that stressed the need to recognize the role of folklore and the danger it faces. Folklore is defined as the totality of tradition-based creations of a cultural community. The recommendation urges measures for the conservation, preservation, dissemination, and protection of folklore.

Cultural workers

In 1980 the UNESCO General Conference adopted a recommendation on the status and position of artists. This instrument deals with the problems of artists in a context of very powerful cultural industries and important changes in the media of reproduction and distribution. Initially, the drafting of the regulation on artists was opposed by Western delegations. They argued that the freedom of the artist would be threatened by state regulation. Also, some of the NGO lobbies, such as the International Federation of Producers of Phonograms and Videograms, opposed the recommendation. Others in the NGO community, such as the International Federation of Musicians, the International Federation of Authors and Composers, and the International Federation of Actors, were in support of efforts to improve the status of artists as cultural workers. "The NGOs concerned were repeatedly to stress their support for urgent adoption of an international instrument; and in so doing were also regularly to proclaim not only the duties of industry towards artists, but their own readiness to accept reference to artistic responsibility" (Wells, 1987: 168). The initial Western opposition mellowed down with the result that the Western amendments weakened the text so that consensus adoption became possible. The Soviet bloc was in favour of regulation (although it wanted a somewhat stronger instrument) but went along with Western preference, as did the Third World, which was supportive although not satisfied with the level of attention to artists and culture in developing countries.

Major issues in global cultural politics

The major issues in connection with culture focus on the diffusion of culture, international cultural cooperation, the preservation and protection of culture, and the defence of cultural identity. Much of the multilateral debates on culture have been embedded in a human rights approach to culture.

There has been a fair consensus in world politics about the importance of multilateral cooperation for the preservation, participation, and promotion of culture. In concrete cases, such as the status of artists, positions have been divided on the need and the strength of multilateral accords. The deepest controversy occurred in connection with the issue of cultural identity. On this issue, the desire of the developing countries to establish solid protective measures was not accommodated. Recent developments suggest that the preference of the most powerful players for a commercial approach will guide the prevailing political practice.

There is extensive multilateral cooperation on the issue of culture. This has been guided by a combination of binding and voluntary accords which are weak. There are binding norms and rules in such treaties as the Beirut and Florence Agreements or the Convention on the Protection of the World Cultural and Natural Heritage. These accords have no effective enforcement mechanisms. Other instruments, such as recommendations and declarations, are of an informal nature. On the issue of cultural identity, multilateral cooperation has been hindered by a basic discord between players defending cultural sovereignty and those promoting unrestricted market access for cultural producers. The issue was very prominent in the 1970s debates on the Third World demand for a New International Information Order. It also figured in the negotiations on satellite television broadcasting. The UNESCO Declaration of Guiding Principles on the Use of Satellite Broadcasting for the Free Flow of Information, the Spread of Education and Greater Cultural Exchanges provides in Article VII that cultural programmes should respect the distinctive character, the value, and dignity of all cultures. The IDTBS (International Direct Television Broadcasting) Principles of 1982 also refer to the respect for the cultural integrity of states.

Cultural rights

The international Bill of Rights (Universal Declaration of Human Rights, International Covenant on Economic, Cultural and Social Rights, International Covenant on Civil and Political Rights) proposed to articulate entitlements in the area of culture as basic human rights. The Universal Declaration of Human Rights (1948) formulated the right to culture in the sense of participation in cultural life. Article 27 provided "Everyone has the right freely to participate in the cultural life of the community". Article 22 of UDHR stated that everyone is entitled to realization through national effort and international cooperation of the economic, social, and cultural rights indispensable for his dignity and the free development of his personality.

Participation in cultural life has raised difficult questions about the definition of communities, the position of sub-cultures, the protection of participation rights of minorities, the provision of physical resources of access, and the links between cultural access and socio-economic conditions. Underlying some of these difficulties is the tension between the concept of culture as public good or as private property. These positions can be mutually exclusive when historical works of art disappear into the vaults of private collections.

189

The inclusive nature of human rights ("everyone") implies a shift away from an elite conception of culture to a view of culture as "common heritage". Actually, the UNESCO Declaration on Racial Prejudice (1978, General Conference Res. 3/1.1/2) founded the right to culture on the notion of culture as "common heritage of mankind" which implies that all people "should respect the right of all groups to their own cultural identity and the development of their distinctive cultural life within the national and international context" (Article 5). The right to culture thus implies, beyond the participation in cultural life, the protection of cultural identity, the need to conserve, develop, and diffuse culture, and the need of international cultural cooperation.

In 1968 a UNESCO conference of experts considered the question of cultural rights as human rights (Paris, July 8–13, 1968). The statement of the conference declared: "The rights to culture include the possibility for each man to obtain the means of developing his personality, through his direct participation in the creation of human values and of becoming, in this way, responsible for his situation, whether local or on a world scale" (UNESCO, 1970: 107). The Intergovernmental Conference on the Institutional, Administrative and Financial Aspects of Cultural Policies (convened by UNESCO in 1970) decided that the right to participate in the cultural life of the community implies the duty for governments to provide the effective means for this participation. A series of regional conferences on cultural policies (in 1972, 1973, and 1975) provided important inputs into the formulation of a UNESCO recommendation on Participation by the People at Large in Cultural Life and Their Contribution to It, approved on November 26, 1976. The recommendation aims to "guarantee as human rights those rights bearing on access to and participation in cultural life". The recommendation questions the concentration of control over the means of producing and distributing culture. Regarding the mass media, the text states that they should not threaten the authenticity of cultures and "they ought not to act as instruments of cultural domination". The preamble proposes that measures are taken against the harmful effect of "commercial mass culture" and recommends that governments "should make sure that the criterion of profit-making does not exert a decisive influence on cultural activities". There was strong Western opposition to various elements of the recommendation, such as the mention of commercial mass culture in a negative sense, and the use of the term "people at large". In the preparatory meetings and during the UNESCO General Conference several Western delegations expressed their concern that the recommendation, if implemented, would restrict the free flow of information and the independence of the mass media. The strongest opponent was the USA.

> The USA asserted a belief from the outset that access to and participation in cultural life were not fit subjects for international regulation, took minimal part of the drafting process, sent no delegation of the intergovernmental meeting, urged the General Conference to turn down the proposed text and, after its adoption, announced that it had no intention of transmitting the Recommendation to the relevant authorities or institutions in the USA. (Wells, 1987: 165)

The Western countries were against, although, in different strength, the developing countries and Eastern European countries supported the text. In the drafting process there was little input from the cultural industries. The vote comprised: 62 for, five against, and 15 abstentions.

The preamble refers to the UDHR, the UNESCO Constitution, and the Declaration of Principles of International Cultural Co-operation and considers cultural development as a true instrument of progress. The recommendation links participation in cultural life with access to culture and claims that "access by the people at large to cultural values can be assured only if social and economic conditions are created that will enable them not only to enjoy the benefits of culture, but also to take an active part in overall cultural life and in the process of cultural development". It is recommended that member states "guarantee as human rights those rights bearing on access to and participation in cultural life", "provide effective safeguards for free access to national and world cultures by all members of society", "pay special attention to women's full entitlement to access to culture and to effective participation in cultural life", and "guarantee the recognition of the equality of cultures, including the culture of national minorities and of foreign minorities".

Regarding the mass media, the recommendation states that they "should not threaten the authenticity of cultures or impair their quality; they ought not to act as instruments of cultural domination but serve mutual understanding and peace". And: member states and appropriate authorities should "promote the active participation of audiences by enabling them to have a voice in the selection and production of programmes, by fostering the creation of a permanent flow of ideas between the public, artists and producers and by encouraging the establishment of production centres for use by audiences at local and community levels". And: "encourage media to pay special attention to the protection of national cultures from potentially harmful influence of some types of mass production".

This line of thought was reinforced by the 1982 World Conference on Cultural Policies held in Mexico City. The Declaration on Cultural Policies adopted by the Conference reaffirmed the requirement that states must take appropriate measures to implement the right to cultural participation. In recommendation 28 on cultural rights the conference participants claimed that governments should take measures "to strengthen the democratization of culture by means of policies that ensure the right to culture and guarantee the participation of society in its benefits without restriction". An assessment of the implementation of the recommendation on participation in cultural life in 1985–1986 showed that little had been done by many states and that these issues remained relevant.

Several factors explain the emergence of cultural rights in the post-Second World War era. There was the rise of post-colonial states which were searching for their identity in the light of both imposed colonial standards and their own traditional values. The issue of cultural identity came up particularly strong in the process of decolonization. The newly independent states saw the affirmation of their cultural identity as an instrument in the struggle against foreign domination. In their earlier battle with colonialism, cultural identity had played a significant role in motivating and legitimizing the liberation movement.

The proliferation of the mass media confronted the risks of cultural uniformity with the possibilities of unprecedented cultural interaction. The spread of a consumer society raised serious questions about the uniformity of a "world culture".

Protection of cultural identity

The protection of cultural identity became an especially hot issue during the 1970s debates on cultural imperialism. In 1973 the Non-Aligned summit at Algiers stated that "it is an established fact that the activity of imperialism is not limited to political and economic domains, but that it encompasses social and cultural areas as well, imposing thereby a foreign ideological domination on the peoples of the developing world".

Cultural domination and the threat to cultural identity was also treated by the MacBride Commission. The Commission saw cultural identity "endangered by the overpowering influence on and assimilation of some national cultures though these nations may well be the heirs to more ancient and richer cultures. Since diversity is the most precious quality of culture, the whole work is poorer" (International Commission, 1980: 31).

In its recommendations the Commission offered very little prospect for a multilateral approach to the issue of cultural domination. Its main recommendation was for the establishment of national policies "which should foster cultural identity. Such policies should also contain guidelines for safeguarding national cultural development while promoting knowledge of other cultures" (International Commission, 1980: 259). No recommendation was proposed on what measures the world community might collectively take. The Commission proposed the strengthening of cultural identity and promoted conditions for the preservation of cultural identity, but left this to be implemented at the national level.

More recently, the South Commission addressed the issue of cultural identity. According to its report, the concern with cultural identity "does not imply rejection of outside influences. Rather, it should be a part of efforts to strengthen the capacity for auto nomous decision-making, blending indigenous and universal elements in the service of a people-centred policy" (South Commission, 1990: 132). The Commission urged governments to adopt Cultural Development Charters which articulate people's basic rights in the field of culture. Cultural policies should stress the right to culture, cultural diversity, and the role of the state in preserving and enriching the cultural heritage of society (South Commission, 1990: 133).

Identity formation in a secular, post-religious world is difficult. Where do we find our authenticity, our uniqueness, our irreplaceability? In our work, our achievements, our products? But these are all replaceable. We can be missed. Religious identity is easier. It is determined by our relationship with God. God sees us as irreplaceable, as unique. The suicidal terrorist act may establish authenticity; it is the definite proof that we were chosen by God. In a paradoxical way, it demonstrates that we are irreplaceable.

Identity formation is inherently a violent process. We define our identity in distinction from the other. This is a very common psychological process; we divide the world into the "Us" versus "Them" and the Them are not as good as Us. There is a strong tendency to define others as inferior, less good, and as threatening! Feeling superior but at the same time threatened is a good base for violence!

The instruments to deal with dissident identities are violent: assimilation, apartheid, but also the more civilized integration policies (the newcomers have to accept the rules and values of the indigenous tribes) use force.

If the core mechanism of your identity formation is ridiculed, this can provoke a violent response.

Cultural imperialism

The word "imperialism" refers to the politics of states to expand their empire and thus their sphere of power and influence. The words "cultural imperialism" refer to the historical fact that in imperial expansion cultural forces have always played a significant role. Illustrations are Christian missionary activities, the introduction of Western-style school systems, forms of colonial administration, modern conceptions of professionalism, and the use of European languages in overseas colonies. The essence of "cultural imperialism" is that in achieving the domination of one nation over other nations, cultural sources of power and influence are of key importance.

Cultural imperialism has different names in the academic literature. It may be called media imperialism (Boyd-Barrett, 1977), cultural colonialism (McPhail, 1987), communication imperialism (Lee, 1988), cultural synchronization (Hamelink, 1983a),[1] or ideological imperialism (Mattelart, 1994).

The combination of culture and imperialism achieved common currency in academic and political debates on North–South relations in the late 1960s and continues to be a recurrent topic on academic and political agendas throughout the 1970s and 1980s, particularly in Latin America (Pasquali, 1963; Beltran, 1976; Matta, 1978). The notion of cultural imperialism played a central activist role in the 1970s debates at UNESCO on the creation of a New International Information Order, later to be renamed a New World Communication and Information Order. Towards the late 1980s cultural imperialism lost its evocative attraction to the notions of globalization and alternative globalization.

Defining cultural imperialism is made difficult by the combination of two highly complex concepts. Culture is defined and interpreted in myriad different ways, as is imperialism. A definition that is often quoted was given by Herbert I. Schiller in his book, *Communication and Cultural Domination* (1976). "The concept of cultural imperialism today best describes the sum of the processes by which a society is brought into the modern world system and how its dominating stratum is attracted, pressured, forced and sometimes bribed into shaping social institutions to correspond to, or even promote, the values and structures of the dominating center of the system." Essential in this definition is the notion of dominance. Cultural imperialism is seen as a process of imperial control that operates through forms of culture and that is more effective than earlier forms of colonial domination through military occupation, foreign administration, and economic dependency.

John Tomlinson (1991) has distinguished different discourses on cultural imperialism.

- Cultural imperialism as a discourse on media imperialism. International media – as producers and disseminators of foreign cultural content – are seen as the key culprits in a process in which foreign cultural contents are imposed upon local cultural traditions. This is contested by scholars who question whether media are the central forces in processes of domination. They ask whether the media are indeed the key cultural points of reference in Western modern societies and whether foreign pressures (particularly from the USA) on structure, ownership, and content of national media effectively constitute a form of foreign domination.
- Cultural imperialism as a discourse on nationality. This is a process by which indigenous cultures are invaded by foreign cultures and either synchronize with the invaders or disappear altogether. This discourse raises critical questions around the notion of national cultural identity.
- Cultural imperialism as a critique of global capitalism. The challenge for this discourse is to demonstrate that capitalism is a homogenizing cultural force and that the global spread of consumerism constitutes a form of domination.
- Cultural imperialism as a critique of modernity. This discourse perceives modernity as a way of life that spreads globally and that creates cultural homogeneity. The critical issue here is that the resistance against modernity may romanticize traditional forms of life

Critics of the "cultural imperialism" perspective have contested what they saw as its main flaw: the assumption that receivers would be passive and non-resisting actors. They have argued that this assumption was empirically falsified in studies that demonstrated that audiences have an active ability to interpret cultural products in their own ways (Liebes and Katz, 1990). According to these authors, the active audience frame of analysis shows that viewers actively produce meaning while consuming foreign TV products.

Critics have also focused on the assumption of the single nature of the invading culture and the single nature of the indigenous culture. They have argued that the cultural imperialism perspective has too little attention for the multiple constructs that cultures are and for the mutuality in processes of influence.

Critics have also addressed the lack of precision, measurability, testability and inconsistence of the cultural imperialism perspective. The response to this has been that cultural imperialism is a macro-theoretical insight into societal processes that by its very nature lacks precision, quantifiability, or consistency. The defenders of cultural imperialism have argued that their macro-analysis could neither be falsified nor verified by the micro-type level of analysis of individual cultural consumption.

Many studies on cultural imperialism have criticized the shortcomings of the cultural imperialism perspective and have suggested that authors defending this perspective have failed to provide empirical support. However, most of the authors who have used the concept "cultural imperialism" in their efforts to understand domination in international relations have argued that they never formulated their work in operational and testable formats.

The cultural imperialism approach connected culture with industrial production but a question that remained unanswered was whether the concentrated industrial control over the production of media content did indeed lead to foreign hegemony over local values, tastes, and beliefs.

Globalization of culture

The global spread of modernity

This is a complex historical process that began in 1648 with the Peace of Westphalia, which formed the basis for European political structures: the sovereign national states. This process was further influenced by the intellectual input of various Enlightenment processes, not only the eighteenth-century European Enlightenment, but also the nineteenth-century Enlightenment periods in the Arab world and in the Ottoman empire. An essential technological dimension of the process began with the industrial revolution in the eighteenth century, and proceeded with the enormous growth of transport and communication technologies in the twentieth century.

What is modernity?

One possible answer refers to the institutionalization and regulation of political and cultural practices.

- Political practices refer to the creation of sovereign and democratic nation-states with the codified legal rules.
- Cultural practices refer to the imagining of an attachment to individual and collective definitions based upon gender, sexuality, ethnicity, and religion,

Identity and modernity

Does the global spread of modernity cause a loss of cultural identity? Global capitalism has certainly been able to spread a specific type of cultural goods around the globe, such as the yellow arch of McDonald's or the Disney icons, but it remains unclear whether a deep existential cultural impact can be inferred from the presence of such goods. Does people's cosmology change when they wear jeans, drink Coke, eat hamburgers, or watch *Sex and the City*?

It can be argued that identity is a typical modern phenomenon and the question whether the global spread of modernity threatens local cultural identities, presumes evidently that there were stable, solid cultural identities before modern times. But did people ever possess this clearly defined individual and collective identity? From the historical record it would seem that in pre-modern times identity was not such a central concern.

An intriguing question is whether there is both a cultural drive towards globality and a drive towards locality. Local personal and communal definitions of identity are increasingly affected by events that take place at a distance (Giddens, 1990) and this may have increased cultural vulnerability. It could also be that the global spread of modernity weakens identities but also causes the emergence of strong but different local identities.

Three views on cultural globalization

The convergence view

In this view cultural globalization successfully spreads the message that the quality of human life can be defined in terms of market value. Everything on earth can be bought and sold. Cultural globalization is present in the global spread of McDonald's fast-food places, and Disney entertainment parks. This is seen as a cultural victory. McDonald's symbolizes the global marketing of the free market ideology, the worldwide export of consumer behaviour, and the global spread of a modern lifestyle. McDonaldization (Ritzer, 1993) goes way beyond the proliferation of fast-food. It introduces worldwide – and with great success – a business formula that is based upon efficiency, calculability, predictability, and rationalization. This formula has worldwide also found its way into such societal sectors as education and health care.

Important instruments of cultural homogenization are entertainment and advertising. These industries showcase an ideal "way of life" in which the availability of consumer goods equals the "good life". Illustrations of cultural convergence or homogenization are found in the global uniformity of media formats (infotainment, for example). The products of News Corporation, Time Warner, and Disney, for example, are found everywhere. There is a globalization of TV culture manifested by similar ways of production and distribution, branding and marketing.

The divergence view

In a 1993 article in *Foreign Affairs* – the precursor of his book *The Clash of Civilizations* (1993) – Huntington wrote: "It is my hypothesis that the fundamental source of conflict in this new world will not primarily be ideological or primarily economic. The great divisions among human kind and the dominating source of conflict will be cultural. ... The clash of civilizations will dominate global politics. The fault line between civilizations will be the battle lines of the future" (Huntington, 1993). The main argument of the thesis is that future world conflict will play out along cultural and religious differences. The problem with Huntington's *Clash of Civilizations* is its assumption that people's identities are based upon civilizations and that people can be brought under civilizational categorizations. The assumption implies the dangerous notion of choiceless singularity (Sen, 2006). Moreover, the thesis is very much representative of US versus THEM thinking. The dangerous "Them" are primarily Muslims.

The hybridity view

The homogenizing effect of cultural convergence meets around the globe with processes in which globalization combines with localization through preferences for local taste in religion, music, or food. Cultural globalization and cultural localization may result in "glocalization", i.e. in hybrid forms of cultural expressions that range from world music to fundamentalist youth on sneakers. Global products are becoming localized in hybrid forms such as the vegetarian burger (in India), the nasi burger (in Indonesia), or McKroket in the Netherlands.

A global mélange emerges in which cultures borrow from one another (Nederveen Pieterse, 2009). The hybridization view offers a synthesis between the perspectives of homogenization (the triumph of McDonald's) and the battlefield of Jihad vs McWorld (Barber, 1995). As Nederveen Pieterse (2009: 59) wrote: "It resolves the tension between purity and emanation, between the local and the global, in a dialectic according to which the local is in the global and the global is in the local." Hybridization recognizes that however cosmopolitan people may feel, in the end the "cultural proximity" of the local language or local jokes remains essential. According to Kraidy (2004: 252), "The 1990s witnessed the rise of hybridity as a multidisciplinary concern over the fragmentation and fusion of cultural forms". This interest found its origin in studies on cultural encounters through the ages and in the observation that cultural mixtures are not necessarily non-hegemonic. Also, in cultural hybridity unequal power relationships continue to play a significant role. Hybridity can, for example, function as a strategy in global advertising to create and control niche markets (Kraidy, 2004: 253).

The understanding of hybridity needs a complexity perspective since it can be articulated from very different perspectives, ranging from hegemonic to progressive (Kraidy, 2004: 256). Articulations of hybridity – especially among diaspora communities – can also be understood from an evolutionary perspective as adaptive answers to new complexities of everyday life.

Bhabha (cited in Straubhaar, 2007: 37) sees hybridity "as an active process ... complex and unpredictable". And Straubhaar asks: "...does the rapid recent push of all these new forces combine to create much stronger impacts on cultures, impacts that might justify the labels or charges of cultural imperialism, homogenization, and destruction of traditional cultures?" (2007: 38).

Hybridity might mean continuity and discontinuity. It may involve resistance to colonialism (Straubhaar, 2007: 39). Local culture may continue to exist in hiding without the colonizers noticing it. Hybridity may be merely superficial and the original indigenous culture survives, such as in India (Straubhaar, 2007: 39). "Complex hybridization seems to have accelerated in the 20th century with postcolonial migration, increased travel, transnational mass media, and economic globalization" (Straubhaar, 2007: 41). There is certainly an increase in cultural encounters out of which has emerged a complex series of stories that narrate about refugees, migrants, diaspora communities, the exiled, and displaced traditional communities.

Intercultural communication

As a result of globalization processes, through the growth of international trade, tourism, migration, and the emergence of diaspora communities, the field of intercultural communication has rapidly expanded. However, in spite of all the publications, "how to" manuals, seminars, and university courses, communication across cultural borders remains a challenge.

? Can you describe your own experiences with intercultural communication?

The study of intercultural communication finds – to an important degree – its origins in the work of Edward T. Hall and the American Foreign Service Institute in the early 1950s. The Institute offered training programmes for US diplomats to be stationed in foreign countries. Hall and his colleague George Trager designed – using antropological, linguistic, and psychoanalytical insights, a matrix to map cultures in terms of their most important dimensions. Hall and Trager identified communication, and especially non-verbal communication, as a crucial dimension. On this topic, Hall wrote in 1959 the famous – and best-selling – book, *The Silent Language*. With this book, a first paradigm for the study of intercultural communication was created. Its core elements were the role of time ('chronemics') and the role of space ('proxemics') in the communicative behaviour of people. The analysis of the use of physical space in *The Silent Language* especially appealed to many readers. Possibly the most cited phrase from the book says, "A US male … stands 18 to 20 inches away when talking face to face to a man he does not know very well; taking a woman under similar circumstances, he increases the distance about four inches. A distance of only 8–13 inches between males is considered … very aggressive. Yet in many parts of Latin America and the Middle East, distances which are almost sexual in connotation are the only ones at which people can talk comfortably" (Hall, 1959).

In the 1960s intercultural communication became part of communication studies at American universities like the University of Pittsburg. A new academic field had emerged that would grow rapidly, especially in the USA and in Japan.

Already, the first paradigm, with its focus on non-verbal communication, signalled that there are big obstacles on the road to effective intercultural communication. With verbal communication such obstacles only increase. People obviously use very different languages. Words can have different meanings in different languages. The syntactic rules that determine the order of words are strongly bound to the cultural histories of communities. Within such communities, people also use their own semantic meaning that they ascribe their own meaning to words and phrases. The same words may have different connotations that are related to the context. An example is the use of the word "no". Some communities use "no" without inhibition whereas others will go out of their way to avoid this word.

The classic academic studies that have tried to contribute to a greater effectiveness in intercultural communication are those by Edward T. Hall and Geert Hofstede. Edward Hall distinguished in his book, *Beyond Culture* (1976), between high-context and low-context cultures. In his analysis, the context of encounters is decisive in the high-context culture. For effective communication, it is essential to give attention to the building of mutual trust and the avoidance of loss of face. The low-context culture prefers direct and efficient exchanges. In Japan the high-context culture is important whereas the Dutch feel better in the low-context culture. For the Japanese, it is important to cultivate long-term, personal relations. The Dutch tend to prefer contractual relations and consider extensive socializing a waste of time. The high-context culture (as in Arab states) presents ideas with elaborate, almost poetic language, whereas in low-context cultures (like in Denmark) the preference is for logical arguments, straight and without too much prudence. In the high context-culture, refusals are avoided or are very carefully worded. In the low-context culture, people have no problem in refusing something without much ado.

Dutch sociologist Geert Hofstede carried out research on the dimensions of national cultures and he identified the variables of power distance, individualism versus collectivism, femininity versus masculinity, avoidance of uncertainty and long-term versus short-term thinking. The results were published in *Culture's Consequences* (Hofstede, 1980, revised in 2001). Power distance refers to the (in)egalitarian natures of societies. Individualism versus collectivism refers to the question of whether people see themselves primarily as individuals or as part of a community. Masculinity refers to the degree in which male values, such as competition and material achievements, are considered more important than female values, and to the question of whether differences in male and female roles are accepted or rejected. Avoidance of uncertainty refers to people's preference for either structured situations or flexibility. Long-term versus short-term thinking reflects obvious differences in approaching the world in which one lives.[2]

Beyond the classics

In the past decades a variety of theoretical (or as I would prefer "conceptual" approaches) have been proposed to understand intercultural communication processes better. Some of these approaches focused on effective outcomes of intercultural interactions.

An example is the cultural convergence theory by D. Lawrence Kincaid that explores how communication can facilitate the convergence to a more mutual understanding of each other's meanings. Barnett and Kincaid (1983) developed a mathematical model on the effect of communication on cultural differences that they based upon the law of thermodynamics. Basically, the model suggests that participants in a closed system will – if communication is unrestricted – converge to a state of cultural uniformity. When communication – due to external stimuli – is restricted, the system tends towards diversity. The model was applied to the study of relations between immigrants and host cultures (Korean immigrants in Hawaii). (Kincaid et al. 1983)

Gudykunst and Hammer (1988) focused on the management of anxiety and uncertainty (the AUM theory). The proposition is that the inability to predict others' attitudes and feelings and the anxiety this causes are basic factors in cultural adjustment and effective inter-group communication. Important for the management of anxiety and uncertainty is the extent to which people are mindful of their communicative behaviour.

Oetzel (1995) focused on effective decision-making in intercultural groups. This approach proposes that the more equal members contribute and the more members are committed to the group, the more effective the decision-making process will be. Hirokawa and Rost (1992) added to this in their Vigilant Interaction Theory: the better members understand the problem and develop many alternatives, the more effective their decisions will be.

Stella Ting-Toomey (1988) developed the cross-cultural theory of face-negotiation and conflict management. For her, "face" is a sense of self-worth that a person wants others to have of him or her. Her proposition is that the more secure individuals are, the more they are open to interacting with members of other cultures and the more resourceful they are in interacting with strangers. The more vulnerable people are (meaning more in need of security), the more anxiety they will experience in intercultural interactions. The more inclusion people need, the more they will value the in-group, and the more differentiation they need, the more distance will they construct between the self and others.

It is crucial to study how people negotiate the secure/vulnerable tension and the differentiation/inclusion dialectics. Cindy Gallois and others (1995) proposed the Communication Accommodation Theory (CAT), which explores an explanation of inter-cultural adaptation. One of their propositions is that the more communicators engage in adaptive behaviour, the more cultural beliefs will change. Young-Yun Kim (1986) has focused upon communication networks and on how individual behaviour is influenced by relationships between individuals. Her interest is to explore how out-group members in personal networks facilitate the competence to communicate with out-groups. In her theory, the adaptive behaviour of strangers is a function of the communication compe-tence of the host. When immigrants are not deviant from norms of the host and engage in assimilative communication, host nationals respond with assimilative communica-tion (they praise the strangers; are available for interaction). When strangers are deviant, hosts will respond with neglectful communication; the immigrants will feel excluded and may develop hostile sentiments.

Social variables, fields and scanning

Nico Vink proposes in his book, *Dealing with Differences* (2005), a new way towards intercultural communication. He resists the temptation to offer a box with useful tricks, but understands that intercultural communication is a complex process and that a variety of variables need to be taken into account to develop an understanding. He argues for the need to look at factors such as power and the realities of social relations for a successful understanding of intercultural communication. He has chosen the felicitous term of "scanning" to discover what happens in communication processes. Sociologist Amitai Etzioni used this term to describe an effective method for planning. The significance of this method is that planners oscillate between the general survey and the details of a situation. This protects the communicator against the effort to comprehensively understand a situation and the risk to get lost in focusing on too much detail.

In this scanning process people fine-tune social variables such as gender, age, societal position, wealth, and education as possible impediments versus possible facilitators for a successful communication process. In the process also, the fields (Vink borrows this concept from French sociologist Pierre Bourdieu) in which people act are crucial factors for understanding and misunderstanding. If people share a field (such as religion, sports, or music) communication across cultural borders tends to be become easier than in cases where they find no matches.

Challenges

The major challenge in all this thinking about cross-cultural or intercultural communications is that most theories and models are developed from a Western and, more particularly, a North-American perspective. There is definitely more research needed by non-US (particularly East-Asian scholars). Another problem is that in most studies (with the exception of the approach proposed by Nico Vink) there is little or no attention for such a crucial variable as "power".

Unfortunately, there is also only limited empirical research conducted to test the theoretical propositions. Most troublesome issue, however, is that although there is a generous labelling of interesting ideas and concepts as "theories", there is little serious scientific theory in the sense of solid coherent sets of ideas, that explain social realities, that predict future outcomes, and that invite new research. It would seem to me that here, as in other studies on communication and culture, important contributions could be made from evolutionary biology and by complexity theory.

Most challenging is the question of how to reflect on cultural differences in an age of globalization or trans-localization. With the growing global interdependence and emerging multicultural societies it becomes questionable whether the convenient thinking in cultural dichotomies, such as individualism versus collectivism, is helpful in understanding cultural differences. Dichotomization is arguably an expression of a largely Western mind-set that prefers the or/or approach over the and/and approach. The latter would seem to match better with an Eastern worldview, in which elements such as Yin and Yang are opposites and yet complementary to each other. The problem with the individualism versus collectivism dichotomy is that individual orientations versus collective orientations are found throughout all cultures and that individuals maybe have both individual and collective orientations and that their relations to the collective may be altruistic or selfish. Social realities are too complex to be categorized into dichotomous opposites. But, does this mean that in the end cultural differences are only marginal and temporary?

For most of my academic career I was partisan to a universalist approach to human thought which suggests that thinking follows the same cognitive processes everywhere and that we use – worldwide – the same tools for causal analysis, categorization, and inference. Scientific reason applies the same processes to different things because it is based upon formal logic and does not tolerate contradictions: if A is the case, then not-A cannot be the case.

Through exposure to students and colleagues from East-Asia, I discovered that in the real world we use different tools and that these differences are particularly clear in the comparison between East-Asians (Chinese, Japanese, Koreans) and Westerners (Europeans and North Americans). The origins of these differences are found in Greek (Aristotelian) philosophy and Chinese (Confucian) philosophy, which represent different ways of thought that people have employed for thousands of years.

The main tool of Greek thought is the syllogism that reaches through formal reasoning to logical solutions from correct assumptions: 1. All human beings are mortal; 2. Socrates is a human being; 3. Socrates is mortal. The main tool of Chinese thought is a form of dialectics that, contrary to Hegelian dialectics, does not resolve contradictions, but uses contradictions: A can imply that not-A is also the case. For Greek thought the world was simple and knowable as long as you understood the attributes of an object and categorized it. For Chinese thought the world was complicated and interdependent. Understanding an object without contextualization does not lead to knowledge. Where for Greek thought individual agency and identity was essential, for Chinese thought collective agency and mutual obligations were crucial. The Greeks were fond of debate, the Chinese preferred harmony and avoided public disagreement. Where the Greek would indulge in abstract speculation, the Chinese focused on the practicality of ideas.

These differences in thinking also translated into different social practices. The fields of law and health provide good illustrations. The Western conception of the legal system is combative and based upon the distinction of winners versus losers. In Chinese law, the role of mediation in the de-escalation of conflicts between people is essential. In the Western judicial system there is one law that is common to all. For the Chinese judge the law should have a personal quality since all cases are different. In the health system, the West takes an analytical and interventionist approach. You identify the problem (e.g. a non-functioning organ) and remove it through surgery. Chinese medicine is holistic and concentrates on finding a balance in the human body rather than removing parts.

The challenge that these differences imply for global communication is whether divergent systems of thought can communicate, whether they eventually may converge, or whether we should find a hybrid mode of communicating and develop the intercultural communication competence to apply this mode. Before we get there we first need to address the specific issues of inter-group communication, the role of religion, and the particularities of human perception.

The group

Intercultural communication encompasses the communication not only between individuals belonging to different cultures, but also among groups. Individuals are always part of a group and individual encounters more often than not also imply communicating with the other group.

Although groups are obviously made up of individuals with their personal psychological characteristic, the collective behaviour of large groups manifests its own specific psychological dynamics.

- All individuals in societies relate to a stronger or lesser degree to groups that are essential in the development of their identity, their existential meaning, and their future perspectives. Groups give answers to such questions as "where do I come from?", "who am I and what is the sense of being me?", and "where do I go, what is my destiny?" The collective answers to such questions render people vulnerable to the manipulation of their collective identity. The more the group cohesion grows, the more individual members of the group will tend to ask ever fewer critical questions and identify with the suggested collective identity. The more cohesive in-groups become, the greater becomes the external disconnectedness to out-groups. As the "Us" versus "Them" dichotomy becomes stronger, the group conflict tends to escalate more quickly. The self-respect of the group members is "tied to believing that their own group is better than other groups" (Pruitt and Kim, 2004: 133). This makes it easier to blame, dehumanize, and ultimately kill members of the out-group. This is especially so in cases where the conflict involves groups with different religions and cultures.
- Individuals in groups develop a strong dependence on social approval and concede to social pressures. An illustration comes from the Japanese kamikaze pilots during the Second World War. We now know that many of them preferred not to kill themselves but found it shameful to disobey orders.
- It is difficult to establish clear accountability for collective acts as they tend to be performed in relative anonymity.
- Most important in group dynamics is that collective violence is difficult to stop. It becomes a mission! Once mass killing and collective humiliation are set in motion, it becomes very difficult to stop the collective violence. Destructive behaviour changes the world vision and the value system of those who participate in it. What people in other times might have seen as impossible, inhuman, and atrocious, now becomes the normal and right thing to do. In the in-group, "groupthink" plays a crucial role and

this discourages members of the group from asking questions, raising objections, or becoming dissidents.

Religion

Most people in the world are religious. Most social groups are religious groups. Religious beliefs represent the sacredness of important values, and it is the mission of the chosen people to defend these beliefs. The non-believers deserve to be discriminated and eventually eliminated. "In today's societies, people cannot escape the confrontation with others who find their deepest convictions absolutely abject and even dangerous. They will inevitably be profoundly hurt" (Hamelink, 2011: 100). In confrontations with religious groups, the ultimate truth may be at stake and mutual understanding may be impossible. When what is held as the most valuable experience in life is ridiculed, criticized, or negated by the "other", this enemy becomes Satan with whom no deals are made. Religious intolerance creates unbridgeable obstacles for intercultural communication.

Human perception

It is obvious that the way human perception works constitutes an important factor in the understanding of intercultural communication.

A first observation is that our perceptions of reality usually start from a hypothesis about what we see, hear, smell, taste or touch. This hypothesis stems from our earlier experiences and from what we learned about reality. Since there is a limit to the insecurity that human beings tolerate, there is a common tendency to the rapid closure of perception. Often, at a first glance ("love at first sight") we establish our definitions of what we perceive (Lippmann, 1922: 81). Because of the multitude of stimuli in our environment we have to filter and select. One way of doing this is through categorization (Tajfel et al., 1971). This makes reality manageable. "For the real environment is altogether too big, too complex, and too fleeting for direct acquaintance. We are not equipped to deal with so much subtlety, so much variety, so many permutations and combinations. And although we have to act in that environment, we have to reconstruct it on a simpler model before we can manage it" (Lippmann, 1922: 16). The most basic categories that we use are the in-group versus the out-group. By applying these categories we contribute to our self-definition, in which we find the images we hold of ourselves usually more attractive than the images of others. We also tend to see US as more heterogeneous than THEM. These images are stereotypes ("pictures in our head" as Walter Lippmann called them) and they can be both positive and negative.

Stereotypical images impede intercultural understanding because they easily lead us into misguided interpretations of how others behave.[3] They preclude our realistic viewing of others. It is very difficult to change them. Intercultural contacts may even reinforce them: "For contact to reduce prejudice, the members of two groups must have equal status, an opportunity to get to know each other, exposure to evidence that disconfirms the stereotypes, shared goals, and active cooperation ... negative stereotypes often resist change" (Kunda, 1999: 363). A mechanism through which we may overcome negative stereotypes *vis-à-vis* individuals is by "fencing them off" from their group and seeing them as a-typical for the group.

Intercultural communication competence

This notion refers to the mastering of those skills that are required to make an intercultural interaction a satisfactory communicative act that participants would like to continue, in which none of the participants feels humiliated, after which participants feel they tried their best to understand each other and to take the other(s) seriously. Chen and Starosta (1996: 358–359) defined intercultural communication competence as "the ability to negotiate cultural meanings and to execute appropriately effective communication behaviors that recognize the interactants' multiple identities in a specific environment".

?
How do you cope with cultural heterogeneity? Is it easy for you to accept views of reality that fundamentally differ from your version of reality? Do you experience such alternative views as a challenge?

Skills that are needed for intercultural communication are:

- The acceptance of multiple identities: the capacity to recognize your own internal dialogues – the symphonies in your head – and the many conversations we conduct with ourselves.
- The self-awareness of one's own cultural identity, cultural biases, values, and practices: the capacity to question how do others see me?
- The social skills to communicate: such as friendliness and openness to others. Do you have the capacity to monitor your own behaviour?
- The capacity to recognize cultural differences, in the sense of empathy, not necessarily sympathy. Can you see the other through his or her eyes? Can you tolerate differences? Is there a basic willingness to understand the values and practices of another culture.
- The capacity recognize one's own cultural luggage: the conceptions, values, assumptions, biases, and stereotypes you carry with yourself.

?
Do you feel that there are boundaries to the respect for other cultures? Do you
think there may be situations in which you have to express criticism against
the cultural practices of social groups you do not belong to?

How to study culture and global communication?

Studying the relation between global communication and culture means that we must try to explore such notions as cultural homogenization, cultural diversity, and cultural hybridity. We must try to understand how cultural expressions are part of current globalization processes and how people across the globe exchange stories both as cosmopolitans and as locals.

We must also explore which research tradition can assist our understanding. The most likely candidate seems to be the field of cultural studies. This approach gives attention to content and focuses on the text and their meaning. A leading question is how production in the cultural industries affects the texts they produce. Whereas the political economy approach questions whose interests are served by the texts the industry produces, the cultural studies approach analyzes what these texts may mean for the identity of the recipients.

A cultural studies approach, then, might involve examining how prevailing patterns of cultural behaviour are reflected in the cultural industries themselves. The cultural studies approach asks us "to consider more carefully how what people want and get from culture shapes the conditions in which these industries have to do business – for example, the way in which music's ability to negotiate the relations between our private and public selves shaped the way the music business has offered musical commodities to us to own in the same way that we own other commodities" (Hesmondhalgh, 2007: 43).

As so often in communication studies our understanding of complex realities requires the synergy of different approaches that complement each other.

Notes

1. In the 1970s the problem of cultural invasion or imperialism was also perceived as "cultural synchronization". (Hamelink, 1983a). This approach made the point that cultural uniformity and threat to cultural identity were not merely the result of imperial processes, they also needed the support of recipient communities. Synchronization also occurs in situations where coercive power is not the main variable. In many developing countries, for example, the local elites have been very helpful to the transnational business corporation in introducing their populations to foreign lifestyles and consumer products.

2. A serious problem with the Hall and Hofstede studies is their unit of analysis. It is questionable whether there are indeed national cultures. There are always many different cultures within the borders of a country. There are sub-cultures, generational cultures, and these are also changing over time.

3. Allport (1954) called a stereotype "an exaggerated belief associated with a category".

Reading spotlight

Culture and Globalization

Featherstone, M. (1995). *Undoing Culture: Globalization, Postmodernism and Identity*. London: Sage.

> In this book Mike Featherstone analyzes the impact of globalization on culture. He explains why culture has gained more importance in people's everyday lives and discusses the significance of non-Western cultural frames in forming today's global modernities. Insightful material on global and local cultures and on cultural identity.

Friedman, J. (1994). *Cultural Identity and Global Process*. London: Sage.

> The author explores the relations between the global and the local and argues that both fragmentation and homogenization are essential dimensions of global developments. Rich in theoretical sources and illustrations from different cultures. A final chapter addresses the complexity of order and disorder in global systems.

Nederveen Pieterse, J. (2009). *Globalization and Culture: Global Mélange* (2nd edition). Lanham, MD: Rowman & Littlefield.

> This book offers a scholarly and well-documented argument (historically and geographically) for the understanding of the current process of hybridisation in global culture. Moving away from easy generalizations about cultural homogenisation or cultural clashes, the author engages with the concept of hybridisation.

Cultural Imperialism

Said, E.W. (1993). *Culture and Imperialism*. New York: A.A. Knopf.

> Edward Said offers a critical and thorough examination of Western culture from Jane Austen to journalistic reporting about the Gulf War. His analysis provides deep insights in the roots of Western cultural imperialism.

Tomlinson, J. (1991). *Cultural Imperialism: A Critical Introduction*. Baltimore, MD: John Hopkins University Press.

> This is a very important guide to the understanding of cultural imperialism. It offers an in-depth introduction to different approaches to and definitions of cultural imperialism. Tomlinson offers critical analytical comments on the cultural synchronization thesis of the author of the present textbook.

Intercultural Communication

Gudykunst, W.B. and Mody, B. (eds) (2002). *Handbook of International and Intercultural Communication*. London: Sage.

This book is an invaluable resource for students of intercultural communication. Four fields – cross-cultural, intercultural, international and development communication are treated through theoretical introductions and reflections on emerging issues. Topics that are examined and critically discussed range from non-verbal communication across cultures, to intercultural communication competence, transnational advertising, and participatory approaches to development communication. Recommended reading.

Online resources

Visit the book's companion website at **https://study.sagepub.com/hamelink** to watch the author discussing the theme of this chapter: **Intercultural Communication**

Visit the book's companion website at **https://study.sagepub.com/hamelink** to access the following journal articles free of charge:

Baraldo, C. (2006). New forms of intercultural communication in a globalized world. *Gazette*, 68(1): 53–69.

Fejes, F. (1981). Media imperialism: an assessment. *Media, Culture & Society*, 3(4): 281–289.

Jin, D.Y. (2007). Reinterpretation of cultural imperialism: emerging domestic market vs continuing US dominance. *Media, Culture & Society*, 29(5): 753–771.

Lee, P.S. (1988). Communication imperialism and dependency: a conceptual clarification. *Gazette*, 41(2): 69–83.

Oliha, H. (2012). Critical questions: the impact and import of the contradictions and epistemic denials in the field of intercultural communication research, theorizing, teaching, and practice. *International Communication Gazette*, 74(6): 586–600.

Sonaike, S.A. (1988). Communication and Third World Development: a dead end? *Gazette*, 41(2):85–108.

Further reading

Asante, M.K. and Gudykunst, W.B. (1989). *Handbook of International and Intercultural Communication*. London: Sage.

Bennett, M. (ed.) (1998). *Basic Concepts of Intercultural Communication*. Yarmouth, ME: Intercultural Press.

Boyd-Barrett, O. (1977). Media imperialism: towards an international framework for the analysis of media systems. In Curran, J., Gurevitch, M. and Wollacotts, J. (eds), *Mass Communication and Society*. London: Arnold. pp. 116–135.

Cohen, R. (1991). *Negotiating across Cultures*. Washington, DC: United States Institute of Peace Press.

Condon, J. and Yousef, F. (1985). *An Introduction to Intercultural Communication*. New York: Macmillan.

Cushner, K. and Brislin, R.W. (1997). *Improving Intercultural Interactions: Modules for Cross-Cultural Training Programs* (Vol. 2). London: Sage.

Friedman, J. (1994). *Cultural Identity and Global Process*. London: Sage.

Gudykunst, W.B. and Kim, Y.Y. (1992). *Communicating with Strangers: An Approach to Intercultural Communication*. New York: McGraw-Hill.

Gudykunst, W.B. and Ting-Toomey, S. (1996). *Communication in Personal Relationships across Cultures*. London: Sage.

Hall, E.T. (1976). *Beyond Culture*. New York: Doubleday.

Hofstede, G. (2001). *Culture's Consequences* (revised edn). London: Sage (1st edn, 1980).

Jandt, F.E. (2012). *Intercultural Communication* (7th edn). London: Sage.

Liu, S., Volcic, Z. and Gallois, C. (2010). *Introducing Intercultural Communication*. London: Sage.

Neuliep, J.W. (2011). *Intercultural Communication: A Contextual Approach*. London: Sage.

Patel, F., Li, M. and Sooknanan, P. (2011). *Intercultural Communication: Building a Global Community*. London: Sage.

Samovar, L., Porter, R. and Stefani, L.A. (1998). *Communication between Cultures*. Belmont, CA: Wadsworth.

Sorrells, K. (2012). *Intercultural Communication*. London: Sage.

Tajfel H. (ed.) (1978). *Differentiation between Social Groups: Studies in the Social Psychology of Intergroup Relations*. London: Academic Press.

Tajfel, H., Billig, M.G., Bundy, R.E. and Flament, C. (1971). Social categorization and intergroup behaviour. *European Journal of Social Psychology*, 1: 149–177.

Tajfel, H. and Turner, J.C. (1986). The social identity theory of intergroup behaviour. In Worchel, S. and Austin, W.G. (eds), *Psychology of Intergroup Relations*. Chicago, IL: Nelson. pp. 7–24.

Ting-Toomey, S. (1999). *Communicating across Cultures*. London: Routledge.

Tomlinson, J. (1999). *Globalization and Culture*. Cambridge: Polity Press.

Vink, N. (2005). *Dealing with Differences*. Amsterdam: KIT Publishers.

Wiseman, R.L. and Koester, J. (eds) (1993). *Intercultural Competence*. London: Sage.

Wiseman, R.L. (ed.) (1995). *Intercultural Communication Theory*. London: Sage.

RESEARCH ASSIGNMENT

Can a valid test for Intercultural Communication Competence Skills be developed?

Think about and discuss with others the possibility of such a test. What precisely would it measure? What essential variables should be used?

What would the test look like? How would it be administered?

GLOBAL COMMUNICATION ONLINE

12

The essential inspiration for this chapter came from that prolific writer and critical analyst of global informational developments, Manuel Castells.

Manuel Castells (1942–)

Castells is a sociologist with a special interest in urban sociology and information society issues. Since 2003 he is professor of communication at The Annenberg School of Communication of the University of Southern California. An important intellectual source for his work on urban issues is Alain Touraine. Castells has introduced important concepts, such as "collective consumption", to refer to services like public transport and public housing, and "space of flows" as crucial components of information networks.

For the study of global communication, his important works are especially: *The Informational City* (1989); the Information Age triology: *The Rise of the Network Society* (1996; 2nd edn, 2010), *The Power of Identity* (1997), and *End of Millennium* (1998); *The Internet Galaxy: Reflections on the Internet, Business and Society* (2001); and *Communication Power* (2009).

For the study of global communication, Manuel Castells taught us to critically reflect on the balance between utopian versus dystopian realities of global networks.

In this chapter I want to explore the most recent development in the field of global communication: the emergence of global digitized networks. In the early twenty-first century global communication has definitely gone online, with the emergence of new social networks that have exponentially expanded the online capacity of global communication. Does this raise new policy challenges and how do the glorious and the dark sides of global online communication interact? The global proliferation of the technologies of social media invites the question whether we are entering a new world?

Global communication goes online

Characteristic in the more than one hundred years' development of global telecommunications are the gradual upgrading of transmission facilities and the addition of switching technology. This emerged when electronic data-processing became available in the late twentieth century, which made telecom networks feasible both on national and international scales. In the course of the 1950s the hitherto distinct technologies of telecommunication and electronic data-processing became fully integrated and computer-communication networks were created both as centralized and decentralized systems. During the 1970s and 1980s innovative technologies (such as modems, optical fibre, packet switching and satellites) rapidly increased the performance capacity, accessibility, and compatibility of computerized telecommunication networks.

Telematics networks became operational that were increasingly interesting for banks and airlines. The pioneer in transnational data flows has been SITA, the Société Internationale des Télécommunications Aéronautiques. SITA was established in 1949 by eleven airlines as a reservations system using a low-speed teleprinter system. Already by 1974, 185 airlines from 90 countries were part of the system. In 2012 SITA served more than 640 members, including 500 airlines and operates the largest global private network that connects 220 countries and territories. It is most probable that today SITA carries the largest volume of data of any computer network.

Among the heavy data traffic users are also the large international banks.

The need for international telecommunication networks has drastically increased with the transnationalization of banking. During the 1960s and at the beginning of the 1970s, US banks, followed by the West European and Japanese banks, spread worldwide. To adequately respond to the communication needs created by this transnationalization, the banks created networks for their individual use and for interbank use. The most important example of a network created for interbank use is SWIFT (Society for Worldwide Interbank Financial Telecommunications). The idea for SWIFT was born in the late 1960s when a group of large West European banks studied the possibility of improved international transaction procedures and came to the conclusion that international banking needed an accurate, rapid, safe, and standardized funds transfer system. As a result of the study and the positive response from the banks, the major West European, Canadian, and US banks established SWIFT in May 1973. Four years later in May 1977 the network became operational. By then, almost US$1 billion had been spent on the network and equipment was procured from Burroughs, ICL, and General Automation. By 1980 SWIFT carried some 250,000 messages daily.

SWIFT connects through operating centres in Belgium, the Netherlands, and the USA over 9,700 banks, brokerage firms, commodity exchanges, securities institutions, and corporate customers in 209 countries. An important feature of the system is that it guarantees absolute confidentiality of message transfer, with all transmissions over international lines being encrypted.

In the early 1990s four important trends became visible in global communication that would have a considerable impact on the daily lives of people around the world. The four trends originated in the 1980s and matured in the 1990s. They were: digitization, consolidation, deregulation, and globalization. They relate to each other both in proactive and reactive ways. The fundamental trend of digitization, which means that more and more cross-border interactions are based upon electronic formats, reinforces both technological integration and institutional consolidation. These integrated technologies and institutions promote the trend towards deregulated environments and reinforce the trend towards globalization. Also, deregulation and globalization are related.

Global operations demand global markets which in turn require deregulation of national markets. Digitization provides the technological basis for globalization as it facilitates the global trading of services, worldwide financial networks, and the spreading of high-technology research and development across the globe. Digitization facilitated since the mid-1980s the shift from public to private corporate networks which have become the backbone of global trade. The group of powerful users and operators of corporate global networks has effectively pushed the shift from public to private ownership of telecommunication structures. Consolidation and globalization are related. Consolidation forms the base from which to globalize and also the movement to global markets forces companies to merge in order to remain competitive on a world market.

The trend towards digitization

Digitization means that technologies for the processing and transmission of information begin to use the same language. This is the computer language of the binary code. This digital language facilitates the convergence of computers, telecommunications, office technologies, and assorted audio-visual consumer electronics. This digital integration offers speed, flexibility, reliability, and low costs. Digitization means better technical quality at lower prices. Channels greatly expand their capacity, the Electro Magnetic Spectrum can be more efficiently used, there is more consumer choice, and more possibilities for interactive systems. Economic efficiency is achieved as conversion to digital forms of storage, retrieval, and editing imply savings in time and labour. Digitization considerably improves the quality of voice and video transmission. For high-quality video, for example, images can be digitally compressed and then transmitted over satellites as computer files. The digital data can be stored on computer disc systems before playback in the original speed. This could be applied in news gathering, as available digital compression and storage systems are light-weight. Digital compression techniques in television offered important economic advantages for satellite TV broadcasting. More TV channels could be put on fewer transponders, which meant considerable savings. Digital technology increased the opportunities for projects like video-conferencing and pay television.

In the process of digitization, earlier analogue modes of information transmission and storage began to be replaced by more powerful, reliable, and flexible digital systems. "The technical foundations of this process lay in the early postwar era, in the innovation of a common language of microelectronics for both computing and, somewhat later, telecommunications" (Schiller and Fregoso, 1991: 195). As digital switches and digital transmission facilities were developed, increasingly around the world the transition from analogue to digital networks began.

As Schiller and Fregoso rightly observed, this process did not merely consist of the shifting from analogue to digital techniques, but beyond the technical transformation, the process was also institutional – "both in its sources and its implications" (Schiller and Fregoso, 1991: 195). The largest users of global communication were demanding broad, affordable, reliable, and flexible electronic highways around the globe. Only a digital global grid could meet these demands. This implied the development of new hardware and software. The digital grid was expected to transport all signals that could be digitized: from the human voice to HDTV imagery. This required the replacement of conventional carriers such as copper wires with optical fibre cables, it meant new switches, and new software to control the unprecedented large flows of information across borders. Digital technology made it possible to send information at the speed of light and at low prices.

In the development of digitization two models have prevailed and collided. The in-house model of corporate plans to integrate their communications capacities. The large corporate users insisted that they need their own private networks translated to digital systems (Schiller and Fregoso, 1991: 196). The second model "emanated mainly from the institutional complex surrounding the public telephone network. It originated in the late 1970s as a design by the supplier's side of the telecommunications service industry for ubiquitous integrated systems within and between subscribing nation-states" (Schiller and Fregoso, 1991: 196). This is the ISDN model that developed from domestic telephone network towards a worldwide connectivity for voice, text, data, and images.

The in-house model became the prominent trend. The growing corporate reliance on cross-border information networks made them articulate demands for accessing networks worldwide. The drive towards a global grid was of necessity accompanied by an equally strong drive to deregulate communication markets around the globe. Political pressures began building up in many countries to transfer public control over telecommunication institutions to private interests.

Although digital technology has been available since the 1960s, only in the 1990s did a strong wave of application, such as Electronic Data Interchange (EDI), emerge that made this technology the essence of more and more cross-border transactions.

The "electronification" of cross-border interactions facilitated the provision of a greater variety of services. At a different pace and with different scope most countries around the world were affected by the application of digital technologies. During the 1980s the process of digitization began to accelerate and by the late 1980s in the advanced industrial market economies between a quarter and half of all central office telephone switches had been digitized. Actually, in the 1980s the international satellite consortium, Intelsat, began to introduce full digital services such as International Business Service (IBS) and Intelnet (digital communications service for use with small terminals). This new commitment to digital technology was seen as essential to Intelsat's future competitiveness on the satellite services market.

During the 1980s digital technology began to be applied in consumer electronics and for such products as the compact disk a rapidly growing market began to emerge. When in 1983 Philips introduced CDs on the Dutch market, sales represented less than 2 per cent of the recorded music market, in 1986 this had risen to over 25 per cent. By 1989 in the USA over 200 million CD units were purchased as compared to some 8 million in 1984 (Robinson, Buck and Cuthbert, 1991: 53).

The latest in consumer electronics was the innovation of smart digital TV sets. Through the deployment of digital technology, HDTV not only improves sound and image, but also facilitates a series of manipulations with the incoming signals (storing, processing, and conversion).

The main feature of digitization is the increasing scale of information-related activities. Information has always been a crucial factor in social processes. Always, people have produced, collected, duplicated, or stolen information. Recent economic and technological developments have, however, significantly changed the scope of these activities. Digitization reinforced a social process in which the production and distribution of information evolved into the most important economic activity in societies in which information technology began to function as the key infrastructure for all industrial production and service provision, and in which information itself became a commodity tradable on a global scale. Digital technology is a "synergetic" technology. This means that its growth leads to growth in other sectors of the economy. It creates an infrastructure around its products and services, similar to the car technology earlier in the twentieth century. As with the transition from manual power to mechanization techniques and later to electro-mechanical innovations, today's shift towards the pervasive application of electronic information techniques has created a number of new industries, such as software production, processing services, time-sharing facilities, semiconductor manufacturing, database management, or electronic publishing. As a result, issues that in themselves may not be new are confronted with the necessity to find new policy responses as many of the current solutions (for example, in criminal law or intellectual property protection) are no longer sufficient.

Digitization demanded exceedingly large investments that were prohibitively expensive for most operators except for a few that were very powerful and resource-rich. The risks implied in such enormous investments in a deregulated, competitive environment were of staggering proportions. One of the inevitable consequences of these large investments in high-risk contexts was to restrict the number of players in the marketplace.

Digitization has raised difficult issues of political economy about access, control, and expense. Who was going to have access to the emerging digital grids, and at what price? Who will control the networks? Where will the intelligence that guides the network be stored and who will own it? The network operator or the end-user? Who pays the bill for the enormous expense the digital process implies? The potential abuse of digital technology and its social consequences are global in nature and require international collaboration and consensus. The optimal protection against abuse and the optimal benefit from use can only be secured multilaterally.

Digitization provided the technological and institutional basis for global online communication that today largely takes place through the Internet. This has deeply influenced thinking about the nature of global communication in modern times.[1] The emergence of this global networking technology seemed to announce a new age of global connectivity and interactivity in which the dominant transmission paradigm would be replaced by an interaction paradigm. As with the earlier announcements of the post-industrial information society, there is the expectation of fundamental changes in people's life-world and in societal power relations. The opportunities the Internet offers for communication in and between societies depend, however, on the recognition of the rights to make use of them in the first place, thus giving people an instrument to call for the public policies that are necessary to exercise them. Even if the Internet may be less troubled by problems of scarcity, inequalities in access, skills, relevant content, or language representation will remain powerful obstacles to any form of empowerment. Also, it would be naïve to assume that the Internet is by its nature "uncontrollable" – the growing power of search machines and software companies, the possibilities of censorship, and the political sensitivities involved in administering the Internet all are issues that need to be considered.

Expanded capacity for human communication?

For the study of global communication, an important question is obviously whether the new possibilities of the Internet, and especially of Web 2.0, such as weblogging, Facebook (one-seventh of the global population has a Facebook profile), Twitter, LinkedIn, YouTube, Pinterest (a very successful and fast-growing site for people who want to collect things that are important to them by pinning them to digital pinboards), ebay (the platform for mom-and-pop vendors), Yahoo, and Flickr, expand human communications capacity to communicate trans-locally? There can be little doubt that this expansion is reality for the global online community that grows rapidly, although it is still unequally distributed around the world. But for a reliable answer to the question of what the socio-political and cultural implications of the expanded communication capacity are, it is in 2014 still too early to say. Some footnotes can be made, however. The notion of "new" suggests not only advances in information and communication technology, but also changes in human behaviour. This reflects a crude determinism that finds no substance in human realities.

The "new" media may be free from the oligopolistic control by the barons of culture, the moguls that gatekeep the news, or the few that belong to a ruling class, an aristocratic elite, or a religious priesthood. The new media may have the many at the helm. There is, however, no historical evidence that the many will be less inclined to the escalation of evil than the few. The "new" media may indeed bring about more freedom to foster, express, disseminate, and receive ideas, but there is no guarantee that the largely expanded and differentiated number of media producers will act more responsibly than the media moguls of the past. It needs to be questioned how far the conventional mass media are past history. Today they continue to be grand players in the global facilitation and dissemination of the basic motives of global and lethal conflict.

An important question that global network technology poses is, according to Castells, "The Internet networks provide global, free communication that becomes essential for everything. But the infrastructure of the networks can be owned, access to them can be controlled, and their uses can be biased, if not monopolized, by commercial, ideological, and political interests. As the Internet becomes the pervasive infrastructure of our lives, who owns and controls access to this infrastructure becomes an essential battle for freedom" (Castells, 2001: 277). Another challenge identified by Castells is the need "to acquire the intellectual capacity of learning to learn throughout one's whole life, retrieving information that is digitally stored, recombining it, and using it to produce knowledge for whatever purpose we want" (Castells, 2001: 278).

It is also important to note that there is a dark side of the Internet. In his book *Net Delusion* (2011), Evgeny Morozov has demystified the Internet and argued that the freedom of the Internet is a delusion and that cybertechnology did not democratize the world. Actually, according to Morozov, the Internet is a popular tool of repressive governments as it can be used for surveillance, propaganda, and censorship. He also calls Facebook and Twitter very helpful tools to the cause of oppressive governments.

? Do you think we can still live offline?

New policy issues?

Global communication online raises the question of whether we have to confront new policy issues. It would seem that all the old policy issues of copyright protection versus creativity, privacy, and confidentiality versus surveillance, freedom versus censorship, security versus risks, and participation versus exclusion are still there. However, they seem to have a more global and urgent presence. How should we deal with them in the twenty-first century? Looking at this from the democratic egalitarian perspective, it makes sense to go back to a recommendation that a meeting of experts (held in 1975 in Geneva) made to the UN General Assembly. The meeting proposed the monitoring and assessment of new technologies from the point of view of human rights. The General Assembly never acted upon the recommendation. More than a quarter-century later, however, the recommendation still makes eminent sense, and it can be regretted that the UN World Summit on the Information Society (Geneva, December 2003, and Tunis, 2005) did not revive it.

The substance and organization of such an assessment could look as follows.

Human rights assessment: the substance

Over a quarter-century ago, Joseph Weizenbaum (1976) suggested criteria that could still be used in a human rights assessment of digital technology today. Special caution is needed in relation to "all projects that propose to substitute a complex system for a human function that involves interpersonal respect, understanding, and love" (Weizenbaum, 1976: 269). Weizenbaum also warns against "computer applications ... which can easily be seen to have irreversible and not entirely foreseeable side effects" (1976: 270). A serious human rights assessment would point to the risks of realizing digital applications that may have not fully foreseeable side-effects and that may be irreversible once they are implemented. A human rights assessment also should be applied whenever digital applications serve to limit human rights. For example, in the context of the so-called "wars" against organized crime and terrorism, telecommunication authorities in many countries can order, on behalf of law enforcement and intelligence agencies, that service providers share customers' personal data. In the majority of situations where this happens, there is no solid base in law. This could be a first test: Are measures that limit civil and political human rights based on a democratically achieved legal provision? Moreover, other criteria for testing could be whether the measures are effective in reaching a consensually defined social purpose, whether they are the only available means to achieve this purpose, and whether they are intended to have a temporary duration only.

Human rights assessment: the organization

Following human rights standards, the assessment process would have to be organized through democratic arrangements. This implies that we should extend the standard of political equality to mean the broadest possible participation of all people in processes of public decision-making. In addition, the democratic process should be moved beyond the political sphere and extend the requirement of participatory institutional arrangements to other social domains. Therefore, forms of participatory democracy have to be designed for policymaking in the sphere of the production, development, and dissemination of digital technologies. This conflicts with the observation that there is presently a widening gap between the domains of technological development and political decision-making (Winner, 1993). As Ulrich Beck (1992: 214) notes, "Faith in progress replaces voting".

The development of biotechnology provides a good illustration. Scientists and investors cooperate to produce artificial tissue, blood vessels, and organs such as hearts and livers. Charles Vacanti, a top scientist in the field of "regenerative" medicine, thinks enough experimentation has been carried out with animals. It is time to begin the

218

renovation of human beings. It is expected that the bio-industry will soon bring a veritable "body shop" with human spare parts on the market ("Bio-Tech Bodies", 1998: 44). Irrespective of possible advantages versus disadvantages, the whole process evolves outside any form of social control. Beck (1992) points out that social concerns and anxieties about developments in genetic technology have no impact on the real decisions in this domain. These decisions have already been taken because the question of whether certain developments were socially desirable was never posed. "One can say 'no' to progress, but that does not change its course at all" (Beck, 1992: 203). This course is determined outside the political domain. Policies on technology are not made by the political system. No votes are taken in parliament on the employment and development of microelectronics, genetic technology, or the like; at most it might vote on supporting them in order to protect the country's economic future (and jobs). It is precisely the intimate connection between decisions on technological development and those on investment which forces the industries to forge their plans in secret for reasons of competition. Consequently, decisions only reach the desks of politicians and the public sphere after being taken (Beck, 1992: 213).

Today, there is a worldwide trend for governments to delegate responsibility for basic social choices to the marketplace. Thus, the democratic control of important social domains is increasingly eroded without any major societal debate. Following their desire to deregulate, liberalize, and privatize, many governments are leaving the governance of the new digital technologies in the hands of private entrepreneurs. One implication is that the realization of the social potential of such technologies comes to depend more on investment decisions than on considerations of common welfare. For anyone who cherishes the democratic ideal, this is a regrettably short-sighted position that demonstrates a basic lack of democratic sensitivity. If democracy represents the notion that all people should participate in those decisions that shape their future welfare, such social forces as digital applications for information and communication cannot just be left to the interests and stakes of commercial parties within the market. If we are serious about the democratic nature of our societies, there is a public responsibility in such a crucial domain as the design, development, and deployment of digital technologies.

Because the choices that are made in this domain have far-reaching impacts on societies, the political process requires the broadest possible participation of all those concerned. In other words, there is an urgent need for an extensive public dialogue about "our common digital future".

Challenges

The essential challenges that global communication online poses are:

- The possibility of global cyberwar
- The growth of global surveillance

- The governance of cyberspace
- The question of how "social" the online networks are

The cyberwar challenge

"The entire phenomenon is shrouded in such government secrecy that it makes the Cold War look like a time of openness and transparency. The biggest secret in the world about cyberwar may be that at the very same time the US prepares for offensive cyberwar, it is continuing policies that make it impossible to defend the nation effectively from cyberattack" (Clarke and Knake, 2010).

- In 1996 there were 250,000 attempts to break into the computers of the Pentagon. Some 75 per cent were successful. The 150 hackers who were eventually prosecuted had managed to get into the central computers of the air force.
- In February 1998 the US Department of Defense was confronted with a forceful digital attack against twelve nodes in the networks for the air force and the navy. Two 16-year-old hackers turned out to be culprits.
- Early March 1998 a computer hacker crashed thousands of computers with Microsoft operating systems in the USA, among them the digital systems of the NASA.
- Also in March 1998 the Israeli police arrested an 18-year-old hacker who had been snooping in Pentagon computers.
- In April 1998 the computer systems of the Pentagon and the NASA were hacked. The hackers (calling themselves "Masters of Downloading") reported their burglary in the cyber magazine *AntiOnline*.

Security is the essential topic in current debates on new forms of warfare. The development of digitally run weapons systems makes "cyberwar" an attractive and "clean" alternative to conventional armed conflicts. A deceptive aspect, however, is that in a digital war there may be fewer victims in the short term than with old-fashioned bombing, but the numbers of victims will rapidly increase as the effects of cyberwar set in. A successful digital attack would, among others things, lead to the disruption of the provision of electricity and water.

The possibility of "cyberwar" implies that states have to design defensive policies to diminish their vulnerability. At the same time, several states, like the USA, actively develop the capacity for digital offensives. The USA has developed an extended digital system for espionage that costs some $30 billion dollars annually. This is justified by the argument that the USA is the target for much industrial espionage and theft of intellectual property. The capacity of this espionage system can also be deployed to secure American economic interests abroad.

Digital weapons systems consist of: (a) software that renders the information networks of opponents inoperational through viruses; (b) advanced bugging devices; and (c) equipment that through electromagnetic pulses can disrupt electronic systems. The Pentagon has this recipe for digital warfare: "Deny, destroy, or intercept adversary computer, network, or communications, while protecting one's own" (Schwartau, 1996: 464).

A cyberattack could close all international communications of a country, render all air traffic impossible, sabotage the provision of electricity and water, and paralyze the country's financial system. A scary prospect is the possibility that organized crime or terrorist groups equip themselves with cyberspace weapons. Societies that apply many digital systems are extremely vulnerable to "cyberterror". With relatively simple tools the key functions of such societies can be disrupted. Clarke and Knake concluded their study on cyberwar with the observations that cyberwar is real, happens at the speed of light, is global, skips the battlefield and has begun: "In anticipation of hostilities, nations are already 'preparing the battlefield'. They are hacking into each other's networks and infrastructures, laying in trapdoors and logic bombs – now in peacetime. This ongoing nature of cyberwar, the blurring of pace and war, adds a dangerous new dimensions of instability" (Clarke and Knake, 2010: 31).

?
There are international agreements for conventional warfare, such as the four Geneva Conventions of 1949, which provide, among other things, rules for the treatment of victims and prisoners of war, or the Hague Conventions (of 1899 and 1907), which deal with the use of weapons in warfare. Should there be international rules for cyberwarfare?

The surveillance challenge

In many countries electronic surveillance is mushrooming, through video-cameras in public spaces, bugging of telephone calls, credit card firms, scanners in supermarkets, "cookies" on the World Wide Web, and international spy satellites. As the scope of "surveillance" in a society grows, the confidentiality of communications diminishes. Digitization renders surveillance easy and attractive. It facilitates what governments have always wanted to do: to collect as much information as possible about those they govern. Because of technological limitations, this was always a difficult job. However, recent technological innovations have made grand-scale spying rather simple. One consequence is that the trading of surveillance technology from rich to poor countries has become an attractive sideline for the world's arms traders.

Digitization facilitates the monitoring of all communications through fax machines, telephones (particularly mobile phones), and computers. It has become technically relatively easy to register all traffic that uses GSM (Global System for Mobile Communication) cellular telephones. Swiss telecom operator Swisscom admitted at the end of 1997 that it registered the communications traffic of more than one million users of cellular phones in the GSM network. Also, in other European countries, police forces use the technical possibility to establish the presence of mobile telephones. The computer systems of telecom service providers can register where mobile phones are, even when they are not used for calls but are switched on to receive voicemail. According to the report, "An Appraisal of the Technologies of Political Control" (published in February 1998), the US National Security Agency (NSA) surveils through the use of intelligent search agents communications traffic of European politicians and citizens. The British research bureau Omega Foundation (in Manchester) prepared this report for the European Commission. The report found that the US espionage computer network "ECHELON" detects keywords in military and political information as well as in economic information used by commercial firms and stores relevant data for later analysis. For a long time there had been indications of eavesdropping on world communication networks by the NSA and the Omega report now provided the evidence. The British-American surveillance programme targets all the Internet satellites that carry the major portion of worldwide telephone calls, fax communications, and Internet traffic. The main justification is the struggle against terrorism and crime. There is, however, little hard evidence that there are indeed positive law enforcement effects. In the meantime, European Parliament members were informed that the NSA, by routine intercepts valuable private commercial data about investments, tenders, and mergers.

Besides ECHELON there is also an EU–FBI surveillance system (for police, security, and immigration services) that facilitates the interception of worldwide communications by the US National Security Agency. In September 1998 the European Parliament discussed the NSA surveillance and adopted a consensus resolution asking for more openness and accountability for electronic spying activities.

Interestingly enough, in early 1999 a working group of the European Parliament proposed the establishment of an extensive tapping network for police and intelligence organizations to intercept all telecommunication traffic among citizens and companies. According to the working group, the permanent surveillance of all data traffic in real time is a "must" for law enforcement purposes. In May 1999 the European Parliament resolved to approve the establishment of a comprehensive surveillance system for all European telecommunications traffic on mobile phones, faxes, pagers, and the Internet. The electronic system that is being designed for this massive interception programme will track data on phone numbers, email addresses, credit card details, PIN codes, and passwords. Also, in 1999 the European Parliament was informed (in the report "Interception Capabilities 2000") about the planning by the NSA, the FBI and the European Union through the International Law Enforcement Telecommunication Seminar of a vast surveillance network that would combine national security and law enforcement activities.

As such plans are made, the very technology of surveillance is making considerable progress. In 1999, for example, a satellite was launched (by a commercial US company Space Imaging) that can detect from space very small objects and that can be used for commercial purposes. A growing number of commercial companies have now acquired licences to launch surveillance satellites.

Since late 1999, the US government uses satellites with the capacity to see objects measuring 8 inches across. Work is also in progress to make the recognition of faces from space possible. Tests have already been done in big cities with the scanning of faces in large crowds and the analysis of the images by databases in remote computers.

Digital bugging devices have become so small that Japanese scientists claim they can build them into cockroaches. Digital miniature cameras and microphones can be constructed in smoke detectors, alarm clocks, hearing aids, ballpoint pens, and spectacles. Most important, however, is the development of increasingly intelligent software for the registering and filtering of information. Using so-called self-learning neural networks, intelligent agents search in vast databases for the specific information that creates complete commercial and political profiles of the objects of their search.

Equipment for surveillance and spying becomes cheaper all the time. Among the big buyers are employers who want to control their employees. In many countries the permanent electronic surveillance of the workforce has become standard practice. This ranges from bugging telephone and email traffic to placing video-cameras in toilets to check for the use of drugs, tracking employee's movements through smart badges, using sensors to monitor whether workers wash their hands after visiting the toilet, and monitoring the use of inappropriate websites. Some companies have installed the "Ascentor" software (designed in 1999 by the British Business Systems group) which reads all the electronic mail traffic in a firm and checks it against certain keywords to assess whether the messages are legitimate company business.

Companies that have intensive telephone traffic with clients (travel agencies, airlines, phone companies, call centres for direct marketing) increasingly use "Big Brother" systems to check the performance quality of their staff. With the help of a computer system, management can register how many clients in a given time frame can be approached, how many transactions are successful, and what operators cost per transaction. Firms may ask their employees to accept forms of surveillance. However, even if staff consents with managerial bugging of their phone traffic, the client will often remain ignorant of the surveillance. Very few firms do indeed announce to their clients that they use surveillance methods. It is therefore advisable, particularly in communications with companies that use "call centres", for clients to always inquire whether the conversation is being recorded, and if so, why is the case, for what purposes, how long the recording will be kept, and whether he/she can get a copy.

In many of the digitally advanced countries, the state has a strong desire to monitor civil electronic communications. The crucial argument is that although this violates people's privacy, it is inevitable to guarantee security. Thus US president George W. Bush authorized the National Security Agency (NSA) after 9/11 to monitor all communications of American citizens who were suspected of connections with terrorism. The NSA surveillance system continues to grow. According to the *New York Times* of August 22, 2012: "It now collects so much digital detritus – emails, text messages, cellphone location data and a catalog of computer viruses – that the NSA is building a 1 million square foot facility in the Utah desert to store and process it".

There is worldwide no serious citizen protest against being invisibly monitored by their governments. Once in a while travellers get very annoyed by the inconvenience of the visible surveillance in airport screening. However, privacy is easily given up when people believe that this improves security against criminals and terrorists. Fortunately, there are around the world groups of privacy advocates that resist the ubiquitous surveillance (Bennett, 2008). There is, however, as Bennett concludes, "no concerted worldwide privacy movement that has anything like the scale, resources, or public recognition of organizations in the environmental, feminist, consumer protection, and human rights fields" (2008: 199).

While Bennett and others explore the possibilities of such a movement, in daily practice millions of people are eager to voluntarily share details of their private lives with the spies in their governments through one of the main instruments of global communication online, Facebook. All the pictures on Facebook, the emails in Gmail and Yahoo are stored in the Cloud. This network of online servers distributed around the globe collects and stores most of our online material with the great comfort that this will not get lost whatever happens to our individual PCs or tablets. The drawback is that US-based intelligence and law enforcement agencies have – on the legal basis of protection of national security – access to the Cloud data of US and non-US citizens.

?
Discuss whether and how anti-surveillance politics could be organized in a globally effective movement.

In the iWorld we are, as Andrejevic (2007: 218) calls it, digitally enclosed in an environment of state and commercial monitoring and peer-to-peer surveillance to which people grow accustomed. "In a world in which we've become used to having details of our daily lives collected and sorted by Web browsers and credit card companies, in which we know that we are surrounded by surveillance cameras in public and private spaces alike, in which our employers can monitor our e-mail correspondence and our online activities, and in which surveillance has become such a popular form of entertainment that the expression 'Big Brother' is just as likely to refer to a game show as to a fading cold war memory of authoritarianism, the government decision to track our phone calls might seem just one more natural extension of the everyday monitoring practices associated with the information age". The real danger lies in the "specter of a benumbed populace" (Andrejevic, 2007: 268): a convenient mental adjustment to practices that seriously undermine the democratic promise of the digital technologies.

The massive intrusion upon corporate and individual privacies through the ECHELON espionage network of the NSA and private data collection projects developed in the early twenty-first century into an unprecedented big data business. Big data – among others through the information that Edward Snowden shared with the world – became one of the hottest topics (both in politics and in publicity) of global communication in the Cloud.

? Read about the Snowden case and argue both for his defence as a human rights lawyer and against his actions as a prosecutor on behalf of the US government.

The Cloud is in fact the global sharing of computer utilities. The recent history of the development of shared computer resources from the early 1950s till the cloud computing of the early twenty-first century is well recorded by Vincent Mosco in his book *To the Cloud* (2014).

Cloud traffic is growing, and more and bigger cloud data-centres are being built around the world. Although cloud advocates often refer to the notion of "public utility", cloud computing is largely private business controlled by only a few transnational corporations, such as Apple, Google, and Microsoft. A very successful leader in cloud computing is Amazon. If you ordered this book through Amazon's service, you are in the cloud. It is even more likely that you are on Facebook and all your virtual friendships are taken to the cloud. The Cloud companies are expanding their market control through purchasing other companies (like Google acquiring YouTube in 2006) or through extending into hardware manufacturing and software development.

The hottest topic is "big data". The analysis of vast amounts of information – extracted from private and public sources and stored in data centres by cloud companies – is largely done by cloud computing. Big data analysis provides information services for political, commercial, and scientific utilization (Mosco, 2014: 188–194). This ranges from the help Amazon Web services supplied to the Obama presidential campaign in 2012 (Mosco, 2014: 177) to their referral to the books you should order next. Leading in governmental use of big data analysis is the NSA, the intelligence agency that aspires to collect data from all global communication traffic.

As Vincent Mosco suggests, "The cloud is an enormously powerful metaphor, arguably the most important developed in the short history of the IT world" (2014: 206). "The cloud is a place of no place; the home of data stored and processed everywhere and nowhere" (2014: 207).

?

Does the monitoring of personal data in your country constitute a contested issue? What position would you take?

- Privacy is a lost cause anyway
- The surveillance society is inevitable
- The right to control information about yourself is a fundamental human right that needs to be protected.

The Internet governance challenge

This issue has now been debated in global meetings for some time and the jury is (in 2012) still out. The main contending parties are governments that want legal control over the Internet, intergovernmental organizations that want control by international agreements, corporations that prefer market control, communities of Internet users that strive towards self-regulation, and the designers of the Internet architecture that argue for technological control over the Internet (van Dijk, 2012: 143). A key issue on Internet governance is posed by the question of net neutrality. This fundamentally addresses the openness and security of the Internet. "The principle of net neutrality holds that all Internet content is treated equally and moves at the same speed over the network" (van Dijk, 2012: 87).

One complicating factor in the debate between those who are in favour net neutrality (and for less regulation for Internet transportation) and those who are against the principle (and for more regulation of tariff structures) is that "those in favour of net neutrality can also be advocates of more regulation to protect Internet privacy" (van Dijk, 2012: 142).

Another challenge is posed by the secret negotiations of an initiative by Russia and China to conclude an international agreement for regulation of the Internet through the United Nations (mainly the International Telecommunication Union). Under the proposed treaty: the UN would distribute and assign all e-names, each country would be notified of the IP addresses of each email user within its borders (allowing China and Russia to track down dissidents), the UN could regulate Internet content, every nation would have the right to censor websites that originate within its borders, and every country could charge a surcharge for access to any websites that originate beyond its borders (Morris and McGann, 2012).

A third challenge relates to the question of the democratic nature of arrangements through which public choices about the governance of the Internet will be made. Democratic arrangements imply that there is the broadest possible participation of all people in the processes of public decision-making. The issue of the democratization of public decision-making in the fields of information and communication has been on the civil society agenda in the recurrent debates on the Right to Communicate, in the initiative for a People's Communication Charter (that started 1992), and in the non-governmental contributions to the United Nations World Summit on the Information Society (2003 and 2005). A democratic arrangement has rules, procedures, and institutional mechanisms to secure public accountability. The principle of accountability logically implies the possibility of remedial action by those whose rights to participation and equality may be violated. Only through effective recourse to remedial measures can fundamental standards be implemented. If those who take decisions engage in harmful acts, those affected should have access to procedures of complaint, arbitration, adjudication, and compensation. The process of establishing the responsibility for decisions taken and demanding compensation for wrongs inflicted should secure the egalitarian nature of the democratic arrangement.

Choices about future Internet rules and practices have to be made under the condition of uncertainty. Effects in the future of choices made today are unknown. The future is open because we have no information about it. If we had such information, there would be no real choice. A serious human rights assessment would point to the risks of realizing choices that may have not fully foreseeable side-effects and that may be irreversible once they are implemented. The possibility of error in public choice making is unavoidable. Therefore, the readiness to learn from past errors and to revise choices already made is essential to the respect for human dignity. Human rights require that Internet governance conquers the insensitivity to error that Barbara Tuchman (1985) has described as the imbecility of government.

The challenge of the social quality of online networks

The global networks such as Facebook, YouTube, Twitter, and Flickr are often referred to as "social" media. In particular, the use of words such as "friends" and "participation" reinforces the suggestion of a cooperative and non-commercial venture that primarily uses the global public sphere to promote democratic values. This may have been true at the beginning in 2004 and 2005, but in her book, *The Culture of Connectivity* (2013), José van Dijck now proposes that "connectivity" media is a more appropriate descriptor for the online networks.

The networks are managed by large corporations in the data business that basically connect users in order to use all the collected data for commercial purposes. Facebook "increasingly serves as a gateway and identity provider to selected services and goods" (van Dijck, 2013: 65). Facebook partnered up with big data companies, such as Acxiom, Epsilon and Datalogix. This allows brands to match data from shopper loyalty programmes with individual Facebook profiles in order to connect Facebook advertisers more effectively to audiences that buy certain products or services. The "sharing", "friending", and "liking" of Facebook are facilitators of commercial connectivity in a global corporate sphere. Facebook connects the globe but does so on the terms of Facebook: "if the world lets Facebook define the norms for sociality online, it will build a world powered by Facebook" (van Dijck, 2013: 67).

Perspectives on global online communication

The evolutionary perspective

This perspective raises serious concerns about global communication online. Our brains are most functional at the relatively low speed that was characteristic for savannah life. If the hunters could cope with the speed of a lion, they had a good chance of surviving. And in those times, the crucial factor was that you could run faster than your fellow-hunters, who were also trying to escape the lion's meal. Today's digital technologies develop at an exponential rate and thus exceed the limits of our bio-brains. This confronts us with a crisis point in cultural evolution. The environment is too fast and too complex for our stone age mind and we can only exploit the Internet galaxy optimally if we expand our bio-brain: an otherwise impressive system, but it is too slow, operates on too few tracks simultaneously, and it is limited in memory and in patterning. The options are for our bio-brain to catch up with technological invention, slow down the rate of technological development or expand our bio-brain with Artificial Intelligence. According to Ray Kurzweil, the ultimate solution has to be the integration of virtual intelligence with our biological system (Kurzweil, 2005).

Herewith, we meet with the challenges of the so-called "convergence technology", which will be discussed in the next chapter on the futures of global communication.

The complexity perspective

Digital systems are usually very complex. This complexity causes unexpected effects because the systems may do things they were not instructed to do. An illustration was the anti-theft detectors in shops that reprogrammed customers' pacemakers, with sometimes fatal consequences.

Can software be less complex? Simpler software is of course possible, but this will diminish the number of functions the systems may perform. If users demand more of their ovens, washing machines, PCs, cockpit-systems, control panels for nuclear reactors, etc., this increases the complexity of operating systems and thus the chances of failure. Even when users do not need all the functions their dishwashers may have, the manufacturers just build them into their systems and suggest a superior quality. Systems may also be so complicated and so user-unfriendly that this causes errors in their use. If, however, systems are made more user-friendly, their security will normally diminish. The system would then, for example, not require that – upon receiving an error message – the user checks all the data put into it before retrial. The protection of complex systems makes systems even more complex. If a system is to anticipate all possible errors, the complexity will inevitably increase. The more complex a system is, the more difficult it becomes to foresee all possible errors. As complexity increases, the margin for surprises also grows.

An additional problem is that software usually steers systems which consist of parts that are interrelated and that influence each other. If one part malfunctions, the whole system may be affected. One of the many components of an electronic system may be a weak element in the chain that impacts the quality of the total system. It is also impossible to predict how components that by themselves may be safe will function when they form a system. Even the application of proven software offers no guarantee for reliability since software that operates in a new system may behave in unexpected ways.

There is a strong suggestion in many writings about emerging forms of online communication that the possibilities of new network technologies would create more communicative equality than former information and communication technologies did. Let us take a closer look at such optimistic expectations.

What would that equality imply?

In general terms there should be equality of access to infrastructures in terms of financial resources and management capability. Here it is important to remember that there was a tendency in the World Summit on the Information Society debates to treat the digital divide mainly as a matter of the globally skewed distribution of information and communication resources. The divide was not primarily seen as a dimension of the overall global "development divide". Since this bigger problem was not seriously addressed, a romantic fallacy prevailed which proposed that the resolution of information/communication problems, and the bridging of knowledge gaps or inequalities of access to technologies, can contribute to the solution of the world's most urgent and explosive socio-economic inequities. This isolated the digital divide from the broader problem of the development divide. In reality, the digital divide is not more than one of the many manifestations of the unequal allocation of both material and immaterial resources in the world, both between and within societies. Its solution has little to do with information, communication, or new network technologies.

An important requirement of the egalitarian perspective is the equal distribution of "information capital". The French sociologist Pierre Bourdieu (1985) has proposed that the position of social actors is not only determined by economic capital, but also by cultural, social, and symbolic capital. Cultural capital is made up of features and skills as knowledge about wines, fine arts, music and literature, good manners, and mastery of foreign languages. Social capital is based upon the social networks that people develop. Symbolic capital represents social prestige and reputation. To these forms of capital, the category of "information capital" should be added (Hamelink, 2000). This concept embraces the financial capacity to pay for network usage and information services, the technical ability to handle network infrastructures, the intellectual capacity to filter and evaluate information, but also the motivation to actively look for information and the skill to translate information into social practice. Just like other forms of capital, information capital is unequally distributed across societies. Its more egalitarian distribution would require an extensive programme of education, training, and conscientization. To just have more "surfers" on the Web does not mean information capital is more equally distributed.

In addition to these requirements of the egalitarian perspective, there should also be equality in the distribution of disadvantages. An fairly common assumption about information and communication technologies is that they have mainly benign effects and that these will be equally distributed. Chapter 8 on inequality and development communication addressed this fallacious assumption.

Note

1. For the history of the internet, see Castells, M. (2001). *The Internet Galaxy: Reflections on the Internet, Business and Society*. Oxford: Oxford University Press. pp. 10–17. For sources on Internet statistics and geography, see www.internet-worldstats.com/stats.htm, www.icann.com, www.isoc.org, www.nua.ie/sirveys/ how_many_online/methodology, www.cybergeography.org/atlas, www.zooknic. com, www.alexa.com

Reading spotlight

Internet

Castells, M. (2001). *The Internet Galaxy: Reflections on the Internet, Business and Society*. Oxford: Oxford University Press.
> "The Internet is the fabric of our lives ... the technological basis for the organizational form of the Information Age: the network" (p.1). "The Internet is a communication medium that allows, for the first time, the communication of many to many, in chosen time, on a global scale"(p. 2).

Morozov, E. (2011). *The Net Delusion: How Not to Liberate the World*. London: Penguin Books.
> The author demystifies the Internet and argues that the freedom of the internet is a delusion and that cybertechnology did not democratise the world. Actually, the Internet is a popular tool of repressive governments as it can be used for surveillance, propaganda and censorship. Facebook and Twitter are very helpful to the cause of oppressive governments.

Slevin, J. (2000). *The Internet and Society*. Cambridge: Polity Press.
> The author offers an easily accessible critical analysis of the impact of the Internet to modern culture. In the book many concrete examples of the use of the Internet are given

to illustrate the examination of such topics as globalization, publicness and regulation. Essential in the text are reflections on the management of risk and uncertainty.

Online resources

Visit the book's companion website at **https://study.sagepub.com/hamelink** to watch the author discussing the theme of this chapter: **Global Communication Online**

Visit the book's companion website at **https://study.sagepub.com/hamelink** to access the following journal articles free of charge:

Ali, S.R. and Fahmy, S. (2013). Gatekeeping and citizen journalism: the use of social media during the recent uprisings in Iran, Egypt, and Libya. *Media, War & Conflict*, 6(1): 55–69.

Dong, F. (2012). Controlling the internet in China: the real story. *Convergence*, 18(4): 403–425.

Himmelboim, I. (2011). Civil society and online political discourse: the network structure of unrestricted discussions. *Communication Research*, 38(5): 634–659.

Lauer, J. (2012). Surveillance history and the history of new media: an evidential paradigm. *New Media & Society*, 14(4): 566–582.

Quandt, Th. (2012). What's left of trust in a network society? An evolutionary model and critical discussion of trust and societal communication. *European Journal of Communication*, 27(1): 7–21.

Wang, H., Chung, J.E., Park, N., McLaughlin, M.L. and Fulk, J. (2012). Understanding online community participation. *Communication Research*, 39(6): 781–801.

Westlund, O. (2010). New(s) functions for the mobile: a cross-cultural study. *New Media & Society*, 12(1): 91–108.

Further reading

Andrejevic, M. (2007). *iSpy: Surveillance and Power in the Interactive Era*. Lawrence, KS: University Press of Kansas.

Braman, S. (2010). Legal globalization and the public sphere. In Gripsrud, J. and Dijck, J. van (eds), *The Culture of Connectivity: A Critical History of Social Media*. Oxford: Oxford University Press.

Burgess, J. and Green, J. (2009). *YouTube*. Cambridge: Polity Press.

Dijk, J.A.G.M. van (2012). *The Network Society*. London: Sage.

Dutton, W. (1999). *Society on the Line: Information Politics in the Digital Age*. Oxford, Oxford University Press.

Gripsrud, J. and Moe, H. (eds) (2010). *The Digital Public Sphere: Challenges for Media Policy*. Göteborg: Nordicom, University of Gothenburg.

Hamelink, C.J. (2000). *The Ethics of Cyberspace*. London: Sage.

Harcourt, W. (ed.) (1999). *Women@internet: Creating New Cultures in Cyberspace*. London: Zed Books.

Peitz, M. and Waldfogel, J. (eds) (2012). *The Oxford Handbook of the Digital Economy*. Oxford: Oxford University Press.

RESEARCH ASSIGNMENT

YouTube was founded in 2000 as a platform for content, not as a producer of content. YouTube may be participatory but is it also diverse? Is it racially diverse? "YouTube pushes up content which receives support from users. While such mechanisms seem democratic, they have the effect of hiding minority perspectives". (Burgess and Green, 2009: 124)

Analyze the supply of minority information provided through YouTube. Does this information reach majority audiences?

How would you methodologically approach these issues?

Marshall McLuhan challenged our notions of the role of media in modern societies and gave us new insights on the human capacity of perception.

Marshall McLuhan (1911–1980)

During his professorship at St Michaels College at the University of Toronto, McLuhan met Harold Innis and adopted Innis' ideas about the impact of the developments in communication media on human history. In this time he also developed his own ideas about media as extensions of human capacities of perception. In 1963 he was invited by the University of Toronto to establish a Center for Culture and Technology. In 1964 he published the book that brought him wide recognition, *Understanding Media*. He became, according to the *San Francisco Chronicle*, "the hottest academic property around".

At the core of his work is the analysis of how human perception changes as a result of the transition from a manual-technical typographic culture to an audio-visual electronic culture. In his book, *The Medium is the Message* (with Q. Fiore and J. Angel, 1967), he wrote that the extension of our capacity of perception through media changes us. With the medium of television, a new non-linear cognitive structure developed that helps our understanding of a complex world. Whereas print media create distance between people, the electronic media bring people in touch with each other. Television will lead to new international relations, national borders will wither away, and the world will become a "global village".

His most well-known aphorism was "The medium is the message", meaning that the impact of media upon society is the consequence of their specific nature rather than of their content. Media are either "cool" (the user plays a crucial role: for example, in telephone or television) or "hot" (the user has little to add: for example, in photos or radio).

(Continued)

(Continued)

The most important sources for the study of global communication are: *Understanding Media* (1964); *Culture is Our Business* (1970); and *The Global Village* (1988).

For the study of global communication, Marshall McLuhan taught us to always critically reflect, to be creative, and courageous as well as caring.

This concluding chapter will examine three themes:

- Futures
- Challenges
- Ethics

If you were to attend the conferences on the World Future Society, where professionals from many disciplines meet to develop foresight, innovation, and strategy, you would find that media and communication scholars are in short supply, if they participate at all. Few of the curricula in communication studies deal seriously with future studies. However, most of what will happen to communication processes and communication institutions will obviously occur in the future. The field of future studies is today no longer the stage of totally non-plausible projections but is developing into an incredibly rich domain of serious methodological and theoretical thinking about the future. Global communication studies could find inspiration from a conversation in *Through the Looking Glass* where Alice says, "I can't remember things before they happen" and the White Queen comments that "It's a poor sort of memory that only works backwards" (Lewis Carroll, 1865/1988: 254). It is an important challenge for communication studies to "remember the future" and to incorporate future studies into teaching and research.

To complete the book I will present the key challenges for the study of global communication – as they emerged from the preceding chapters – and will discuss a possible approach from a global ethics view for global communication.

Futures

Most of us are concerned about the future. We want to know what will happen next. We avidly read forecasts by experts on population explosions, climate changes, imminent wars, and economic crises. The future is important for us because, as Einstein once remarked, "I intend to live in it!" The future is the only part of human life we can do something about. The past has gone and the present is, as we speak, already past. The future is the only time in life that you can try to change. What is irritating about the future is the uncertainty. Most human beings have difficulties with uncertainty. In an increasingly complex world we would prefer to have knowledge about what is in store for us and we find it unsettling to admit that we are ignorant about the future. Therefore, we are inclined to make forecasts and to believe forecasts, especially those that are produced by experts.

Can we forecast the future?

Is there a way to remember the future? Can communication studies help us to remember the future and thus be better prepared for it so that we are not all the time taken by surprise. How can we provide useful knowledge for decision-making about the future?

Most efforts at forecasting in the field of communication can be criticized from several angles. Here are some critical footnotes.[1]

Forecasting often departs from an inductivist base. It is guided by the assumption that one can make statements about the future on the basis of a limited number of observations in the past. Against this inductivism, David Hume proposed in his treatise on human nature that there is no logical argument for the conclusion that phenomena we have no knowledge about would resemble those we do know about (Hume, 1739/1975). Inductivism has to assume an inherent continuity of the historical process. It forecasts the future with linear extrapolations based upon inductive reasoning. It needs to accept that history is a process of continuity and that there are unalterable laws of historical destiny. Such laws may be formulated by the physical sciences for the regularities in the physical environment, but there is no empirical indication that similar regularities are valid to the social environment.

Certainly, there are trends to be observed in human social history, but these are distinct from natural laws that determine the movement of a society and thus provide a valid prediction about society's future. Trends depend upon the specific configuration of historical conditions which themselves are not unequivocally determined. It is possible to establish correlations between trends and historical conditions, but these cannot in any way guarantee that a prediction based upon them is valid. This is caused by another flaw in the forecasting of social developments: the poverty of social scientific theory.

It is possible to provide a theoretical explanation for the relationship between certain trends and certain historical conditions. However, if one refuses the notion of unyielding laws in the historical process, any explanation can be contested. A characteristic of social scientific theories is that they are "underdetermined", that is, there are always several theoretical perspectives that concur with the empirical observation of social reality (Harding, 1978). This implies that empirical observation does not provide an arbitration among divergent theories.

The explanatory poverty of social scientific theory invalidates technology forecasting because this is based upon the assumption of the possibility of a valid explanation of the modes of interaction between technology and society. There is no theoretical perspective on technology and society available that could provide the basis for a solid prediction about their future interaction. Given the essential contestability of theory in the social sciences, there is no prospect of such a prediction emerging shortly, either. This may be disguised by the sophisticated nature of some forecasting techniques, but this basic flaw makes them no better than ancient astrology.

Forecasts have a tendency to rely on expert opinions. However, this may be a risky business since predictions by experts are often wrong (Cerf and Navaskym, 1984; Garner, 2011). Illustrative are the cases of Albert Einstein, who was convinced (in 1932) that nuclear energy was impossible; of Thomas Alva Edison, who claimed (in 1880) that the phonograph had no commercial value; of Lord Kelvin, the famous mathematician and president of the British Royal Society, who announced (in 1878) that radio had absolutely no future; or Paul Ehrlich's prediction of massive famines in the 1970s (Ehrlich, 1969). One problem with experts is that they tend to be so confident about their opinions that they hardly listen to criticism and focus too much on one idea only. There are the experts that media love most: "The sort who delivers quality sound bites and compelling stories. The sort who doesn't bother with complications, caveats, and uncertainties. The sort who has One Big idea. Yes, the sort of expert typically found in the media is most likely to be wrong" (Garner, 2011: 27).

Communication and information technology forecasting is based upon a social model in which technology is an independent variable, and social effect is a dependent variable. This does not take into account that the social accommodation to an artefact itself is conditioned by a variety of social factors. Consequently, what emerges as an effect may not be a consequence of the technology at all. The interaction between social conditions and artefacts (that themselves stem from these conditions) implies a complex chain process of unpredictable outcomes and consequences. The difficulty starts with the conception of technology and society as separate phenomena. This is equally as unwarranted and unproductive as the separation of such variables as crime and society or television behaviour versus other behaviour. In all such cases, social research tends to construct connections between variables that are artificially created in the first place.

As was already observed in Chapter 1, part of the contemporary context of global communication is the proliferation of serious risks. It would therefore seem advisable to engage in future risk evaluation. Developments in global communication confront us with the need to weigh present benefits against future risks. There are, however, a number of difficult problems with the use of risk analysis. There is the implied suggestion that the causes of undesirable events can be known and that the probability of their occurrence can be estimated – assuming that we could identify all or most of the events that could stem from particular choices in the politics of global communications. The question then is how good are human beings at the estimation of probabilities? Even if we were good at estimating probabilities, we would also have to be good at assessing the utilities of various consequences.

Risk can be seen as the index of the probability that an undesirable consequence may occur. The evaluation of risk is pertinent because choices (even transactional choices) always entail risk, that is, an above-zero possibility that the preferred course of action does not lead to the objective, that the outcome may be unexpected, and that the consequences may be undesirable. The main concerns of risk analysis have been the social hazards in fields such as health, occupational safety, and environment.

Risky choices are often made by small groups, although they may affect large collectivities. This has led to various modalities of risk evaluation, such as governmental commissions, public advisory boards, and referenda. In its various modes, risk evaluation performs three functions: (a) regulatory (the definition of standards); (b) political (the reconciliation of different interests); and (c) legitimation (the justification of choices already made).

Broadly speaking, risk evaluation can be conceived in a dualistic or a holistic manner. The dualistic mode proposes that risk problems have objective components and subjective components. The objective components are scientific observations that are value-free and are the domain of experts. The subjective components are the policy choices that are guided by social values. This two-pronged process involves two sets of decision-makers. The holistic mode argues, against this position, that facts and values cannot be separated. Also, the expert's analysis of the facts is laden with value judgments, and even the facts themselves are constructs based on preconceived visions of reality. On the methodological level, risk evaluation proceeds either as risk estimation or as risk assessment.

Risk estimation is the measurement of the probability of the occurrence of risks and their magnitude. These probabilities can be based on the past and/or present occurrence of events. The factual occurrence of an event is taken as the basis for projection, for example, the number of victims in plane crashes per year or the number of lethal car accidents per 100,000 population in a country. Probabilities can also be based upon the subjective judgment of experts or lay people. The key notion is probability. The basic assumption is that it is possible to assign a numerical value to the probability of the occurrence of an event.

One source of probability is the observed frequency of events. This is often used in so-called fault-tree analyses, in which the possible failures of a system are listed, branching out into ever further detailed failures that may cause higher-order failures. The mirror technique to this backward analysis is the so-called event-tree analysis, which starts with an initial event and identifies, forward, possible outcomes and consequences. Based upon a known frequency analysis, probabilities can be assigned to the failure of the system components and to the simultaneous failure of various components.

Another source are theoretical probabilities. Going beyond the extrapolation from past events, probabilities are, in this case, based upon scientific theory. This involves the complexity of assigning probability value to the level of the correctness of theories when, as often happens to be the case, a field has several competing theories to offer. The problem is that here are no impartial judges. Moreover, as Dagfinn Follesdal (quoted in Elster, 1983: 198) suggests, the larger the number of competing theories, the larger the probability that they are all false. Probabilities can also be subjective. This assumes that experts and occasionally, lay people can estimate with reasonable reliability the probable occurrence of events. This, in turn, assumes that in such cases people do not operate in complete ignorance and that their estimates are calibrated, that is, that there is a similarity between their assigned probabilities and the actual occurrences of events.

The assessment of risks aims at the identification of acceptable levels of risk. It involves the ranking of risks according to a hierarchy of social values and implies a degree of social consensus about these rankings. In the ranking of future risks the following techniques are employed:

- Revealed preferences. On the basis of statistical data, observations are made about the kinds of risks people take and accept. An attempt is made to identify the internalized cost–benefit analysis a society has made in the past. This assumes that what was valid in the past will also be true in the future.
- Expressed preferences. People are asked their opinions about risks through questionnaires and interviews. This assumes that people fully understand the questions they respond to, that they know what they want, and that their responses are consistent. There also has to be the assumption that attitude measurement tells us something about people's actual behaviour.
- Cost–benefit analysis. This implies the assigning of probabilities to the occurrence of risks and the estimation of their costs in some market measure. The same is done for the likely benefits of desirable consequences of choices. On this basis, a cost–benefit ratio is calculated. Cost–benefit analysis assumes that all outcomes and consequences can be known, that probability assignments are valid, and that costs versus benefits can be translated into monetary terms. As a solution to unreliable probability estimates, a technique called sensitivity analysis is offered which makes it possible to take account of possible errors. This is done through estimating outcomes when varying the levels of probability, for example, by considering what the difference would be if there was a 20 per cent error (Slovic and Fischoff, 1980).

In a somewhat more elaborate format, cost–benefit analysis is also called decision analysis. This is better suited to deal with costs and benefits that cannot be put in monetary terms and in situations which have multiple alternative courses of action. Decision analysis first identifies possible courses of action, then the utility value of various outcomes is determined, and the probability of conditions under which outcomes occur is estimated. The outcome with the highest expected value is chosen. To detail the multiple options, fault trees or event trees can be used. The probability assessments are based on the assumptions mentioned earlier. The utility estimates do assume that people know what they prefer, that they subscribe to coherent value systems, and that they are not trapped by the manner in which a problem has been framed.

Risk evaluation would seem pertinent to the global application of digital technology. The technology is complicated and difficult to understand for lay people. Adverse events of some magnitude may have a low probability of occurrence but, if they occur, the consequences may be extremely hazardous to society. A problem with the application of risk evaluation is the suggestion that the causes of undesirable events can be identified. Actually, risk evaluation only makes sense if all risks can be known and the probability of their occurrence can be estimated. This ignores the possibility of unanticipated risks. It may be, however, that truly massive risks belong to the category of the non-imaginary. Risk evaluation cannot really deal with the representation of the unthinkable.

The technique for detailing with all the possible factors leading to a fault is the fault-tree analysis. However, this decision-analytical tool has serious shortcomings. A common problem are the errors caused by elements that were left out, the omission of which even experts did not notice. Even the most detailed fault tree cannot deal with all the possible contingencies. And exactly these may turn out to be the cause of the great disaster. If one analyzes disasters, such as Bhopal, Harrisburg, Chernobyl, or major crashes, the cause is often a convergence of unthinkable factors. The disaster that can be predicted rarely occurs. Accidents are caused by failures that were absolutely "impossible". The two totally independent systems did turn out to be interdependent. Forty extremely small, insignificant things went wrong in the same time span and all converged to cause a major calamity. This is very realistic in large and complex systems for which the only valid law is indeed Murphy's famous law that if anything can go wrong, it will. And specifically, with complex systems, experts do not really know how hundreds of thousands of components will influence each other under varying conditions over long periods of time. Moreover, a crucial cause of faults is human error, which can hardly (or not at all) be foreseen. If the probability estimation of technical failure is very difficult and error-ridden, the calculation of human error is practically impossible, given the numerous factors that influence human behaviour. Let us assume we could identify all or most of the events that could stem from a particular technology choice. The next question would then be how good are human beings at the estimation of probabilities?

The simplest problem would seem to be the approach by objective probabilities. This is based on the occurrence of known events. This assumes that data about such factual occurrences are correct, and it assumes that choices of data can be value free. The choice of any set of data, however, reveals some preconceived notion and implies a value judgment. For example, crises in traffic may be estimated based upon the numbers of deaths or may include cases of seriously injured and, among those, cases of lifelong handicaps may be included or excluded. These choices affect the outcome considerably. In the calculation of probability based on past occurrences, a choice has to be made on the unit of measurement. Both the choices of a time frame or of the comparative figure (e.g. per 100,000 population) are arbitrary. The decision to base risk evaluation in air traffic on crash victims over the past 10 years per 100,000 inhabitants of a country is merely a subjective preference. Any attempt to justify such a choice objectively is utterly misleading.

Many risk analyses are based upon subjective probabilities. The problem with them is that both experts and lay people turn out to be very bad at the job. In judging probabilities, people are consistently misled by the heuristic tricks they apply in their estimation. Like in the question of whether cause A will lead to event B, the probability is a causal connection judged to be larger, the more similar A and B are. This neglects prior base-rate frequencies, such as traffic accidents. Another judgmental heuristic is the gambler's fallacy. This is the

belief that, after a long series of event A, the chance of occurrence of B increases significantly. Also, the availability of some event (e.g. through mass media publicity) influences
the estimation of the probability of its occurrence. Sensationalizing certain accidents in
newspapers will lead people to estimate the probability of their occurrence as much higher
than for accidents they hear less about. Another important factor is the strong tendency for
people to underestimate the probability of failure in complex systems. Even if the failure
chance of one component is considered high, people will estimate the likelihood of the
overall system failing as very low. This also raises the issue of how to deal with the very low
probability of an event that, at its occurrence, is extremely serious. This is difficult because
even low probabilities will increase over time. An event which has a probability of occurring once in 100 years sees its probability over those 100 years increase some 63 per cent.
However, the tendency is not to take low probabilities very seriously. Very low probabilities
may easily be underestimated and consequently may totally disappear.

As psychological research demonstrates, people are in general risk-averse. This leads
to neglect of low probabilities or to an overweighing of such unlikely losses that extensive risk-averse behaviour and related measures may be implemented, which lead to the
neglect of much more likely causes of failure. Also deceptive is the fact that people tend to
systematically underestimate personal risk. They prefer to believe that they are immune to
disaster. It is always some other airplane that may crash and some other driver that dies in
an accident. Related to this is the observation that people overestimate their own talents.
Many car drivers think they are pretty good drivers.

Even if people were very good at estimating probabilities, they would also have to be
good at assessing the utilities of various consequences. This evidently assumes that people
know their preferences and treat them consistently.

The first problem here is that in any society there is substantial disagreement among
experts and lay people over what constitutes risk and how acceptable risks are. The assessment of risk would imply some a priori consensus on the basis of which risks could be
ranked. The perception of risk is, as Mary Douglas and Aaron Wildavsky (1983: 8) claim, a
social process: "Each form of social life has its own typical risk portfolio."

Moreover, in risk assessment, people would be asked to rank preferences and the
responses could easily be determined by the framing of the questions. Questions framed in
different ways elicit very different responses. Additionally, there is the question of whether
or not people do understand what they are being asked to respond to. This is important
because research findings suggest that interviewees also tend to provide answers on topics
they really know nothing about. This situation is compounded by the fact that opinions
also tend to be stronger the less someone knows about the topic. Further, people are often
unclear about what they want and err about their own preferences.

The estimation of utilities is also influenced by human risk behaviour. There is a general risk aversion which leads to an underestimation of the utility of a reduced probability
of a hazard compared to the complete elimination of that hazard. Equally, people tend

to overestimate the negative utility of highly unlikely losses. This explains the success of insurance companies. If people were to calculate the expected value of risks versus the cost of premiums, they might easily conclude to buy less insurance. However, their subjective values dominate and they agree to pay high premiums for the profit of the companies. People are particularly risk-averse when they stand to gain important benefits or when they are confronted with unlikely losses. They may turn out to be risk-seeking, however, when they stand to lose considerably or when they are confronted with unlikely benefits. This risk behaviour influences the ways in which people assess values in risky situations. Even if people could coherently assign utility values, there would have to be a process of weighing. The eventual choice, in order to be justifiable, would have to be based on comparing risk utilities with gain utilities. Apart from all the other assumptions, this introduces the problem of the skewed distribution of risks and benefits. For those to whom benefits may accrue, the risks will seem less significant. This makes any cost–benefit calculation a dubious proposition because any judgment of costs is strongly biased by the prospect of likely benefits. The better the benefit prospect, the more the cost will be neglected. This is further biased because of people's tendency to overrate benefits because they can be more easily imagined than costs (Fischoff et al., 1981).

The assessment of future impacts of technology

The origin of technology assessment is a concern about the future social impact of advanced technology. In particular, the development of supersonic air travel and the problems of environmental pollution led the US Congress in 1982 to establish the Office of Technology Assessment (OTA). The principal idea was that, instead of finding harmful effects after the introduction of technology, such effects would be forecast in extensive studies and consequently be avoided. "The fear of technology would be sublimated into a positive act of will to avoid unwanted effects by foreseeing them. Foresight would substitute hindsight" (Braun, 1984: 98).

Emilio Daddario, the first director of the OTA, defined technology assessment as "...a form of policy research which provides a balanced appraisal to the policymaker. Ideally, it is a system to ask the right questions and obtain correct and timely answers. It identifies policy issues, assesses the impact of alternative courses of action, and presents findings. It is a method of analysis that systematically appraises the nature, significance, and merit of a technological progress" (quoted in Hetman, 1973: 54).

There are many other definitions of technology assessment (TA) but, as Ernst Braun concludes, "Whatever the precise wording of the definition, TA is generally understood to mean an attempt to discover all the ramifications and effects which a technology is likely to have when it is in full use at some future date" (Braun, 1984: 100). Crucial to TA is the generation of information for decision-makers, "in the hope that better information will lead to better decisions" (Braun, 1984: 105).

Specific techniques employed in TA are the Delphi technique, scenario writing, cross-impact analysis, or trend extrapolation. The Delphi technique is a communications process among experts aimed at establishing a consensus opinion about the future. It involves several rounds of questioning with regular feedback. The participants are anonymous. After each round, the panellists can revise their estimates on the basis of the information provided by others. Anonymity avoids the traps of group decision-making. Basic to the Delphi technique is forecasting on the basis of subjective probabilities.

In scenario writing, descriptions of different future developments are elaborated. This approach takes account of the implications of alternative futures and allows the development of contingency plans. Usually, future developments under various conditions are described in the form of "if Condition A..., then Future B..." statements. In scenario writing, several forecasting techniques can be applied.

Cross-impact analysis analyzes the interacting impact of various trends. It can be employed to analyze the impact of one future development upon another development. Its basic assumption is that a model of the future can be developed and that models provide insights into the future impact of choices.

Trend extrapolation is a forecasting technique based upon mathematical calculations. It determines the future of a variable based on the past values of the variable. It basically uses time-series data and plots them as value versus time. The assumption is that past and present trends in the future will develop in the same direction and at the same rate as in the past.

In all cases, the technique has three dimensions: it can be exploratory, speculative, or normative. The exploratory projection of trends is based on the assumption that the future is surprise free and on the expectation that a consequence in the past will replicate itself in the future. The speculative technique is based on the calculation of probability and implies the related assumptions. The normative technique describes desirable futures in scenarios.

To all these reservations about the meaningfulness of forecasting we need to add the problem of living in complex environments. The world around us – and certainly the world of global communication – can be described with the metaphor of the tropical rainforest. All elements of the forest are interrelated, there are no linear processes, and small causes may have massive consequences. This combination of interdependence, non-linearity and the Butterfly Effect[2] challenges the limited capacity of the human brain (in itself a complex system in which some 23 billion neurons interact in numerous and unpredictable variations) to deal with complexity as it is risk-averse, prone to make mistakes, and often misleads human perception.

The question that now emerges is can we prepare – without achieving perfect certainty – for surprises?

Scenarios for plausible futures

What method can we use to base decisions upon (in politics, in business, or in the military) that take the future into account? One possibility is to write stories about plausible, possible futures. The initiators of this approach to the future were Hermann Kahn and Gaston Berger. In the 1950s Kahn developed for the US military stories about what would happen in the case of a nuclear war between the USA and the USSR. He called them the "what-if" stories scenarios. In Paris, Gaston Berger created La Prospective, a centre for studies of the future, and designed normative scenarios for public policy. In his thinking, the future had to be invented as something new and unpredictable. The development of future scenario building really began in the 1960s and came into full swing in the 1970s when the emergence of the OPEC cartel and the environmentalism movement made future thinking particularly important for energy companies such as Shell.

Writing plausible scenarios for global communication futures

An exercise in scenario writing explores what might be plausible answers to the question: what could happen in the future? What decisions will have to be made for the future in the domains of commerce and economy, law and politics, public advocacy and social intervention. The crucial element of the exercise is learning how to make decisions about the future.

A simple method for the writing of scenarios is to select (after a good deal of discussion and analysis) two key variables (these could be political, social, economic, or cultural) that seem essential in future developments. Once these have been placed on two axes, four stories about possible futures emerge. Now try to establish what could be your preferred versus your undesirable futures.

Preferred future scenarios describe desirable future outcomes. For these scenarios the leading question is: If things went well, being optimistic but realistic, what would the desirable outcomes look like? What actions (e.g. more regulation versus deregulation?) would have to be taken to achieve such desirable future outcomes? It is important in this scenario to make underlying values and norms explicit and argue their relevance. If one was to develop a preferred futures scenario for the mega metropolitan cities of the future, one could describe the optimistic vision as The Green City, where ecological concerns are dominant factors, material needs have been satisfied, and people enjoy peaceful human interaction, community solidarity, and egalitarian relations.

Undesirable futures are described in early-warning scenarios. These are intended to assist in contingency planning. What plans have to be prepared in case undesirable – even unlikely – outcomes are projected? For early-warning scenarios the leading question is:

If things went wrong, what developments and outcomes would the consultants worry about? It is important in this scenario that the negative developments and outcomes are coherently argued. This scenario needs an additional advice on how worst-case developments and outcomes may be prevented.

ILLUSTRATIONS OF GLOBAL COMMUNICATION SCENARIOS

1. The wired globe: towards an integrated planet

A scenario based upon extrapolation of present trends that continue, possibly in exponential ways. In the wired globe everyone is online, operates on fast digital tracks. Information and knowledge are extensified and are processed largely through artificial intelligence.

Current trends in global communication are towards increases in conflicts about basic resources (such as water), about tribal and religious identities, and about living in urban contexts. The ensuing confusion and anxiety will lead to strong demands for centralized authoritarian governance institutions that will largely operate along the lines of corporate management if they are not already themselves fully privatized.

2. The wired globe: towards a fragmented planet

A scenario based upon the assumption that exponential change will not occur as current trends flatten towards a global society characterized by decreasing levels of consumption, acceptance of cultural differences, formulation of individual responsibilities, and a techno-sceptical attitude that steers policies on information and communication technology. Crucial segments of public choice will be managed through widely accessed referenda.

The creation of plausible scenarios for possible futures is urgently needed in view of the major challenges that you as a student of global communication will have to reflect upon.

The major challenges for global communication futures

From McLuhan's thinking, existential questions emerge in connection with the extreme extensification of knowledge in areas such as nano-technology, artificial intelligence, robotics, biochemistry, and neuroscience. Will the acquisition of knowledge in the future predominantly occur through digital

---

> copying, pasting, and searching? There is a massive volume of knowledge
> available for the twenty-first-century person but how does this impact upon
> the intellectual capacity to understand ourselves better? Could it be that
> this capacity does not evolve at the same rate as the extensification of
> knowledge to intelligent tools? The ultimate consequence of this process
> could be that the carriers of knowledge are no longer human beings but
> intelligent artefacts. In this case, the human being loses his/her role as
> actor in future knowledge societies. Just like McLuhan predicted!

The most challenging concerns for the futures of global communication are as follows.

Global access to information and knowledge

There is an unprecedented growth of information and knowledge in today's world. However, millions of individuals and entire countries are not equipped to access and use these crucial resources. The ability to effectively process and use information and knowledge that are relevant to people's needs is inadequately developed across the world. There remains a highly unequal access to such essential information media as daily newspapers, radio receivers, TV sets, and the Internet. Information disparity exists between countries and regions, but also within most countries there are gaps that follow the frontiers of gender, age, ethnicity, social class, and the urban/rural divide. The current information/knowledge divide fits into the general patterns of social, economic, cultural, and environmental fractures between and within the world's countries. Serious obstacles need to be overcome. In shorthand, it can be stated that the whole project of broadening access to information and knowledge has little meaning if, in the next 10–15 years, the international community fails to make serious progress in the following areas: solving global poverty, creating basic literacy, providing facilities for primary and secondary education, providing special educational and technical resources for girls and women, retaining public interest information in the public domain, preventing that protection of intellectual property rights becomes an obstacle to the free flow of information, solving the problems of governmental and commercial censorship, providing global access to telecom infrastructures, creating sustainable information structures, and developing adequate programmes of information and knowledge management.

Global Billboard Society

Worldwide advertising has become ubiquitous. In many countries there are hardly any advertising-free zones left. In spite of the political declarations that we live in a Global Information/Knowledge Society, it seems more realistic to expect a Global Billboard Society!

Whatever its local variation, advertising proclaims to the world a single cultural standard: consumption fulfils people's basic aspirations, fun shopping is an essential cultural activity. It subjects the world's cultural differences to the dominance of a consumption-oriented lifestyle. A person's fundamental cultural identity is to be a consumer. Advertising teaches children around the world the values of materialism and the practices of consumerism. The dominant neo-liberal political agenda has a strong interest in the expansion of advertising. This implies, among others things, more commercial space in media (conventional mass media and the Internet), new target groups (especially children), more sponsorships (films, orchestras, exhibits), and more public places to be used for advertising (the ubiquitous outdoor billboards). If advertising can be seen as global commercial propaganda, there is also – worldwide – a strong propagandistic movement inspired by political interests. A highly professional breed of "perception managers" and "spin doctors" provides much of the fabricated and/or distorted information that the world's media broadcast to their audiences.

Global governance

It is problematic that the world's communication and cultural issues should be primarily discussed in a global trade forum, the World Trade Organization (WTO). The WTO is generally more focused on the trading interests of the major industrial countries than on the world's cultural interests. Most of its economic and financial rules are made by self-selected policy groups that exclude the majority of national governments and that consult only a select number of developing countries. The decision-making processes in these elite groups lack transparency, formal mechanisms of civil representation, or procedures for public accountability. It would be preferable to have an open global forum where all the stakeholders (government, business, civil society) can participate in shaping the world's common information/communication future. A lot of pressure from civil society organizations (CSOs) is needed to move the United Nations System in the direction of democratic governance structures that make common deliberation and decision-making possible.

The late American historian, Barbara Tuchman, argued in *The March of Folly* (1985) that human history can be described as a march of fools. This foolishness is particularly demonstrated in the unwillingness to learn from history. Human beings repeat the same mistakes throughout history and find it impossible to change course. Therefore, a real challenging issue for the governance of global communication is whether such global platforms as the United Nations can engage in critical reflection on all those laudable proposals and action plans that the UN General Assembly has adopted time and again but never implemented.

Global news

The provision of news raises the question of how informed or disinformed the global citizen will be. The development of global news networks such as CNN, BBC World Service and Al-Jazeera raised the prospect of a global public sphere in the sense of a space for rational and informed communication. As gaps in time and space shrank and news began to happen 24/7 and the citizens could always be there "on the spot" (a possibility strengthened by the development of online news), the optimism that global news flows and democratization are partners seemed very realistic. Interactive communication with news media emerged and readers could talk back to their newspaper. Access for large numbers of non-professionals became possible as thousands of blogs were run by non-journalists. A closer look, however, showed that global flows remained largely dominated by only a handful of voices and that the rampant commercialization of news stories formed an obstacle for the development of independent global news media. Yet, the appearance of Wikileaks brought back the expectation of the global news networks as the fourth estate: controlling worldwide the abuse of power.

Global participation

Do social media like YouTube create a participatory culture? What possibilities for participation do alternative sites for contestation in global communication offer? There are sites such as the Mideast Youth platform for a series of websites that provide an opportunity for young people to discuss matters that are largely taboo in the region, such as homosexuality, and that attract large numbers of visitors. Do such media have a sustainable future? Among the essential challenges are questions such as: Can a commercial enterprise such as YouTube accommodate the growing diversity in public participation? Can the scale and measure of present growth be maintained? Will the future of global communication be conversation (social networks) or distribution (broadcasting)? Will the funding (largely through advertising) for the social networks determine their contents? Can the pressures of big media in the field of copyright be resisted? What will happen with the growing popularity of local content in China and South Korea? What will be the result of competition from the growth of the distribution of user-generated content by not-for-profit institutions, such as the BBC or public libraries?

Money in global communication

Global flows of digital currency may undermine the state monopoly on currencies and facilitate the private issuing of money. Also, small savers can go off-shore with their financial transactions and escape governmental control. There could be an exodus from regulated retail banking to unregulated off-shore banking. Governmental control will demand Big Brother scenarios or threats of physical sanctions. Enforcing taxes in the digital age and securing privacy may be impossible! A possible scenario is that you have a stored-value card (like the prepaid phone card) on which you have a bank balance that you downloaded from an ATM teller that is the on-shore affiliate of the off-shore branch of a reputable Swiss bank.

Convergence technology and human communication

Possibly the most critical challenge is posed by the ways in which the exponential growth of convergence technology affects the ways in which human beings communicate.

Humans have an almost unlimited desire to communicate, even with angels, trees, and dolphins. The converging technologies promise to open up further opportunities to expand this communicative compulsion. Enormous benefits could be in store, such as the removal of all the obstacles that during most of human history limited the effectiveness of message transfer. Such obstacles were the restrictions of distance, speed, volume, and reliability. Another essential impediment to human communication across borders has always been the existence of different languages. The advent of communications steered by machine intelligence will almost certainly offer the solution of this problem through advanced speech recognition and instant translation. Although one may easily be carried away with such prospects, it needs to be realized that it is unlikely that the availability, accessibility, and affordability of these emerging technologies would be globally and equitably shared. Given the reality of unequal socio-economic positions in the world, one can foresee that such divides as the development divide, the information divide, and the digital divide will be succeeded by a convergence-divide. And, as with the other gaps, this divide will be exploited to consolidate positions of power and privilege.

What different modalities of impact on human communication could we possibly expect in the not too distant future? I will briefly discuss:

- human–machine communication
- machine-to-machine communication
- communication between living and deceased people
- brain-to-brain communication
- cross-species communication.

Human–machine communication

People will increasingly communicate with the assistance of machine intelligence and the machines will have ever more human features.

Developments in the converging technologies will produce machines with an intelligence that far exceeds human intellectual capabilities. In order to co-exist with these machines humans will have to learn to communicate by being gifted with superior intelligence. The deepest impact of this development will be the necessity to rethink the whole concept of what it means to be 'human'. As Bill Joy (2000) wonders, "Given the incredible power of these technologies, shouldn't we be asking how we can best coexist with them? And if our extinction is a likely, or even possible, outcome of our technological development, shouldn't we proceed with great caution?" A crucial question is whether humans are ready for a peaceful co-existence with such beings.

Machine-to-machine communication

Among the new forms of communication that humans will be exposed to is the communication among intelligent nanobots in our biological systems. The introduction of

248

machine intelligence in our biological systems implies the prospect of longevity and even immortality. "Billions of nanobots will travel through the bloodstream of our bodies and brains. In our bodies, they will destroy pathogens, correct DNA errors, eliminate toxins, and perform many tasks to enhance physical well-being. As a result, we will be able to live indefinitely without aging" (Kurzweil, 2005 43). The convergent technologies may well create a future, as Bill Joy argues, that does not need humans anymore. Humans in the world of convergence may still communicate with each other, but it may not matter anymore. How to deal with a new Copernican change that positions humans no longer at the centre of the universe?

Cyberimmortality

The development of the converging technologies might open up the possibility of communicating across the barrier of human mortality. Artificial intelligence technology is likely to make it possible that people continue their lives after death as archived personalities. "The Convergenists' agenda is aimed at improving human performance without limit, and many of the anticipated technological spin-offs would be useful for recording, preserving, and reanimating human personalities – ultimately creating cyberimmortality" (Bainbridge, 2006: 28). With this development, a realistic expectation would be that living people can communicate with persons that have died but are electronically "archived". This represents a challenging prospect for religious reflection. It is interesting to note that converging technologies have not yet caused a similar concern as human cloning has. It remains to be seen how religious leaders and theological experts will respond to humanoid, intelligent robots with the personality characteristics of people who have died.

Indicative for the nature of this development may be the observation of the strong emotional bonds that elderly lonesome people have with such intelligent artifacts as the Sony dog Aibo. Although Aibo is clearly a metallic toy, experiments demon-strate that people quickly grow attached to their electronic pet, with which they share problems and very private concerns. Imagine how they would relate to the deceased partner with whom communication remains possible and who would not only listen like the digital dog, but who would respond with advice and understanding as he or she did when still alive.

Telepathic communication

Converging technologies will make communication between human brains possible. As Kurzweil proposes "the age of telepathic communication is upon us" (Kurzweil, 2006: 43).

Communication between human brains and machine intelligence and between human brains may significantly alter the way human brains operate through the exponential expansion of our memory and cognitive capacities. An intriguing question is whether effective human communication is not largely influenced by our failing memories. Try to imagine that in human encounters we would have full recollection and cognition of all the interlocutors in the conversations we conduct.

Cross-species communication

Humans have demonstrated throughout history a tendency to treat non-human animals in very destructive ways. This has always been rationalized and legitimized by referring to the fundamental divides between the different species. This position has been reinforced by the impossibility of trans-human communication. We know that whales communicate with each other over great distances (over hundreds of miles) and with voluminous contents (anywhere between 1 and 10 million "bits" per 30 minutes). Humans cannot communicate with them, which makes killing them and industrially processing them easier. It is interesting to observe that when people can communicate (even in the sense of giving orders that are understood) with their pets, they are less inclined to murder and consume them. This would lead to the conclusion that human treatment of other sentient beings (animals and even plants) would change once communication – or at least hearing the "others" – is possible.

Research in photo-acoustics demonstrates that plants are not as silent as is commonly assumed. Most plants make sounds. If one registers – through advances audio-technology – the sounds of a rose that wakes up, there is a regular succession of chords that reminds the listener of Bach's toccatas (Berendt, 1987: 62). Biological research has also demonstrated that different sounds have a different impact upon the growth and well-being of plants.

It has also been empirically demonstrated that different types of music cause different crystal patterns in frozen water. It seems a realistic expectation that the further development of converging technologies will allow humans to hear sounds where they assumed only silence existed (like in the deep seas) and to produce sounds that are beneficial to other living beings. Admittedly, it is a very rudimentary basis for inter-species communication, but it is a beginning nevertheless!

The human dimension

We are already well on our way to losing the human dimension in many of our communication processes. Even the plain old telephone is increasingly going virtual and it is an ever rarer experience to talk to a live human being instead of communicating with a machine. Virtual voices welcome our telephone calls, direct us through a maze of numbers and options, tell us that all human operators are too busy, and when we are on the verge of strangling the virtual respondent, kindly thank us for our business. Is this still human communication? If it can be called communication at all, it certainly falls in the narrow category of the "transfer of messages" model and does not fit in a conception of communication as "interaction".

Can we still communicate in the sense of Martin Buber's relational communication? (Buber, 1958). What happens to human communication when all "I–Thou" relations are technically mediated? We will certainly expand and upgrade our communicative transmission practices, but can we ever listen to the "otherness" of the other in communication processes mediated by the converging technologies?

Solutions?

If we think this is an undesirable development, should we try to limit technological development? Can we limit "our pursuit of certain kinds of knowledge" (Joy, 2000)? In a modern world that is largely inspired by the Enlightenment ideals of human improvement through science and technology, this is difficult to imagine. The holy mantra of our era seems to be that knowledge in itself is good and that acquiring more knowledge is even better. And, indeed, the search for knowledge satisfies a fundamental human desire to "fly away from ignorance", as William Shakespeare elegantly put it.

However, as we acquire more knowledge, we should also become aware of the dark sides to an uncritical reverence for scientific and technological development. In the past decades science and technology brought humankind close to the destruction of the planet and the emerging converging technologies make the extinction of humanity a very real possibility. You may object that humans as individuals have a strong desire to survive. This may be true, but it does not guarantee that the collective of humans as a species will not be guided by an equally strong negligence towards its future. The nuclear arms race of recent history does not provide a very reassuring picture. Humankind has collectively a great capacity for irresponsible and destructive action. Technology has rarely ever been invented, developed, and applied under the guidance of normative, moral principles. Engineerability was and remains, in combination with military and commercial interest, the essential driving force. The question is whether we can still afford this in the twenty-first century? Should not the development of the converging technologies be tested against the human rights standards of human dignity, security and autonomy? If the human dimension is chosen as the normative yardstick, we would have to seriously consider the observation that the tools people make are rapidly outpacing their mental capacities. For their survival, human beings may not be very well equipped, but they are streetwise in designing constructs (such as languages, technologies) that compensate innate inadequacies.

Amid the impressive array of human cultural constructs the question comes up whether these may wander too far away from human nature. Could it be that the distance between construct and nature grows so big that what seemed a solution turns out to be a danger? The development of advanced, sophisticated armaments is a good illustration. Modern arms (such as computer-steered fighter planes) no longer match the human capacity to understand what we are doing and what the consequences may be. The fighter pilot is morally so distant from his victims that he may as well be playing a computer game rather than destroying human lives. But even if he tried to understand and reason morally about his acts, he could not possibly begin to imagine what the effects of his actions are. Whereas our minds still travel in the age of horse-drawn carriages and spears, our bodies travel in super-fast cars and airplanes, and we have the devastating power of nuclear arms at our disposal. Can minds catch up with bodies? The mind-boggling developments in science and technology inspired the belief that the rational, conscious, and free human mind that the Enlightenment projected was capable of dealing with these developments in a humanitarian way. This illusion was fundamentally challenged by the twentieth-century horrors of Auschwitz and Hiroshima. To regain the human dimension we have to contemplate how we could bring the different paces of mind and body into harmony. Maybe the aboriginals in Australia can help us by what they do during long journeys: before they reach the destination of their walks they take time for their souls to catch up with their bodies.

The challenge of the ethics of global communication

Whatever position you may have in relation to the futures of global communication, there can be little doubt that finding a humane perspective for your preferred future demands making moral choices. During our lives we constantly make choices and many of them have a moral dimension. This is the case when we have to make choices among conflicting moral principles, when our choices have significant impact on the well-being of others, or deviate strongly from prevailing moral standards.

We cannot leave the world of global communication without reflection on the right and the wrong in this field of study. All human societies have – to varying extents – moral intuitions about right versus wrong. Worldwide there are conflicts about moral judgments and great differences in resolving moral issues. In spite of the complexity of global moral disputes, all those involved, be they researchers, policymakers, practitioners or ordinary users, will have to engage with a continuous reiterative process of finding what – temporarily – can be identified as a best possible choice.

Kwame Appiah writes, "there are some values that are, and should be, universal just as there are lots of values that are, and must be, local" (2006: xxi). Since there is no way to reach a consensus on ranking these values, we should be open to "conversation between people from different ways of life" (Appiah, 2006: xxi). I found no better way to describe the core of global communication as the cosmopolitan conversation with strangers about our ways of life in order to find common futures that share human universals and that respect differences. Global communication (its technical infrastructure, its connectivity, and its contents) is in ethical perspective the project of a global conversation among strangers. This conversation is a moral challenge because of its post-colonial nature, the lessons to be learnt from differences, the tension between universalism and bounded nationality, and the public space the global conversation requires.

Post-colonial cosmopolitanism

The essential issue of cosmopolitanism is the conversation with the other. The question is how will this global conversation be conducted? On whose terms? Often the engagement with the other is managed by a dominant, missionary culture and thus remains a colonial adventure. A serious moral dialogue requires a post-colonial cosmopolitanism that accepts that others are different and yet equal in human dignity. A problem with the notion "post-colonialism" is that it might suggest that colonialism is past history. This may be true in the sense of direct administrative control by mother countries over exploited countries. However, in reality the key aspects of colonial rule continue to shape global relations of power. Most colonizers never really gave up and many of the colonized became accomplices in continued external domination. Efforts to "civilize" the savages and pagans abound under the umbrella of developmental interventions. In much global discourse, the Western image of how humanity should live continues to be standard. A sensible interpretation of the notion "post-colonial" refers to the intellectual space to interrogate what colonial regimes did and do to the minds and bodies of exploited people and investigate on what assumptions these regimes were based.[3] As Mohan Dutta (2011: 5) writes: "One of the key threads of the postcolonial approach to communicative processes is its examination of colonial discourses that circulate and reify the material inequities across the globe."

Differences

Kwame Appiah tells us that "…the cosmopolitan knows there is much to learn from our differences" (Appiah, 2006: xv). A moral dilemma that has great urgency in today's world is the question of how moral universalism and moral relativism can co-exist. Our world has a tremendous diversity in moral norms. This necessarily implies the difficult question of how tolerant and flexible we can be in the confrontation with differences in normative judgments. The universalist position would argue that moral standards, as codified in the Universal Declaration of Human Rights, have universal validity.[4] Philosophers as different as Immanuel Kant, David Hume, Jeremy Bentham, John Rawls, Jean-Paul Sartre, and Jürgen Habermas "agree that ethics is in some sense universal … that the justification of an ethical principle cannot be in terms of any partial or sectional group" (Singer, 1979: 11). There is, however, always the danger that universalism adopts a missionary and imperialist attitude by perceiving a preferred normative position as superior to all alternative positions. This represents a "colonial universalism" that imposes the moral judgments of the in-group on the members of the out-group and coerces "Them" to accept the standards of "Us", excludes Them from the dominant moral universe or teaches Them how to assimilate. This form of colonialism strengthens the relativist argument that all morality is relative to local cultural preferences. Attractive as moral relativism may seem, it may ultimately lead to moral indifference for events beyond the confines of a local catalogue of normative principles. This could imply that you can never criticize moral choices by people in other cultures and thus would have to condone whatever others do, including rape, murder, torture, and child abuse. The relativist position is rightly concerned about the respect due to differences in morality within and between societies. This cannot, however, absolve us from resolving pressing moral issues (such as poverty, health care, education, genocide, and climate change) in a way that supports a sustainable global society. Universalists and relativists need to engage in serious dialogue about the shift from a "colonial universalism" and an "indifferent relativism" towards a cosmopolitan sense of universalism and a caring sense of relativism.

For "cosmopolitan universalism" the principles of communal responsibility and collective welfare stress the need to accept reciprocal obligations among the members of a society. "Caring relativism" searches – while respecting differences in judgment – with compassion to deal with such common human experiences as suffering and death. It acknowledges a cross-cultural desire to avoid harm. Throughout the world's religious and ethical systems we find a powerful motivation to limit human suffering. The motive to avoid avoidable harm to others and to diminish people's suffering is a key concern in Confucianism, Taoism, Hinduism, Judaism, Christianity, and Islam.

?

How would a cosmopolitan universalism and a caring relativism cope with stories in the media that lead to serious clashes between those who defend freedom of opinion and those who defend the protection of religious values (use material on the Danish cartoon controversy in 2005; among other sources, see Jensen, 2010: 160–163).

Conversation as dialogue

Morality has a social nature and this implies that in moral choice-making there is the permanent need of a discursive, reiterative, and participatory process with all those involved. The optimal form for this process would seem the collective, inclusive discussion that searches for the best ideas and legitimate arguments. That is a non-combative procedure that makes progress in the moral dialogue while acknowledging the existence of basic differences.

Moral choice and moral intuition

How many times did you not wonder why the choice you intuitively made in situations often turned out to be the better one, even if rational consideration advised you to take a different route? We should realize that in many situations the choice we arrived at through rational processes is the lesser one. Unfortunately, it often escapes us how intuitive and seemingly irrational important choices are in our lives, which may range from the selection of a partner for life to the military invasion of a foreign country. That is because we often rationalize our emotion-driven choices after the fact and then begin to believe that these rationalizations were our real motives in the first place.

Taking our emotions and intuitions seriously, it is also good to realize that our basic moral intuitions already existed before we codified them in religious and legal instruments. We know from our cousins, the primates, that they act in line with fundamental values, such as cooperation (and reciprocal altruism), fairness (and a feeling of justice), reconciliation (and consolation) after conflict, and the capacity to empathize (and have compassion) (de Waal, 2013). In our deliberations on moral choice these intuitions may guide us through the complexities of today's and future global communication.

The global conversation requires global public space

Public spaces are all around us in the localities where we live (marketplaces, city halls, parks, and terraces). These are physical spaces that can be touched. Next to this, virtual spaces have developed – we can also meet albeit without touching – in cyberspace without recognition of time, place, and other constraints. An intriguing question remains in how far global communication infrastructures and processes facilitate the emergence of a genuine global public space. Just like the public marketplace is today around the world transformed into the private shopping mall, virtual spaces are most often domains whose infrastructures are controlled by private interests with impressive capabilities of surveillance and censorship. If a public space should not be under the control of private interests, can there be a genuinely public global virtual space? Here Robert W. McChesney helps us to understand the reality of that global space called the Internet. He suggests that "with enlightened public investments, the Internet can provide the greatest journalism and public space ever imagined". However, he adds, "left on their current course and driven by the needs of capital, digital technologies can be deployed in ways that are extraordinarily inimical to freedom, democracy, and anything remotely connected to the good life. Therefore, battles over the Internet are of central importance for all those seeking to build a better society" (McChesney, 2013: 232).

? "In a hybrid space like YouTube, it is often very difficult to determine what regimes of truth govern different genres of user-generated content. The goals of communicators can no longer be simply read off the channels of communication" (Burgess and Green, 2009: 122). How would you propose to deal with truth-finding on YouTube?

Post-scriptum

Here ends our journey along the various dimensions of global communication. There is much more to explore and investigate. My teacher's hope is that you will do that. Ask new questions, look with new eyes, and make discoveries. The best that seniors can do is to expect that juniors will move far beyond their knowledge and insights on their own way to a permanent global dialogue in which we share our similarities and our intriguing differences as cosmopolitan strangers. In this dialogue I do hope you will be guided by what Kwame Appiah calls "cosmopolitan curiosity".

Notes

1. The following text is largely based upon an earlier study on technology choice in C.J. Hamelink (1988). The Technology Gamble. Norwood: Ablex.
2. Meteorologist Edward Lorenz (1963 & 1969) developed a computer to study weather patterns and discovered that very small variations in initial conditions would result in very divergent patterns. He called this the Butterfly Effect: a butterfly in Brazil flapping the wings can after some time cause a tornado in Texas. He discovered that linear statistical models were not suited to measure non-linear atmospheric conditions. Predicting the weather of tomorrow may be possible but forecasts for a week or more are inevitably inaccurate.
3. Very helpful for an understanding of the post-colonial approach is the book by Childs and Williams (1997).
4. The United Nations World Conference on Human Rights in 1993 has reaffirmed the universality of human rights. The Final Declaration states "The universal nature of human rights is beyond question".

Reading spotlight

Ethics

Fortner, R.S. and Fackler, P.M. (eds) (2011). The Handbook of Global Communication and Media Ethics (Vols 1 and 2). Oxford: Blackwell Publishing.
This book brings together the contributions of some 60 scholars on media and communication ethics. It is a really unique project that instructs, challenges, provokes and teaches.

Hamelink, C.J. (2000). The Ethics of Cyberspace. London: Sage.
Denis McQuail wrote about this book "Cees Hamelink has written an indispensable pioneering guide to the moral maze of cyberspace. It is at the same time an informative,

critical and practical response to the global challenges of information communication technology for all who care about human rights and citizenship".

Future Studies

Schwartz, P. (1998). *The Art of the Long View: Planning for the Future in an Uncertain World*. New York: Wiley & Sons.

Schwartz provides the reader with essential tools for the art of scenario building. He describes new techniques for strategic visions as developed by the Royal Dutch Shell energy company, and uses his first-hand experience with many real-life scenarios.

Online resources

 Visit the book's companion website at **https://study.sagepub.com/hamelink** to watch the author discussing the theme of this chapter: **The Future of Global Communication**

Visit the book's companion website at **https://study.sagepub.com/hamelink** to access the following journal articles free of charge:

Humphreys, L. (2013). Mobile social media: future challenges and opportunities. *Mobile Media & Communication*, 1(1): 20–25.

Kurzweil, R. (2010). Merging with the machines: information technology, artificial intelligence, and the law of exponential growth. *World Future Review*, 2(1): 61–66.

Rao, S. and Wasserman, H. (2007). Global media ethics revisited: a postcolonial critique. *Global Media and Communication*, 3(1): 29–50.

Saniotis, A. (2009). Future brains: an exploration of human evolution in the 21st century and beyond. *World Future Review*, 1(3): 5–11.

Wasserman, H. and Rao, S. (2008). The glocalization of journalism ethics. *Journalism*, 9(2): 163–181.

Further reading

Bell, W. (1997). *Foundation of Future Studies*. New Brunswick, NJ: Transaction Books.

Genosko, G. (ed.) (2004). *Marshall McLuhan: Critical Evaluations in Cultural Theory*. London: Routledge.

Gordon, W.T. (1997). *McLuhan for Beginners*. New York: Writers and Readers Publishing.

Heijden, K. van der (1996). *Scenarios: The Art of Strategic Conversation*. New York: Wiley & Sons.

Hughes, B.B. (1999). *International Futures: Choices in the Face of Uncertainty*. Boulder, CO: Westview Press.

Kahn, H. (1976). *The Next Two Hundred Years*. New York: Quill.

Marchand, Ph. (1989). *Marshall McLuhan: The Medium and the Messenger*. Toronto: Random House of Canada.

Masini, E. (1994). *Why Futures Studies?* London: Grey Seal.

Masini, E. and Sasson, A. (eds) (1994). *The Futures of Cultures*. Paris: Unesco.

May, G.H. (1996). *The Future is Ours*. London: Adamantine.

Ringland, G. (1998). *Scenario Planning: Managing the Future*. New York: Wiley & Sons.

Schwartz, P. (1998). *The Art of the Long View: Planning for the Future in an Uncertain World*. New York: Wiley & Sons.

Strate, L. and Wachtel, E. (eds) (2004). *The Legacy of McLuhan*. Cresskill, NJ: Hampton Press.

Tough, A. (1991). *Crucial Questions about the Future*. Lanham, MD: University Press of America.

Wagar, W.W. (1999). *A Short History of the Future* (3rd edition). Chicago, IL: University of Chicago Press.

Zingrone, F. and McLuhan, E. (1995). *Essential McLuhan*. Toronto: House of Anansi Press.

Further reading on universalism versus relativism

Ayton-Shenker, D. (1995). *The Challenge of Human Rights and Cultural Diversity: United Nations Background Note*. New York: United Nations Department of Public Information.

Clayton, J. (1995). Religions and rights: local values and universal declarations. In An-Na'Im, A.A., Gort, J.D., Jansen, H. and Vroom, H.M. (eds), *Human Rights and Religious Values*. Grand Rapids, MI: William Eerdmans Publishing Company. pp. 259–266.

Donnelly, J. (1999). A defense of 'Western' universalism. In Bauer, J. and Bell, D. (eds), *The East Asian Challenge for Human Rights*. Cambridge: Cambridge University Press. pp. 60–87.

Freeman, M. (2000). Universal rights and particular cultures. In Jacobsen, M. and Bruun, O. (eds), *Human Rights and Asian Values*. Richmond: Curzon Press. pp. 43–58.

Nickel, J.W. (1987). *Making Sense of Human Rights*. Berkeley, CA: University of California Press. Chapter 4, 'Universal Rights in a diverse world', pp. 61–81.

Renteln, A.D. (1990). *International Human Rights: Universalism versus Relativism*. London: Sage.

RESEARCH ASSIGNMENT

Design the preferred and undesirable scenarios for futures of global communication using a time span of some 30 years. Create the scenarios from the perspective of different global actors, such as the United Nations, the Disney Corporation, or the Google company.

Discuss the methodological approach and the theoretical framework that you might want to use for these scenarios. How would you identify the most important contemporary trends and drivers of societal and technological developments without making forecasts?

REFERENCES

Allport, G.W. (1954). *The Nature of Prejudice*. Reading, MA: Addison-Wesley.

Amin, S. (1976). *Unequal Development*. New York: Monthly Review Press.

Amin, S. (2000). Economic globalism and political universalism: conflicting issues? *Journal of World-Systems Research*, VI(3): 582–622.

Andrejevic, M. (2007). *iSpy: Surveillance and Power in the Interactive Era*. Lawrence, KS: University Press of Kansas.

Appiah, K.A. (2002). Citizens of the World? *Biblio: A Review of Books*. Special issue: March–April: 6–10.

Appiah, K.A. (2006). *Cosmopolitanism: Ethics in a World of Strangers*. New York: W.W. Norton & Company.

Asante, M.K. (2011). De-Westernizing communication. In Wang, G. (ed.), *De-Westernizing Communication Research: Altering Questions and Changing Frameworks*. London: Routledge. pp. 21–27.

Bainbridge, W.S. (2006). Cyberimmortality: science, religion and the battle to save our souls. *The Futurist*, 40(2): 25–29.

Barber, B. (1995). *Jihad vs McWorld*. New York: Times Books.

Barbero, J.M. (1988). Communication from culture: the crisis of national and emergence of the popular. *Media, Culture & Society*, 10: 447–465.

Barnett, G.A. and Kincaid, D.L. (1983). Cultural convergence: a mathematical theory. In W. Gudykunst (ed.) *International Intercultural Communication Annual VII*. Beverley Hills: Sage. pp. 171–194.

Beck, U. (1992). *Risk Society: Towards a New Modernity*. London: Sage.

Bell, D. (1973). *The Coming of Post-Industrial Society: A Venture in Social Forecasting*. New York: Basic Books.

Beltran, L. (1967). Communication: forgotten tool of national development. *International Agricultural Development*, October, No. 36.

Beltran, L. (1970). Communication in Latin America: Persuasion for Status Quo or for National Development. PhD thesis, Michigan State University.

Beltran, L. (1976). Communication for development in Latin America: a forty years appraisal. In Nostbakken, D. and Morrow, C. (eds), *Cultural Expression in the Global Village*. Penang: Southbound.

Beltran, L.R. (1978). Communication and cultural domination: USA–Latin America case. *Media Asia*, 5(4): 183–192.

Beltran, L. (1980). A farewell to Aristotle: horizontal communication. *Communication*, 5: 5–41.

Beltran, L. (1993a). *Que comunicacion para el desarrolo?* Lima, Peru: IPAL.

Beltran, L. (1993b). *La communication para el desarrollo en Latinoamerica*. Lima, Peru: IPAL.

Bennett, C.J. (2008). *The Privacy Advocates*. Cambridge, MA: The MIT Press.

Berendt, J.-E. (1987). *Nada Brahma: The World is Sound*. London: Destiny Books.

Berridge, G.R. (1994). *Talking to the Enemy*. New York: St Martin's Press.

Bhabha, H. (1994). *The Location of Culture*. London: Routledge.

Boulding, K. (1959). National images and international systems. *Conflict Resolution*, 3(2): 120–131.

Bourdieu, P. (1985). Social space and genesis of classes. *Theory and Society*, 14: 723–744.

Bouwhuijsen, H. van den (2010). *In de schaduw van God* [*In God's Shade*]. Kampen: Klement.

Boyd-Barrett, J.O. (1977). Media imperialism: towards an international framework for an analysis of media systems. In Curran, J., Gurevitch, M. and Woollacott, J. (eds), *Mass Communication and Society*. London: Edward Arnold. pp. 116–135.

Braun, E. (1984). *Wayward Technology*. London: Frances Pinter.

Buber, M. (1958). *I and Thou*. New York: Scribner.

Burgess, J. and Green, J. (2009). *YouTube*. Cambridge: Polity Press.

Business Week, (1998). 'Bio-Tech Bodies', 27 July, 42–49.

Carroll, L. (1865/1988). *Alice in Wonderland: Through the Looking Glass*. Harmondsworth, UK: Penguin.

Castells, M. (1989). *The Informational City*. Oxford: Blackwell Publishers.

Castells, M. (1996). *The Rise of the Network Society*. Oxford: Wiley-Blackwell.

Castells, M. (1997). *The Power of Identity*. Oxford: Wiley-Blackwell.

Castells, M. (1998). *End of Millennium*. Oxford: Wiley-Blackwell.

Castells, M. (2001). *The Internet Galaxy: Reflections on the Internet, Business and Society*. Oxford: Oxford University Press.

Castells, M. (2009). *Communication Power*. Oxford: Oxford University Press.

Castells, M. (2010). *The Rise of the Network Society* (2nd edition). Oxford: Wiley-Blackwell.

Cavalli, J. (1986). *Le Genèse de la Convention de Berne pour la Protection des Oeuvres Littéraires et Artistiques du 9 Septembre 1886*. Lausanne: Imprimeries Reunies.

Cerf, C. and Navaskym, V. (1984). *The Experts Speak*. New York: Pantheon.

Chapple, S. and Garofalo, R. (1977). *Rock 'n' Roll is Here to Pay*. Chicago, IL: Nelson Hall.

Charmaz, K. (2006). *Constructing Grounded Theory: A Practical Guide through Qualitative Analysis*. Thousand Oaks, CA: Sage.

Chen, G.M. and Starosta, W.J. (1996). *Intercultural communication competence*. *Communication Yearbook*, 19, 353–384.

Childs, H. and Whitton, J.B. (1942). *Propaganda by Short Wave*. Princeton, Princeton University Press.

Childs, P. and Williams, R.J. (1997). *An Introduction to Post-Colonial Theory*. London: Prentice Hall.

261

Chomsky, N. and Herman, E.S. (1988). *Manufacturing Consent. The Political Economy of the Mass Media*. New York: Knopf Doubleday.

Chomsky, N. (1989). *Necessary Illusions: Thought Control in Democratic Societies*. Boston, MA: South End Press.

Chomsky, N. (2002). *Media Control: The Spectacular Achievements of Propaganda*. New York: Seven Stories Press.

Christians, C., Glasser, Th.L., McQuail, D., Nordenstreng, K. and White, R. (2009). *Normative Theories of the Media: Journalism in Democratic Societies*. Urbana, IL: University of Illinois Press.

Clarke, R.A. and Knake, R.K. (2010*). Cyber War: The Next Threat to National Security and What to Do About It*. New York: Harper Collins.

Collingridge, D. (1982). *Critical Decision Making*. London: Frances Pinter.

Cottle, S. (2006). *Mediatized Conflict: Developments in Media and Conflict Issues*. Maidenhead, UK: Open University Press.

Couldry, N. (2012). *Media, Society, World*. Cambridge: Polity Press.

Creel, G. (1920). *How We Advertised America: The First Telling of the Amazing Story of the Committee on Public Information that Carried the Gospel of Americanism to Every Corner of the Globe*. New York: Harper.

Cyert, R.M. and March, J.G. (1992/1963). *A Behavioural Theory of the Firm*. Englewood Cliffs, NJ: Prentice-Hall (1st edn, 1963).

Dahl, R.A. (1956). *A Preface to Democratic Theory*. Chicago, IL: University of Chicago Press.

Daly, M. and Wilson, M. (1988). *Homicide*. New York: De Gruyter.

Dijk, J., van (2012). *The Network Society* (3rd edition). London: Sage.

Dijck, J., van (2013). *The Culture of Connectivity*. Oxford: Oxford University Press.

Douglas, M. and Wildavsky, A. (1983). *Risk and Culture*. Berkeley, CA: University of California Press.

Dutta, M.J. (2011). *Communicating Social Change*. London: Routledge.

Dworkin, R. (1985). *A Matter of Principle*. Cambridge, MA: Harvard University Press.

Ehrlich, P. (1969). *Eco-catastrophe*. San Francisco, City Lights Book

Ekecranz, J. (2009). Media studies going global. In D.K. Thussu (ed.),. *Internationalizing Media Studies*. London, Routledge. pp. 75–90.

Elster, J. (1983*). Explaining Technical Change*. Cambridge: Cambridge University Press.

Falk, R.A. (1993). The making of global citizenship. In Brecher, J., Childs, J. and Cutler, J. (eds), *Global Visions: Beyond the New World Order*. Boston, MA: South End Press. pp. 39–50.

Fischoff, B. et al. (1981). *Acceptable Risk*. Cambridge: Cambridge University Press.

Flournoy, D. and Stewart, R. (1997). *CNN: Making news in the global market*. Luton: University of Luton Press.

Fortner, R.S. (1993). *International Communication: History, Conflict and Control of the Global Metropolis*. Belmont, CA: Wadsworth.

Foucault, M. (2003). *Society must be Defended: 1975–1976. Lectures at the College de France*. New York: Picador.

Frank, A.G. (1969). *Latin America: Underdevelopment or Revolution*. New York: Monthly Review Press.

Friedland, L. (1992). *Covering the World: International Television News Services*. New York: Twentieth Century Fund Press.

Gallie, W.B. (1956). Essentially contested concepts. *Proceeding of the Aristotelian Society*. 56: 167–198.

Gallois C., Giles, H., Jones, E., Cargile, A.C. and Ota, H. (1995). Communication Accommodation Theory: Elaborations and Extensions. In R. Wiseman (ed.), *Intercultural Communication Theory*. (Intercultural and International Communication Annual). Beverly Hills: Sage. pp. 330–342.

Galtung, J. (1980). *The True Worlds*. New York: The Free Press.

Galtung, J. (1984). *Johan Galtung: There are Alternatives*. Nottingham: Spokesman.

Galtung, J. (1988). *Essays in Peace Research* (Vols 1–6). Copenhagen: Christian Ejlers.

Galtung, J. (1994). *Human Rights in Another Key*. Cambridge: Polity Press.

Galtung, J. (1997). *Economics in Another Key*. Cambridge: Polity Press.

Galtung, J. and Vincent, R. (1992). *Global Glasnost: Towards a New World Communication Order?* Cresskill, NJ: Hampton Press.

Garner, D. (2011). *Future Babble*. New York: Penguin.

Garnham, N. (1990). *Capitalism and Communication*. London: Sage.

Gerbner, G., Gross, L.P. and Melody, W. (eds) (1973). *Communications Technology and Social Policy: Cultural Indicators – The Third Voice*. New York: John Wiley & Sons. pp. 555–573.

Gerbner, G., Mowlana, H. and Nordenstreng, K. (eds) (1993). *The Global Media Debate: Its Rise, Fall and Renewal*. Norwood, NJ: Ablex Publishing.

Gerbner, G., Mowlana, H. and Schiller, H.I. (eds) (1992). *Triumph of the Image: The Media's War in the Persian Gulf – A Global Perspective*. Boulder, CO: Westview Press.

Gerbner, G., Siefert, M. (eds) (1984). *World Communications: A Handbook*. New York: Longman.

Giddens, A. (1990). *The Consequences of Modernity*. Cambridge: Polity Press.

Gilboa, E. (2000). Mass communication and diplomacy: a theoretical framework. *Communication Theory*, 10(3): 275–309.

Ginneken, J. van (1998). *Understanding Global News*. London: Sage.

Gowing, N. (1994). Real-time TV coverage from war: Does it make or break government policy? Paper given at British Film Institute, London.

Gould, C.C. (1988). *Rethinking Democracy: Freedom and Social Cooperation in Politics, Economy, and Society*. Cambridge: Cambridge University Press.

Grossman, D. (1995). *On Killing: The Psychological Cost of Learning to Kill in War and Society*. New York: Little, Brown and Co.

Gudykunst, W.B. and Hammer, M.A. (1988). *Strangers and Hosts: An uncertainty reduction based theory of intercultural adaptation*. In Y.Y. Kim and W.B. Gudykunst (eds). *Cross-cultural adaptation: Current Approaches*. Newbury Park (CA): Sage. pp. 106–139.

Gumucio-Dagron, A. and Tufte, T. (eds) (2006). *Communication for Social Change Anthology: Historical and Contemporary Readings*. South Orange, NJ: Communication for Social Change Consortium.

Hackett, R.A. and Schroeder, B. (2008). Does anybody practice peace journalism? A cross-national comparison of press coverage of the Afghanistan and Israeli-Hezbollah wars. *Peace & Policy*, 13: 26–61.

Hall, E.T. (1959). *The Silent Language*. New York, Doubleday.

Hall, E.T. (1976). *Beyond Culture*. New York: Doubleday.

Halloran, J.D. (1970). *Mass Media in Society: The Need of Research*. UNESCO Reports and Papers on Mass Communication, No. 59. New York: UNESCO.

Halloran, J.D. (1973). Research in forbidden territory. In Gerbner, G., Gross, L.P. and Melody, W. (eds), *Communications Technology and Social Policy*. New York: John Wiley and Sons. pp. 547–554.

Halloran, J.D. (1981). The context of communication research. In McAnany, E.G., Schnitman, J. and Janus, N. (eds), *Communication and Social Structure: Critical Studies in Mass Media Research*. New York: Praeger. pp. 21–57.

Halloran, J.D. (1986). International democratization of communication, the challenge for research. In Becker, J., Hedebro, G. and Paldan, L. (eds), *Communication and Domination: Essays to Honor Herbert I. Schiller*. Norwood, NJ: Ablex Publishing. pp. 241–248.

Hamelink, C.J. (1983a). *Cultural Autonomy in Global Communications*. New York: Longman.

Hamelink, C.J. (1983b). *Finance and Information*. Norwood, NJ: Ablex Publishing.

Hamelink, C.J. (1984). *Transnational Data Flows in the Information Age*. Lund: Studentlitteratur.

Hamelink, C.J. (1986). *Militarization in the Information Age*. Geneva: World Council of Churches.

Hamelink, C.J. (1988). *The Technology Gamble*. Norwood, NJ: Ablex Publishing.

Hamelink, C.J. (1994a). *Trends in World Communication*. Penang: Southbound.

Hamelink, C.J. (1994b). *The Politics of World Communication*. London: Sage.

Hamelink, C.J. (2000). *The Ethics of Cyberspace*. London, Sage.

Hamelink, C.J. (2011). *Media and Conflict: Escalating Evil*. Boulder, CO: Paradigm.

Harding, S. (1978). *Can Theories Be Refuted?* Dordrecht: Reidel.

Headrick, D.R. (1991). *The Invisible Weapon: Telecommunications and International Politics 1851–1945*. New York: Oxford University Press.

Hesmondhalgh, D. (2002). *The Cultural Industries*. First ed. London: Sage.

Hesmondhalgh, D. (2007). *The Cultural Industries*. Second ed. London: Sage.

Hetman, F. (1973). *Society and the Assessment of Technology*. Paris: OECD.

Hofstede, G. (1980/2001). *Culture's Consequences*. London: Sage (revised in 2001).

Holwerda, H.H. and Gershon, R.A. (1997). The Transnational Advertising Agency: global messages and free market competition. In Gershon, R.A. (ed.), *The Transnational Media Corporation*. Mahwah, NJ: Lawrence Erlbaum Associates.

264

Hudson, H. (1984). *When Telephones Reach the Village: The Role of Telecommunication in Rural Development*. Norwood, NJ: Ablex Publishing.

Hudson, H. (1990). *Communication Satellites: Their Development and Impact*. New York: The Free Press.

Hudson, H. (1997). Converging technologies and changing realities: toward universal access to telecom in the developing world. In Melody, W.H. (ed.), *Telecom Reform: Principles, Policies and Regulatory Practices*. Lyngby: Technical University of Denmark. pp. 395–404.

Hudson, H. (2009). *From Rural Village to Global Village: Telecommunication in the Information Age*. London: Routledge.

Hume, D. (1739/1975). *A Treatise of Human Nature*. Oxford: Oxford University Press.

Huntington, S.P. (1993). *The Clash of Civilizations and the Remaking of World Order*. New York: Touchstone Books.

Innis, H. (1950). *Empire and Communication*. Oxford: Clarendon Press.

International Commission for the Study of Communication Problems (1980). Many Voices, One World. Paris, UNESCO.

Inter Press Service (1997). *Articles of Association*. Rome, Inter Press Service.

Irvan, S. (2006). Peace journalism as a normative theory: premises and obstacles. *Global Media Journal: Mediterranean Edition*, 1(2): 34–39.

ITU (1997). *World Telecommunication Development Report 1996/97: Trade in Telecommunications*. Geneva: International Telecommunication Union.

ITU (1998a). *General Trends in Telecommunication Reform 1998: World* (Vol. 1). Geneva: International Telecommunication Union.

ITU (1998b). *World Telecommunication Development Report: Universal Access*. Geneva: International Telecommunication Union.

Jakobsen, P.V. (1996). National interest, humanitarianism or CNN: What triggers UN Peace Enforcement after the Cold War? *Journal of Peace Research*, 33(2): 205–215.

Janus, N. (1981). Advertising and the mass media in the era of global corporation. In McAnany, E., Schnitman, J. and Janus, N. (eds), *Communication and Social Structure*. New York: Praeger. pp. 290–303.

Jensen, K.B. (2010). *Media Convergence*. London: Routledge.

Johnson, N. (2010). *Simply Complexity*. Oxford: Oneworld Publications.

Jowett, G.S. and O'Donnell, V. (1986). *Propaganda and Persuasion*. London: Sage.

Joy, B. (2000). Why the future doesn't need us. *Wired*, 8: 04.

Kaplan, A. (1999). *The Development Capacity: NGLIS Development Dossier*. Geneva: Non-Governmental Liaison Service.

Kim, Y.Y. (1986). *Interethnic communication: Current research*. International and Intercultural Communication Annual. Vol. 10: 9–18. Newbury Park, CA: Sage.

Kincaid, D.L., Yum, J.O., Woelfel, J. and Barnett, G.A. (1983). The cultural convergence of Korean immigrants in Hawaii: An empirical test of a mathematical theory. In *Quality and Quantity*, 18: 59–78. Amsterdam: Elsevier Science Publishers.

Klein, J.T., Grossenbacher-Mansuy, W., Häberli, R., Bill, A., Scholz, R.W. and Welti, M. (2001). *Transdisciplinary Joint Problem Solving among Science, Technology and Society: An Effective Way for Managing Complexity*. Basel: Birkhäuser Verlag.

Knightley, Ph. (2000). *The First Casualty: The War Correspondent as Hero and Myth-maker from the Krimea to Kosovo*. London: Prion.

Knightley, Ph. (2003). *The Second Oldest Profession: Spies and Spying in the Twentieth Century*. London: Pimlico.

Kraidy, M.M. (2004). From culture to hybridity. In Semati, M. (ed.), *New Frontiers in International Communication Theory*. Oxford: Rowman & Littlefield. pp. 247–262.

Kraidy, M.M. (2011). Globalizing media and communication studies. In Wang, G. (ed.), *De-Westernizing Communication Research: Altering Questions and Changing Frameworks*. London: Routledge. pp. 50–57.

Kubka, J. and Nordenstreng, K. (1986). *Useful Recollections. Part I and Part II*. Prague: International Organization of Journalists.

Kuhn, T.S. (1996). *The Structure of Scientific Revolutions*. Chicago, IL: University of Chicago Press.

Kunczik, M. (1990). *Images of Nations and International Public Relations*. Bonn: Friedrich Ebert Stiftung.

Kunda, Z. (1999). *Social Cognition: Making Sense of People*. Cambridge, MA: The MIT Press.

Kurzweil, R. (2005). *The Singularity is Near: When Humans Transcend Biology*. New York: Penguin.

Kurzweil, R. (2006). Reinventing humanity: the future of machine–human intelligence. *The Futurist*, 40(2): 39–46.

Lasswell, H.D. (1927). The theory of political propaganda. *American Political Science Review*, 21(3): 627–631.

Lasswell, H.D. (1971). *A Pre-View of Policy Sciences*. London: American Elsevier.

Lazarsfeld, P. (1952). The prognosis for international communication research. *Public Opinion Quarterly*, 16: 482–490.

Lee, P.S. (1988). Communication imperialism and dependency: a conceptual clarification. *Gazette*, 41(2): 69–83.

Lerner, D. (1958). *The Passing of Traditional Society*. New York: Free Press.

Liebes, T. and Katz, E. (1990). *The Export of Meaning: Cross-cultural Readings of "Dallas"*. Oxford: Oxford University Press.

Lippmann, W. (1922). *Public Opinion*. New York: Harcourt Brace.

Loasby, B. (1976). *Choice, Complexity and Ignorance*. Cambridge: Cambridge University Press.

Lorenz, E.N. (1963). Deterministic Nonperiodic Flow. *Journal of the Atmospheric Sciences*, 20(2): 130–141.

Lorenz, E.N. (1969). Atmospheric predictability as revealed by naturally occurring analogues. *Journal of the Atmospheric Sciences*, 26(4): 636–646.

Lorenz, E.N. (1969). Three approaches to atmospheric predictability. *Bulletin of the American Meteorological Society*, 50: 345–349.

Luhmann, N. (1971) Selbststeuerung der Wissenschaft. In Niklas Luhmann (ed.) *Soziologische Aufklärung*. Opladen: Westdeutscher Verlag. pp. 232–252.

Luther, S.F. (1988). *The United States and the Direct Broadcast Satellite*. Oxford: Oxford University Press.

Mansell, R. (1999). The politics of designing information networks. *Media Development*, 46(2): 7–11.

Mansell, R. and Wehn, U. (1998). *Knowledge Societies: Information Technology for Sustainable Development*. Oxford: Oxford University Press.

March, J.G. and Simon, H.A. (1958). *Organizations*. New York: Wiley.

Matta, F. (1978). *La Información en el Nuevo Orden Internacional*. Mexico: ILET.

Mattelart, A. and Dorfman, A. (1975). *How to Read Donald Duck: Imperialist Ideology in the Disney Comic*. New York: International General.

Mattelart, A. (1979). *Multinational Corporations and the Control of Culture. The Ideological Apparatuses of Imperialism*. Sussex: Harvester Press.

Mattelart, A. (1983). *Transnationals and the Third World: The Struggle for Culture*. South Hadley, MA: Bergin and Garvey.

Mattelart, A. (1984). *International Image Markets. In Search of an Alternative*. (with Michèle Mattelart and Xavier Delcourt). London: Comedia.

Mattelart, A. (1991). *Advertising International: The Privatisation of Public Space*. London: Routledge.

Mattelart, A. (1994). *Mapping World Communication: War, Progress, Culture*. Minneapolis MN: University of Minnesota Press.

Mattelart, A. (2010). An archaeology of the global era. In Thussu, D.K. (ed.), *International Communication: A Reader*. London: Routledge. pp. 313–328.

McAnany, E.G. (2012). *Saving the World: A Brief History of Communication for Development and Social Change*. Champaign, IL: University of Illinois Press.

McChesney, R.W. (2000). *Rich Media, Poor Democracy*. New York: The New Press.

McChesney, R.W. (2010). The media system goes global. In Thussu, D.K. (ed.), *International Communication: A Reader*. London: Routledge. pp. 188–220.

McChesney, R.W. (2013). *Digital Disconnect: How Capitalism is Turning the Internet against Democracy*. New York: The New Press.

McLuhan, M. (1964). *Understanding Media*. London: Routledge & Kegan Paul.

McLuhan, M. (1970). *Culture is Our Business*. New York, McGraw Hill.

McLuhan, M. (1988). *The Global Village: Transformations in World Life in the 21st Century*. Oxford: Oxford University Press.

McLuhan, M., Fiore, Q. and Angel, J. (1967). *The Medium is the Message*. New York: Bantam/Random House.

McPhail, T.L. (1987). *Electronic Colonialism: The Future of International Broadcasting and Communication*. Newbury Park, CA: Sage.

McPhail, Th.L. (2002). *Global Communication*. London: Allyn and Bacon.

McQuail, D. (1983). *Mass Communication Theory: An Introduction*. London: Sage.

McQuail, D. (2010). *McQuail's Mass Communication Theory*. London: Sage.

Melkote, S.R. and Steeves, H.L. (2001). *Communication for Development in the Third World: Theory and Practice for Empowerment* (2nd edn). London: Sage.

Mitchell, J.M. (1986). *International Cultural Relations*. London: Allen and Unwin.

Mjos, O.J. (2010). *Media Globalization and the Discovery Channel Networks*. London: Routledge.

Mooij, M. de (2013). *Global Marketing and Advertising: Understanding Cultural Paradoxes*. London: Sage.

Moor, L. (2007). *The Rise of Brands*. London: Bloomsbury Academic.

Morozov, E. (2011). *The Net Delusion: On How Not to Liberate the World*. London: Penguin.

Morris, D. and McGann, E. (2012). *Here Come the Black Helicopters! UN Global Governance and the Loss of Freedom*. New York: HarperCollins.

Mosco, V. (1996). *The Political Economy of Communication*. London: Sage.

Mosco, V. (2009). *The Political Economy of Communication*. London: Sage.

Mosco, V. (2014). *To the Cloud*. Boulder, CO: Paradigm.

Muto, I. (1993). For an alliance of hope. In Brecher, J., Brown Childs, J. and Cutler, J. (eds), *Global Visions: Beyond the New World Order*. Boston, MA: South End Press. pp. 147–162.

Nederveen Pieterse, J. (2009). Media and global divides: representing the rise of the rest as threat. *Global Media and Communication*, 5(2): 1–17.

Nordenstreng, K. (1997). Beyond the four theories of the press. In Servaes, J. and Lie, R. (eds), *Media and Politics in Transition*. Leuven: ACCO.

OECD (2011). *Communications Outlook 2011*. Paris: OECD.

Oetzel, J.G. (1995). Intercultural small groups: An effective decision-making theory. In R.L. Wiseman (ed.), *Intercultural Communication Theories*. Thousand Oaks, CA: Sage. pp. 202–224.

Pasquali, A. (1963). Teoría de la Comunicación: las implicaciones sociológocas entre información y cultura. In Gumucia-Dagron, A. and T. Tufte (eds). Antología de Comunicación para el cambio social. South Orange, NJ: Communication for Social Change Consortium. pp. 60–80.

Pateman, C. (1970). *Participation and Democratic Theory*. Cambridge: Cambridge University Press.

Pavlik, J.V. (1987). *Public Relations: What Research Tells Us*. Newbury Park, CA: Sage.

Picard, R.G. (2002). *The Economics and Financing of Media Companies*. New York: Fordham University Press.

Pinker, S. (1994). *The Language Instinct*. New York: William Morrow.

Pinker, S. (2011). The Better Angels of Our Nature: The Decline of Violence in History and Its Causes. London: Penguin.

Popper, K. (1959). *The Logic of Scientific Discovery*. London: Hutchinson.

Pruitt, D.G. and Kim, S.H. (2004). *Social Conflict: Escalation, Stalemate, and Settlement*. New York: McGraw-Hill.

Rantanen, T. (2010). Methodological inter-nationalism in comparative media research. In Roosvall, A. and Salovaara-Moring, I. (eds), *Communicating the Nation*. Gothenburg: Nordicom. pp. 25–39.

Ritzer, G. (1993). *The McDonaldization of Society*. London and Thousand Oaks, CA: Pine Forge Press.

Robertson, A. (2010). *Mediated Cosmopolitanism: The World of Television News*. Oxford: Polity Press.

Robinson, D., E. Buck and M. Cuthbert (1991). *Music at the Margins: Popular Music and Global Cultural Diversity*. London: Sage.

Rogers. E. (1962). *Diffusion of innovations*. New York: Macmillan.

Rosenblum, M. (1993). *Who Stole the News?* New York: John Wiley & Sons.

Said, E.W. (1978). *Orientalism*. New York: Pantheon.

Said, E.W. (1993). *Culture and Imperialism*. New York: A.A. Knopf.

Sassen, S. (2001). *The Global City: New York, London, Tokyo*. Princeton, NJ: Princeton University Press.

Sassen, S. (2009). The Global City: strategic site/new frontier. *American Studies*, 41(2/3): 79–95.

Schiller, D. and Fregoso, R.L. (1991). A private view of the digital world. *Telecommunications Policy*, 15(3): 195–208.

Schiller, H.I. (1969). *Mass Communication and American Empire*. Boston, MA: Beacon Press.

Schiller, H.I. (1973). *The Mind Managers*. Boston, MA: Beacon Press.

Schiller, H.I. (1976). *Communication and Cultural Domination*. New York: International Arts and Sciences Press.

Schiller, H.I. (1981). *Who Knows: Information in the Age of the Fortune 500*. Norwood, NJ: Ablex Publishing.

Schiller, H.I. (1984). *Information and the Crisis Economy*. Norwood, NJ: Ablex Publishing.

Schiller, H.I. (1989). *Culture Inc., The Corporate Takeover of Public Expression*. Oxford: Oxford University Press.

Schiller, H.I. (2000). *Living in the Number One Country*. New York: Seven Stories Press.

Schramm, W. (1964). *Mass Media and National Development*. Stanford, California: Stanford University Press.

Schramm, W. and Rivers, W.L. (1969). *Responsibility in Mass Communication*. New York: Harper & Row.

Schumpeter, J.A. (1942). *Capitalism, Socialism and Democracy*. London: Allen & Unwin.

Schwartau, W. (1996). *Information Warfare*. New York: Thunder Mouth's Press.

Sen, A. (2006). Identity and Violence: The Illusion of Destiny. New York: W.W. Norton & Co.

Servaes, J. (2008). *Communication for Development and Social Change*. London: Sage.

Siebert, F., Peterson, T. and Schramm, W. (1956). *Four Theories of the Press*. Urbana: University of Illinois Press.

Singer, P. (1979). *Practical Ethics*. Cambridge: Cambridge University Press.

Shinar, D. (2008). Why not more peace journalism? The coverage of the 2006 Lebanon War in Canadian and Israeli media. *Peace & Policy*, 13: 8–25.

Sinclair, J. (2012). *Advertising, the Media and Globalisation*. London: Routledge.

Sirois, A. and Wasko, J. (2011). The political economy of the recorded music industry. In Wasko, J., Murdock, G. and Sousa, H. (eds), *The Handbook of Political Economy of Communications*. Oxford: Blackwell Publishing. pp. 331–357.

Slovic, P. and Fischoff, B. (1980). How safe is safe enough? In Dowie, J. and Lefrefe, P. (eds), *Risk and Chance*. Milton Keynes: Open University Press. pp. 121–147.

Smith, A. (1979). *The Newspaper: An International History*. London: Thames and Hudson.

Sontag, S. (2002). *Regarding the Pain of Others*. London: Hamilton.

South Commission, (1990). *The Challenge to the South: the Report of the South Commission*. Oxford: Oxford University Press.

Speier, H. (1944). *German Radio Propaganda*. London, Oxford University Press.

Stein, D.E. (2012). The scientific method after next. *World Future Review*, 4(1): 34–41.

Stephens, M. (1988). *A History of News: From the Drum to the Satellite*. London: Penguin.

Stiglitz, J.E. (2012). *The Price of Inequality: How Today's Divided Society Endangers Our Future*. New York: W.W. Norton & Co.

Straubhaar, J. (2007). *World Television: From Global to Local*. London: Sage.

Tajfel, H., Billig, M.G., Bundy, R.E. and Flament, C. (1971). Social categorization and inter-group behaviour. *European Journal of Social Psychology*, 1: 149–177.

Taylor, P.M. (1990). *Munitions of the Mind: War Propaganda from the Ancient World to the Nuclear Age*. Wellingborough: Patrick Stevens.

Taylor, P.M. (1997). *Global Communication, International Affairs and the Media since 1945*. London: Routledge.

Temkin, L.S. (1993). *Inequality*. Oxford: Oxford University Press.

Thussu, D.K. (2000/2006). *International Communication, Continuity and Change*. London: Hodder (2nd edn, 2006).

Thussu, D.K. (ed.) (2007). *Media on the Move: Global Flow and Contra-flow*. London: Routledge.

Ting-Toomey, S. (1988). Intercultural conflict styles: A face-negotiation theory. In Y.Y. Kim and W. Gudykunst (eds). *Theories in intercultural communication*. Newbury Park CA: Sage.

Toffler, A. (1980). *The Third Wave*. New York: Bantam Books.

Tomlinson, J. (1991). *Cultural imperialism: A Critical Introduction*. Baltimore, MD: Johns Hopkins University Press.

Tuchman, B. (1985). *The March of Folly*. London: Sphere Books.

Tunstall, J. (2008). *The Media Were American: US Mass Media in Decline*. Oxford: Oxford University Press.

UN Commission on Global Governance (1995). *Our Global Neighbourhood*. New York: Oxford University Press.

UNCTAD (1985). *The History of UNCTAD 1964–1984*. New York: United Nations.

UNDP (1999). *Human Development Report*. New York: Oxford University Press.

UNESCO (1961). *Mass Media in Developing Countries*. Paris: UNESCO.

UNESCO (2005). *International Flows of Selected Goods and Services*. Paris: UNESCO.

UN Habitat (2011). *State of the World's Cities 2010/2011*. Nairobi: UN Habitat.

Van Dinh, T. (1987). *Communication and Diplomacy in a Changing World*. Norwood, NJ: Ablex Publishing.

Venturelli, S. (1998). Cultural rights and world trade agreements in the information society. *Gazette*, 60(1): 47–76.

Vink, N. (2005). *Dealing with Differences*. Amsterdam: KIT Publishers.

Waal, F. de (2010). *Tijd voor Empathie*. Amsterdam: Contact.

Waal, F. de (2013). *The Bonobo and the Atheist: In Search of Humanism among the Primates*. New York: W.W. Norton & Co.

Wang, G. (ed.) (2011). *De-Westernizing Communication Research: Altering Questions and Changing Frameworks*. London: Routledge.

Weizenbaum, J. (1976). *Computer Power and Human Reason*. San Francisco, CA: Freeman and Co.

Wells, C. (1987). *The UN, UNESCO and the Politics of Knowledge*. London: Macmillan.

Whitton, J.B. (1979). Hostile international propaganda and international law. In Nordenstreng, K. and Schiller, H.I. (eds), *National Sovereignty and International Communication*. Norwood, NJ: Ablex Publishing. pp. 217–229.

Wikström, P. (2009). *The Music Industry*. Cambridge: Polity Press.

Wilcox, D.L., Ault, Ph. and Age, K. (1989). *Public Relations: Strategies and Tactics*. New York: Harper & Row.

Wilkins, K., Tufte, T. and Obregon, R. (eds) (2014). *The Handbook of Development Communication and Social Change*. Oxford: Wiley-Blackwell.

Williams, W. (1971). *The Shaping of American Diplomacy*. Chicago, IL: Rand McNally.

Winner, L. (1993). Citizen virtues in a technological order. In Winkler, E.R. and Coomb, J.R. (eds), *Applied Ethics*. Oxford: Blackwell. pp. 46–48.

Winseck, D.R. and Pike, R.M. (2007). *Communication and Empire: Media, Markets and Globalization, 1860–1930*. Durham, NC: Duke University Press.

Wright, A.F. (1979). On the spread of Buddhism to China. In Lasswell, H.H., Lerner, D. and Speier, H. (eds), *Propaganda and Communication in World History* (Vol. I). Honolulu: The University of Hawaii Press.

World Commission on Culture and Development (1995). *Our Creative Diversity*. Paris:

World Trade Organization (1998). *World Telecommunications Agreement*. Geneva: WTO.

INDEX